Education and the law

second edition

edited by Robert Morris

LONGMAN

Longman Information and Reference,
Longman Group UK Limited,
The High, Harlow, Essex, CM20 1 YR, England.
Telephone Harlow (0279) 442601; Fax Harlow (0279) 444501; Telex 81491 Padlog

First edition published 1986

A catalogue record for this book is available from the British Library

ISBN 0-582-08809-7

Typeset by Communitype Communications Ltd, Leicester
Printed and bound in Great Britain by
Biddles Ltd, Guildford and King's Lynn

Contents

Foreword

The period since 1988 has seen an unprecedented flurry in the development of the legislation which affects the provision made by the public education service through the school system, colleges of further education and the higher education sector. New laws have invariably given the Secretary of State for Education wide powers to control the detail of the service, which find expression in the plethora of Statutory Instruments, Regulations, Orders, and Circulars with which institutions and local education authority officers need to interpret.

This compilation provides ready access to the law. As such it is to be much welcomed by all who require a clear understanding of the law as a basis either for the advice they give or as a source of authority for the action they take.

Christopher Farmer
President, Society of Education Officers 1993–94
Chief Education Officer, Coventry City Council

Contributors

Chris Brooks is a former Principal at the Department of Education and Science, and was closely associated with the early development of the Certificate of Pre-Vocational Education. He was also appointed as the Department's Parliamentary Clerk and, later, as Private Secretary to schools Minister Mrs Margaret Beckett MP. He is now County Adult Education Officer with Lancashire, having previously been responsible for the planning, resourcing and marketing of further education in the county. He was an adviser to the Association of County Councils on the FHE Bill (1991/92).

Michael Brunt spent eight years teaching German and French, rising to the level of head of department, before joining educational administration with Walsall Metropolitan Borough Council in 1978, where he successively took on the roles of Assistant Education Officer (Secondary), (Primary) and (Special). He then moved to Solihull as Assistant Director (Common Services), which included responsibility for personnel and local financial management. He is now Deputy Director of Education with Doncaster MBC, a position he has held since 1990 and a member of the Council of the Society of Education Officers.

John Dobie is a Depute Director of Education with Lothian Regional Council, based in Edinburgh. He is in charge of the Finance, Personnel and Computer Systems Support Division. He is also a Management Side adviser to the Scottish Joint Negotiating Committee (Teaching Staff in School Education), and Assistant Secretary to the Association of Directors of Education in Scotland. He is the Convener of the Convention of Scottish Local Authorities Officer Advisers Liaison Group, and a member of the UK Centre for European Education. Before joining Lothian in 1979, he taught in secondary schools in Cheshire and Liverpool, and served in the directorates of Manchester and Stockport LEAs.

Neil Gill is Director of Education for Barnet and Chairman of the South-East Region of the Society of Education Officers. Educated at school in Sheffield and at Cambridge University, he had varied teaching experience in grammar and comprehensive schools and in teacher education before entering administration with Hertfordshire in 1971, joining Barnet three years later. He serves on the General Synod Board of Education and the National Society's Legal Committee, is Vice-Chairman of the St Albans Diocesan Board of Education and represents the SEO on the Council of the Christian Education Movement.

Kathleen Higgins is Group Director of the newly-merged Education and Social Services Department in Hillingdon, having previously worked in metropolitan and county authorities from the north to the south-west of England. Miss Higgins is a member of several national organisations, including the Council of the Society of Education Officers and the Social Policy Forum of the National Children's Bureau. She is an adviser to the Royal Society of Arts Committee on Early Years Education, and was formerly an adviser on early years to the Association of Metropolitan Authorities. She chairs the SEO *ad hoc* group on grant-maintained schools.

Bob Morris is Visiting Senior Research Fellow at the Centre for Educational Policy and Management in the School of Education, the Open University. He is also a tutor, on the university's newly-launched course E326 *Managing Schools: Challenge and Response.* Dr Morris took early retirement from the post of Education Officer of the Association of Metropolitan Authorities in 1992.

Graham Platts studied at the universities of York, Birmingham and Nottingham. Over the years, he has taught pupils and students of all ages in a variety of contexts, but mainly through community colleges in Leicestershire. More recently, Dr Platts has been serving as an education officer for Suffolk LEA. He is a member of the Council of the Society of Education Officers.

Brian Unwin is a field officer for the Secondary Heads Association, having been until retirement Headteacher of Connahs Quay High School, Clwyd LEA. He is the immediate past Legal Secretary of SHA, and is a section editor of Croner's *School Governor's Manual.*

Geoffrey Williams is Assistant Director (Parent and Student Services) for Hertfordshire. His previous posts with the county entailed responsibility for primary and for secondary education as Senior Education Officer. He is Chair of the Management Development Committee of the Society of Education Officers. He contributes on management matters to *Education*, and has most recently contributed to and edited a resource manual for education officers, published by Longman as a joint venture with the SEO.

1 The present state of affairs

Bob Morris

Purposes of this edition of *Education and the law*

I do not apologise for, but shall explain, the fact that this is a book by educators rather than lawyers. We number the latter amongst our close colleagues, and some lawyers have been consulted in preparation of parts of this work. The spirit of the times, of litigation as well as frenetic legislative activity, has brought educators and their legal advisors in ever-greater contact with each other. Nevertheless, I cling to the principle summed up by Sir Michael Kerry, former Treasury Solicitor:

> In general . . . administrators as a whole do not approach their legal advisors at every turn . . . There are many administrators and few lawyers. The former still operate, for the most part on the assumption that the standards of reasonableness and fairness which they apply are adequate. (Kerry 1986)

The purpose of the present edition does not differ very much from that of its predecessor, to provide an overview with analysis, but this time some more commentary. It is intended as a guide, which we hope people will read at home and in the library as well as at the office. It should be of interest to the new entrant into what used confidently to be called educational administration, and to the experienced manager; and we offer it also to students and other academic commentators. The balance of kudos seems to have swung from 'administration' to 'management' recently, but I am unsure whether the shift is more than semantic. At any rate, I hope that this book will be of use to both managers and administrators, whether in LEAs, schools, colleges — or the new magistracies and new commissariats (on which there is more below).

The end of stability

The first edition of *Education and the law* went to press in October 1985 and was published in 1986. To say simply that there have been great changes in the subject since then would be an understatement. The first edition set out its information and commentary in a format implying stability and even a hierarchy in the ordering of the chapters: central government, local education authorities (LEAs), schools, governors, parental rights and duties, employment of teachers, school administration, the teacher's duty of care, 'ancillary arrangements', special educational needs, and Scotland. This time, the order is to set the scene, initially for England and Wales, and then to look at the changing patterns of education in Scotland, before passing to Brian Unwin's chapter on the schools, the importance of which is being heavily underscored in the legislation. The term 'the autonomous school', which Kathleen Higgins (Chapter 6) uses while exploring the concept, has passed into the currency of the service.

The political policies which intended the transformation of the public education service are described elsewhere (eg Morris and Griggs 1988, Morris 1990, Simon 1991, Lawrence 1992), but a note on the means by which ministers have sought to alter both the constitutional set-up and ways of doing things is wholly relevant here. Since 1944, there have been (for England and Wales) some 34 statutes on education, 15 of them in the past 13 years and under successive Conservative administrations. Some of the Education Acts of the period have been in the tradition of straightforward repeal, as in the intention of the 1979 Act to negate the requirement of the Labour government's Act of 1976 that LEAs should submit plans for reorganising all their secondary schools on the comprehensive principle. Others were to tidy up: the Education (Fees and Awards) Act 1983 regularised the financial position of students from overseas, and the first two Acts of 1986 (there were three in all that year) respectively increased the proportion of education expenditure that could be covered by specific grant and made a technical reform to the procedures of pooled expenditure.

Of the larger Acts, two early ones of Mrs Thatcher's first administration also fell into the classic type: the 1980 Act was partly based on the 1977 Taylor Report on school governance (*A New Partnership for Our Schools*), and the 1981 Act largely implemented the recommendations of the 1978 Warnock Report (*Special Educational Needs* Cmnd 7212). The Taylor Committee had been set up by the Labour Government in 1975 and the Warnock Committee by the Conservatives in 1972. The 1980 Act also reflected policies on which the Conservative Party had been working in Opposition, on the theme of a charter for parents, though the provisions on the parents' right to receive information and to express preferences as to the schools their children should attend were only a little stronger than those set out in Labour's Education Bill (clauses 7, 10) presented by Secretary of State Shirley Williams in November 1978 (legislation which fell with the election of 1979 and the Conservative victory). The Warnock Report had been widely welcomed at the time of its publication, and the 1981 Act picked up a principle enunciated in the Act of 1976, but not implemented, that children with special educational needs should be educated in ordinary schools unless that would, in the particular cases, interfere with good education or prove excessively costly.

Sir Keith Joseph's Education (No. 2) Act 1986 was the culmination of traditional consultations and public discussion of policy, and had been preceded by a Green (consultative) Paper, *Parental Influence at School* (Cmnd 9242) in 1984 and a White Paper, *Better Schools* (Cmnd 9469) in the following year.

The shift in policy which produced non-consensual legislation occurred with the appointment of Kenneth Baker as Secretary of State in the summer of 1986, in succession to Sir Keith Joseph. The Teachers' Pay and Conditions Act, of early 1987, marked the failure of attempts by the Burnham Committee to reach agreement on an explicit set of contractual obligations for schoolteachers. The Act created an Interim Advisory Committee on School Teachers' Pay and [other] Conditions, and contained provision for its own expiry at 31 March 1990 unless renewed by an order subject to the affirmative resolution procedure, i.e. a positive vote in each House. The subsequent narrative is taken up in Busher and Saran's *Teachers' Conditions of Employment* (1992), but the legislative culmination was in the School Teachers' Pay and Conditions Act 1991, which has established a Review Body, unique among such bodies in two important respects: the employment group covered are not government employees, and the body's scope ranges beyond pay into all the key conditions of duties, working days and hours, and even professional relationships. The details are explained in Chapter 8 of the present book; there Michael Brunt also illustrates in detail the peculiarities of the employment position of teachers in LEA-maintained schools, and of non-teaching staffs, for whom the formal arrangements are somewhat different again.

The Education Reform Act 1988 (ERA) was intended to introduce a 'programme of reform . . . the most far-reaching since the war' (Baker 1987). It introduced the National Curriculum, local management of LEA-maintained schools and colleges, grant-maintained schools, and the definition of more open enrolment; it provided for the establishment of a separate sector of higher education (HE), to be funded by the Polytechnics and Colleges Funding Council, and for transfer of the polytechnics and other large HE colleges from LEA ownership, maintenance and control to corporate status; the largest LEA in England and Wales, the Inner London Education Authority, was marked down for abolition in 1989; and two statutory quangos, on curriculum and examinations, were to be set up to replace the School Curriculum Development Committee and the Secondary Examinations Council (established by Secretary of State Sir Keith Joseph when he abolished the Schools Council in 1984).

Mr Baker's speech at the Second Reading of his Education Reform Bill was designed to set the measure in a context which included also the Acts of 1902 (Balfour's) and 1944 (Butler's), and to contrast it as action with the mere debate stimulated by the Prime Minister of the day Mr (now Lord) Callaghan in his famous remarks at Ruskin College in October 1976 on the shortcomings of the public education service (though, as Graham Platts reminds us in Chapter 5, the teachers were the main butt of prime ministerial criticism). What Mr Baker did not claim for his legislation, however, was lapidary permanence of the sort which the 1944 Act acquired, despite amendments and partial repeals, over several decades.

More legislation, of a radical nature, has already followed. In 1992, two Bills reached the statute book shortly before the general election, the Education (Schools) Act, which provides for regular full inspections of schools by registered inspectors who will have successfully tendered for their assignments, and the Further and Higher Education Act. Under the latter, all mainstream colleges of further education (FE) will have acquired corporate status under the Further Education Funding Council, as from April 1993; the polytechnics have become universities, PCFC and its counterpart the Universities Funding Council are to have merged into the HE Funding Council; and — a smaller but significant point — the governing bodies of LEA-maintained schools have been empowered, from September 1992, to provide adult education classes at their schools without prior consultation with the LEA.

The significance of that modest new power is that it signals a further identification of the school as an entity separate from its LEA, a process which can be traced back to some of the thinking that gave separate duties to LEA and school in respect of special educational needs (1981 Act). It can be said to have culminated in the opting-out provisions of the ERA and the proposal in the Education Bill presented in October 1992 that, on a day to be appointed, governing bodies of LEA-maintained schools should be incorporated.

The scale and pace of primary legislation

Table 1.1 charts in outline the Education Acts since Butler's. The pattern shows that there was little statute-making activity in the fifteen years following the 1944 Act; and, indeed for the 25 years thereafter, primary legislation was mostly of the single-subject kind — to use an educator's term in a legal context. Where innovation could be achieved only after legitimation (such as the establishment of middle schools or encouraging pupils to experience in school time the disciplines of adult work before school-leaving age), the necessary legislation was passed. Some of the Acts were responses to crises: over teachers' pay, or as the result of challenges at law to the Secretary of State's intervention in controversial schemes of school reorganisation.

Table 1.1   Education Acts 1944–1993

1944	●		The Principal Act
1945			
1946	●		'to amend and supplement'
1947			
1948	●		Miscellaneous provisions
1949			
1950			
1951			
1952			
1953	●		Miscellaneous provisions
1954			
1955			
1956			
1957			
1958			
1959	●		more help for aided schools
1960			
1961			
1962	●		awards; school-leaving dates
1963	‡●		first RTA
1964	●		middle schools
1965	‡●		second RTA
1966			
1967	●		voluntary schools
1968	●	‡●	schools, size and character; college government

Table 1.1 (cont'd)

1969		
1970	‡●	handicapped children
1971	‡●	milk
1972		
1973	●●	trusts, awards; work experience
1974		
1975	●	awards, voluntary schools
1976	†● ●	school-leaving dates; comprehensivisation
1977		
1978		
1979	●	repeal of comprehensivisation
1980	●	school government, admissions, reorganisations
1981	●	special educational needs
1982		
1983	●	overseas students
1984	●	education support grants (ESG)
1985	●	FE — goods and services
1986	●●●	ESG; pooling; training grant, school government
1987	‡●	TPCA
1988	●	Education Reform Act
1989		
1990	●	student loans
1991	●	STPCA
1992	●●	FHE; Schools: inspection, information
1993	*●	*Choice and Diversity* legislation

● an Act
‡ now repealed in full
† Education Bill (1992) would repeal
* subject to the will of Parliament

RTA   Remuneration of Teachers Acts 1963, 1965
TCPA   Teachers' Pay and Conditions Act
STCPA School Teachers' Pay and Conditions Act

By contrast, the reformist zeal of ministers in the later 1980s was reflected in the bewildering succession of statutes, specifying in some instances the fine detail of new administrative arrangements, such as procedures for opting out, whereas the detail of the National Curriculum was left in the conventional way for subordinate legislation, in the form of Orders. A process of consolidation was under way by 1987 (Hooper 1987), but had little likelihood of Parliamentary time under a Prime Minister scornful of the very word (Thatcher 1987). The Education Bill of October 1992, however, was avowedly consolidatory in intent as regards two of its largest elements, re-writing of and addition to the special educational needs legislation of 1981 and the grant-maintained procedures of 1988, together with consolidation of school-attendance provisions which the Secretary of State has traced back through the legislation to 1944 (Patten 1992). Politically, Secretary of State Mr Patten seemed freer than Mr Baker to imply a commitment to the longer term; Mr Patten's 'new framework for primary and secondary schools . . . will endure well into the next century'. (Secretaries of State 1992).

Some re-writing was needed in any case. The ERA had been produced in a hurry, and looked like it. Hugo Young had summed it up:

> Hundreds of amendments, most of them the minister's own, were introduced during the parliamentary passage . . . But, as a demonstration of the radical imperative — action before words, decision before debate, the presumption of guilt exceeding all possibility of innocence in the previous way of doing things — the Education Reform Act 1988 had few equals in the first Thatcher term and none in the second.
> (Young 1989)

The Education Acts 1944–1992 (and, prospectively, 1993) now look ragged; the principal Act has been considerably altered and reduced, and some statutes remain in force only because of a few unspent sections in otherwise superseded legislation. 'Construction as one' with the 1944 Act becomes progressively harder as the formulations change over time. As one solid manifestation of the effects of change, the standard work of reference, *The Law of Education*, has grown into a three-volume loose-leaf compilation, the authors (Liell and Saunders 1992) of which consulted the readership about the desirability of going into a third volume. That has now appeared. The ninth edition of what had been through the previous eight, since 1944, single volumes under the title *The New Law of Education* has undergone 22 revisionary supplements and inserts between 1984 and 1993.

Kenneth Poole, whose masterly narrative *Education Law* was published after enactment of the ERA but on a timescale which prevented inclusion of commentary on that Act, argued strongly for consolidation, and drew attention to a much earlier request for just that. In the Second Reading debate on what was to become the Act of 1946, that is, the first amending legislation after Butler's own Act, Butler as Opposition spokesman on education called for consolidation, in order not to confuse the reader. The junior Minister's response was that there was no time for the Parliamentary draftsman to do the necessary groundwork. Poole (1988) comments: 'Governments have found time to innovate but not to consolidate.'

Work continues on an Education (Consolidation) Bill (Mackay 1989). If it is now being prepared for early presentation after the 1992 Bill, the event would imply an end for the time being to controversial lawmaking on education. Conventionally, a consolidation Act is non-controversial, and normally, if there are significant changes in the law to be consolidated, they have to be passed separately and previously. To many that will be a relief, as overload has left little time to ponder over or even properly meet the requirements of the Acts of the past few years. Local management of FE colleges was required under the ERA from 1989, and that Act allowed for incorporation of a college by agreement with its LEA and upon successful application to the Secretary of State, but within four years all this has been overtaken by statutory incorporation of the colleges (and the removal of just over £2bn of relevant expenditure from local government); in Chapter 9, Chris Brooks conveys the sense of shock felt across LEAs at the largely unexpected announcement of the new policy on FE in March 1991 and its rapid translation into law. Grant-maintained schools opted out for a variety of reasons, but one of them must have been a wish to escape, as they perceived their situation, from bureaucratic control; the proposals in the Education Bill will establish funding authorities, one for England and one for Wales, to perform a range of duties, including executive responsibility for the distribution of grant to individual schools and the power to propose significant changes to the character or size of those schools. Though s.52 of the ERA roundly declared it to be the duty of the Secretary of State to maintain the grant-maintained school, the Bill has been equivocal; it is only the detailed wording that shows the funding authority to be acquiring that responsibility.

The legislative changes have come thick and fast:

> and the mazed world,
> By their increase, now knows not which is which.

Further reform before consolidation?

On the other hand, there are educational reforms which promoters outside government would like to see enacted, such as getting to grips with the injustices in the student-awards systems, establishment of a general teaching council for England and Wales, putting a duty upon LEAs to provide nursery education, or, at a more mundane but urgent level, clearing up the uncertainties of the law on home-to-school transport. These are simply items from my shopping list, and other commentators will have their own, as — crucially — will politicians. I suggest, however, that the four examples will feature on several lists, and it is mainly the cost implications which deter Ministers from tackling some widely-identified anomalies.

In a study (1992) I wrote for the Gulbenkian and Sir John Cass's Foundations, I drew attention to several authoritative surveys of the disjunction between mandatory awards for (largely) first-degree courses undertaken (very largely) by students in their late teens and early twenties and, on the other side, the patchy discretionary support available to (sometimes) older and (often) part-time students pursuing courses of a vocational nature, or taking Open University, or other distance- and flexible-learning courses. There was a huge contrast between the 'state' system of mandatory awards, supported by 100 per cent specific funding by the Government, and the discretionary arrangements of 116 LEAs, with much diversity as to availability, coverage and duration. Though it could be argued that there should be scope for the exercise of local discretion, the LEAs themselves had advanced the contrary. As the Council of Local Education Authorities had put it in 1979: 'It is at least questionable whether support on courses necessary for the completion of basic career qualifications should be the subject of local discretion'. The representative body of LEAs of England and Wales was arguing that this was a matter on which the continued exercise of local discretion was open to challenge.

On the proposed general teaching council, the shopping lists of some influential organisations have been published. Creation of a GTC for England and Wales featured as an item in the election manifestos of the Labour and Liberal Democrat parties (Labour Party 1992, Liberal Democrat Party 1992), and was also a recommendation of the House of Commons Education, Science and Arts Committee (ESAC 1990). The Government's response (1990) to the report avoided complete rejection, but 'With a considerable number of new bodies recently created and new initiatives being undertaken, the Government does not consider that the creation of a GTC would in the near future contribute to the success of its education reforms or to an improvement in teacher supply [this being the overall subject of the committee's report]'. Promoters of a statutory GTC, for which that operating in Scotland under the Teaching Council (Scotland) Act 1965 is seen as an analogue rather than a template, have published their proposals, complete with a draft Bill (GTC 1992). John Dobie's chapter in the present book includes commentary on the Scottish GTC.

The 1944 Education Act (s.8(2)(b)) had contained a requirement that the LEA have regard *inter alia* to the need to secure provision of education for the under-fives, but in language that came closer to that of power and discretion rather than duty. Despite lobbying by political, social and educational interests, who drew attention to the great disparities of practice across England and Wales, amendment to the law came, in 1980, by clarification that the provision might be provided by exercise of a power, but that there was no duty (1980 Act, s.24(2)).

The law on home-to-school transport was to have been reformed in what became the 1980 Act, following growing dissatisfaction with the imprecise provisions of the 1944 Act and an authoritative report from DES (Hodges 1973) showing their anachronism. Linkage of transport duties and powers to a defence against prosecution for failing to secure a child's attendance, a position depending on inference from, rather than straightforward reading of, the law, and reliance on the 1944 concept of reasonable walking distance — all make the present statutory provisions look ripe for change. But the Government's preferred vehicle for reform, a discretion for LEAs to charge generally for home-to-school transport, was rejected by the House of Lords, where denominational interests were fully represented, and so the Government dropped the proposal (Howard 1987). Indeed, the junior Minister responsible for schools has frankly admitted:

> [Transport] is a difficult subject, on which there are many different views . . . [An] effort that was made some years ago to alter the arrangements got into dreadful difficulty . . . I remain to be convinced that there is a demonstrably better way of dealing with the entire subject . . . than we have at present . . . I do not say that it is flawless or that it could not be improved, but nobody has yet presented to me a suggestion that is workable, clearly an improvement and containable within any reasonable resource provision.
> (Forth 1992)

It is also worth considering in some depth an area of education where a fundamental review had been promised but not in the event delivered.

Special educational needs: a case study for reform

Though the 1992 Bill offers some greater clarity in its wording of the procedures for assessing special educational needs and where appropriate making, acting upon and maintaining statements of such needs, the Bill stops far short of the kind of review which some of their Lordships were envisaging in a debate Baroness Warnock initiated (House of Lords 1991). The Bill introduces the Special Educational Needs Tribunal, a reform in that which represents a single appeal mechanism for parents to use. It replaces recourse, of at least two separate stages, to the Secretary of State, and to the LEA's own appeals committee. It does not, however, rule out a complaint to the local government ombudsman (the Commissioner for Local Administration), or an action to seek judicial review. Another change for the better is that parents of a statemented child will have the right to express a preference as to the school the child should attend; this should be a formal improvement in most cases, as proper regard to the 1981 Act and the regulations will already have entailed full involvement of the parents in assessing the problems and drafting the prescribed response. In that the 1981 Act envisaged in effect a negotiation with the parents, they already had a stronger power to register preferences than did the generality of parents.

Outstanding problems, however, are great. They include the philosophical: Baroness Warnock admitted to the House that the report of her committee had made 'a rather trendy mistake' in seeking to do away with categories of special need (House of Lords 1991). There were also problems specifically of children whose behaviour disrupted school: they could be regarded, in some cases, as pupils with emotional or behavioural problems — and the very phrase reads as an embarrassing euphemism for the cruel categorisation 'maladjusted' — or simply very badly-behaved children whom the school might exclude and the LEA have difficulty in placing elsewhere.

Very shortly after implementation of the 1981 Act, Baroness Warnock had labelled as 'the fatal weakness' one of the basic principles set out in the report and embedded in the legislation (Warnock 1982). That was the liberal concept of the continuum of special educational needs affecting up to one-fifth of schoolchildren in their careers, one-sixth at any stage, and about one-fiftieth to an extent that would necessitate specific action from outside the mainstream school's resources. The fiftieth, the 2 per cent, might be expected to be covered by statements of special educational need. The statement can be seen as protection in the sense that, in theory, it guarantees the provision which should be made for the child; it can also attract resources for the school where the statemented child is being educated, or, conversely, it can be seen as the means of ensuring removal of a child for whom the school cannot make proper provision to a place which might. The judgement whether or not to make a statement is made within an open-ended framework: the LEA may make a very large number of statements, or very few, or, conceivably, make them in inappropriate cases. The DES guidance in the first few years of the legislation on this sensitive area has been unusually unhelpful. Circular 8/81, of 7 December 1981, virtually subverted Warnock's liberal principle from the start. Of the probable number of statemented children, it said: 'It is expected that the number of such children will correspond approximately to those children now ascertained as handicapped under section 34 of the 1944 Act.' (DES 1981).

The more detailed guidance in Circular 1/83 (since withdrawn) was somewhat more positive and less prejudicial. The Secretary of State, it said, expected that children would have the protection of a statement if they had 'severe or complex learning difficulties which required . . . extra resources in ordinary schools' or if they were to be placed in a special school or unit or an approved independent school. The circular went on, however, to say:

> Formal procedures are not required where ordinary schools provide special educational provision from their own resources in the form of additional tuition and remedial provision, or, in normal circumstances, where the child attends a reading centre or unit for disruptive pupils. (DES 1983)

Before local management of schools, it was difficult to identify a school's 'own' resources; and the phrase 'in normal circumstances' sat in a connotatively unhappy position in a document on special needs.

The Department's advice was improved and updated in Circular 22/89, of 29 September 1989 (DES 1989). The formulation quoted above was not repeated, and the revised guidance wisely focused upon the words of the 1981 Act and the circumstances in which the LEA might 'determine' the special provision to be made for a particular child. There was, however, an inept new wording, insufficiently soundly based upon the Court of Appeal judgement in *R v Secretary of State for Education and Science ex parte Lashford* (1988), which was cited; the Department now implied that not only the LEA but also the headteacher and governing body of a school had the duty, in a particular case, to 'determine' provision. The false impression was corrected in a further revision, in an Addendum (*sic*) issued on 19 March 1992 (DES 1992).

The judgement in *Lashford* is illuminating, and confirms the logical coherence of the Warnock thinking incorporated into the 1981 Act: most children do not have special educational needs (and, indeed, the Act specifically excludes both giftedness or having a language other than English as first language as a cause for identifying special educational needs); where a child has such needs, however, the school may cope with them, within its ordinary work; the child may, however, be considered to require assessment by the LEA; and the assessment may produce evidence on which the LEA concludes that it should determine the provision to be made; in that case, a statement will be drawn up.

Besides these fine distinctions, there has been a cruder source of trouble, not directly to do with the nature of the law. Baroness Warnock has been among many other commentators who have deplored the unavailability of resources specifically to implement the 1981 Act. As a result, some LEAs have been accused of instructing their officers not to proceed to make statements, or to temper the advice given within them, or of allowing the wholly non-statutory concept of a waiting list of children needing forms of special provision. The ombudsman has been involved in some well-publicised cases including the award of monetary compensation, and has produced the charge against one LEA with proportions of statemented children far below the national average that 'a culture had evolved which mitigated (*sic*) against the proper application of the Act' (Pyke 1992a).

Though the Education Bill will empower the Secretary of State to draw up 'a code of practice giving practical guidance' on LEA responsibilities in respect of special needs, that will be on the basis of the 1981 Act as replaced by the Bill's provisions rather than a fundamental review or radical revision of the law's demands. Lady Warnock had argued, at the Second Reading of Lord Campbell of Alloway's Education (Amendment) Bill in the summer of 1992, for reconsideration of the 1981 Act and review of the location of responsibilities for children with special educational needs (Warnock 1992). The Bill was withdrawn after ministerial assurances that there would be Government measures, within the forthcoming legislation, to produce the kinds of reform for which Lord Campbell was calling. As I have suggested above, however, the Education Bill of October 1992 did not equate to the outcome of fundamental reappraisal.

Nor, short of a successful amendment in Parliament, will the consolidated provisions of 1993 on special needs resolve another real problem — real, that is, in the sense of actually experienced — that was made the cause of litigation and then left to local resolution. This is another difficulty of resources, though this one is directly linked to the legislative requirements. The provision which the statement identifies as needed in a particular case may include non-educational as well as educational provision. The most problematic forms of the non-educational are those for which another body has the main statutory responsibility, and speech therapy has proved so far to be the most troublesome example.

Most speech therapists are employed by district health authorities (DHAs) and trusts. From the start of implementation of the 1981 Act, LEAs assumed that the effect of s.5 of the National Health Service Act 1977, and the partnership of DHA colleagues in the procedures and processes of statementing would ensure that any speech therapy required would be provided. In general, that was how things worked. But there were hard cases, especially where the DHA could not meet the full extent of the provision specified, either through lack of cash or because of a shortage of speech therapists (or both). A family in Oxfordshire brought a case against their LEA when the DHA provided only three sessions of speech therapy a week for their child, who had been statemented as requiring five; following judgement for Oxfordshire in the Divisional Court, it was reported that a neighbouring LEA had decided to cut out its provision of such therapy as being a DHA, not LEA, responsibility; the Oxfordshire parents appealed to the Court of Appeal, but the action was abandoned in 1987 when the DHA was able to make the specified provision and the LEA for its part provided the necessary transport (*The Independent* 1987).

One, but only one, element of the problem had been that the 1983 Special Education Regulations (SI 1983/29 as amended, reg. 10(1)(c) (1.)) allowed the LEA to specify in a statement non-educational provision '. . . which unless proposed to be made available by the education authority, [the LEA is] satisfied will be made available by a [DHA] . . .' The LEA had to be satisfied that the DHA would make the provision, but the former authority had no power of direction over the latter, which had no explicit or exclusive statutory duty to make the provision.

Following debates in Committee on the Education Reform Bill, the Government tabled an amendment which was duly included as paragraph 83 of Schedule 12 of the ERA, amending s.7 of the 1981 Act so as to insert reference to a power of the LEA to 'arrange any non-educational provision specified in the statement . . . in such manner as [the LEA considers] appropriate'.

It was established in *R v Lancashire CC ex parte CM* (1989) that speech therapy could be essentially educational or non-educational in character, according to the circumstances. But neither the judgement then nor the 1988 amendment could deal with the practical matter of DHA resources, human or financial, and a 1990 amendment of the 1983 regulations still left the LEA without the power to direct a DHA or anyone else to make non-educational provision.

The LEA thus has either a duty to make provision in a case in which speech therapy appears to be needed for educational reasons, or a discretion to exercise if another authority, the DHA or health service trust, omits to make provision. In circumstances such as the latter, the LEA's power comes very close to a duty, but neither the grant mechanisms for funding LEAs and DHAs nor the numbers of qualified therapists in post have yet been improved to the point at which the LEA could readily meet the likely obligation.

I have dwelt on these problems in the area of special needs at some length, because of their intrinsic importance; the likelihood that, after the 1993 legislation, such matters will feature even more prominently among the remaining responsibilities of LEAs; and because they illustrate the limitations of lawmaking as instruments of national educational policy. As to the first two of those considerations, it is interesting that the Chairman of the ESAC (Sir Malcolm Thornton MP, Conservative, Crosby) called in December 1992 for a delay in the passage of the Education Bill so that there could be some general agreement on securing resources for special needs (Pyke 1992b). His committee had been over the subject before, in a report (ESAC 1987) which is (again, unusually) cited with apparent approval in DES Circular 22/89.

Reflections on common law

As to the intrumentalist approach to legislation, that has been criticised in the overall context of local government but with particular reference to financial devices in two articles by Professor Martin Loughlin (1990, 1991); he doubts whether our legal system is equal to the public-law litigation resulting from the sharp change in the Government's legislative approach of the 1980s. These thoughts are a reminder that the law of education does not exist in a vacuum, but is affected immediately by changes in local authority law and practice, including the continuing instabilities of the financial régimes and now even new structural change.

The common law has not stood still. Here, perhaps, one of the most significant developments for education since 1985 has been the continued growth of judicial review, in which education itself has been an important contributor in the area of the requirements of public consultation, for example over schemes of school reorganisation, and the clarification of the doctrine of legitimate expectation on the part of the public to be consulted in a meaningful way. Leading cases are *R v Brent LBC ex parte Gunning and Ors* (1985) and *R v Sutton LB ex parte Hamlet* (1986). In the former, the LEA was found at fault because of perfunctory consultation on inadequate information, and because the proposals which the LEA adopted were materially different from those on which there had been consultation: it should have discussed the revised proposals in public consultations. The authority was also faulted for not having received and considered, as required by paragraph 7 of part II of the Second Schedule of the 1944 Act, a report from its education committee before reaching its decision. In *Hamlet,* Mr Justice Webster distinguished between the statutory requirement to consult expert bodies which would be able to give technical advice to central government and the more democratic obligation to meet the legitimate expectation of the public to be fully consulted and listened to.

The limitation of the principle of legitimate expectation was further refined by the Court of Appeal in *R v Gateshead MBC ex parte Nichol* (1988): the LEA had not been at fault in consulting on the detail of proposals already formulated still counted as consulting at a formative stage. To go out with no preferred proposals would be like holding a referendum rather than a consultation.

It is for the moment a matter of speculation how the funding authorities (in England the Funding Agency for Schools, and the Schools Funding Council for Wales) which the Education Bill proposes will exercise their functions in respect of school reorganisations. The quangos will lack the background of the local and multi-service authority, whose consultations include detail of non-educational implications such as transport, road safety, welfare, leisure services and town planning — as well as specific educational and financial issues. Kathleen Higgins registers some speculative enquiries in Chapter 6.

Constitutional implications of change: the new commissariats

In 1981, I proposed, and nine years later, elaborated, the concept of the 'new magistracies' in education (Morris 1990). The term was meant both in a classical Roman sense and as in the functions of the Justices of the Peace in county areas until the late nineteenth century. The term connoted not only adjudicatory but also administrative functions, and I applied it to locally-established statutory bodies formed from the LEA but taking to themselves some of the authority's decision-making, or discretion. The original four examples were: the revivified school governing bodies; bodies set up under arrangements subject to the Secretary of State's approval to hear and 'dispose of' complaints about curricular matters under s.23

of the ERA; appeals committees; and the standing advisory councils for religious education (SACREs), mandatory since the 1988 Act.

I identified as main characteristics of the new magistracies their relative smallness (in comparison with education committees or major sub-committees), their being mostly appointed rather than elected, their dependence on the LEA for their servicing, their operating where the LEA had overall or concurrent responsibilities, their inclusion of an outside element in their membership (which is essentially lay), their exercise of powers by delegation or prescription, and their being a buffer or filter between LEA and the Secretary of State. In that analysis, I concentrated on purely educational bodies, but would since have added the training and enterprise councils (TECs), which, though not specified in legislation, have been created under the very broad powers which the Secretary of State for Employment enjoys under the Employment and Training Act 1973.

The new magistracies have been active. In Chapter 3, Brian Unwin gives the picture seen from inside of the governing body's exercise of its responsibilities for the conduct and — as ministers persist in adding (Patten 1992) — management of the schools; and Brian goes into some of the consequences of the blurred distinction. Neil Gill outlines in Chapter 4 the importance of the SACRE, and Graham Platts in Chapter 5 puts the SACRE in context of quality-assurance mechanisms, and he also refers to the workload implications of those and other bodies such as those charged with dealing with curricular complaints. Although relatively few such complaints have been handled formally under section 23 of ERA, each one is nevertheless time-consuming and therefore expensive. Apart from the Education Bill's replacement of the local appeals committee, in cases involving special needs, by a local tribunal of the Special Educational Needs Tribunal, and the evidence from the National Consumer Council that the complaints machinery is underused because its existence is insufficiently known (Harris 1992), the new magistracies have had their responsibilities expanded.

Professor John Stewart has picked up the phrase 'new magistracies' and has run with it (Stewart 1992). It is noteworthy that national newspapers at the end of 1992 gave some prominence to his comments on the constitutional implications of the growth of the new magistracies (Wintour 1992, Timmins 1992).

But I now believe that an additional tier has to be described, that of the new commissariats in education. This category comprises the two funding agencies, the FE Funding Councils (one for England, with regional advisory committees and their offices, and one FEFC for Wales), and the education associations whom the Secretary of State may appoint, in the words of the Bill, 'to secure, so far as it is practicable to do so, the elimination of any deficiencies in the conduct of a school' found to be failing. Characteristics of the commissariats are that: they — or at least their chairs and chief executiveships — are paid offices (it was tempting otherwise to label the education associations as stipendiary magistracies); the Secretary of State appoints the commissaries; the funding comes from the national exchequer; and the commissariats have their own offices and staffs.

The commissariats exercise powers in place of the LEA, though there is some concurrence. For example, the Funding Agency for Schools (FAS) and its Welsh counterpart will be involved in a spectrum of responsibility alongside the LEA before the 'exit point', and thereafter the LEA has powers to act where the FAS has a duty to secure the provision of school places. The Further Education Funding Council (FEFC) and LEA are linked in a *chiasmus* of powers and duties in respect of FE; Chapter 9 gives the detail. Both the Funding Agency for Schools (FAS) and the FEFC are given statutory functions for their areas, a phrase which the 1944 Act applied to the operations of the LEA, but, in the case of either quango, the 'area' is the whole of England. Both quangos, astonishingly, have responsibilities for individuals, the FEFC for students with special needs, and the FAS for children whose placement at a school has to be the subject of a direction.

I have chosen 'commissariat' as a label, since its connotations are Continental and sufficiently various. 'Commissions' would mislead, since it is a term of art in our systems, including the area of central government control over the functions of local authorities where directions to act or to cease certain activities have failed. 'Commissars' would have been unnecessarily pejorative.

It would probably be correct to place the School Curriculum and Assessment Authority (SCAA) in the new commissariat category, even though its antecedents go back to the Secondary Schools Examination Council, the Curriculum Study Group and the Schools Council. The character of the most recent forbears, the tightening statutory remit, and the close attention apparently paid by ministers in selecting members — and the facility to correspond directly with schools over executive functions and policy matters — surely imply a commissary role.

The Lord Chancellor is to appoint to the SEN Tribunal those of its members who are required to be legally qualified, and the Secretary of State appoints the lay panellists. The constitutional and procedural detail will be set out in regulations. As a constitutionally more dignified body than the LEA appeals committee sitting on an SEN case, the Tribunal surely ranks as a new commissariat.

Most, but not all, of the new commissariats are quangos. They have to take instruction as deemed necessary by the Secretary of State. For example, the Further Education Funding Council and the FEFC for Wales, and the HE Funding Councils for England and for Wales, may have imposed upon them by sections 7 and 68 respectively of the FHE Act 1992 grant conditions which in turn will place conditions on the funding allocated by the councils to institutions. The Funding Agency for Schools and its Welsh counterpart may be directed by the Secretary of State to cease funding a particular school. Also under the Education Bill, the SCAA will have to comply with any directions made by the Secretary of State.

Table 1.2   New magistracies and commissariats

New magistracies
   school governing bodies
   admissions and exclusions appeals committees
   SACREs
   bodies to deal with s.23 ERA complaints

New commissariats
   the HE funding councils
   the FE funding councils
   the funding authorities for grant-maintained schools
   the SEN Tribunal
   education associations
   the SCAA
   OFSTED

Additional notes
1   Since 1989 HE, and since 1993 FE, colleges have enjoyed a greater measure of autonomy, with corporate status under the funding councils. Their detachment from LEA administration and location in national funding arrangements imply commissary status, though the Secretary of State's interest in gubernatorial appointments lapses after inauguration. I am inclined to regard grant-maintained school governing bodies as magistracies, because of their essentially local role.
2   TECs resemble new magistracies in their local nature, and the fact that the Secretary of State for Employment was involved in setting them up, but their functions in administering national training schemes and disbursing departmental resources, and their having offices of their own, imply commissary status.
3   At the risk of being accused of fancifulness, I propose a third category: the janissaries. The Turkish origin of the word approximates to 'new militia', which seems apposite for the registered inspectors and their teams.

A parallel requirement is placed upon Her Majesty's Chief

Inspectors in England and in Wales by sections 2(6) and 6(6) respectively of the Schools Act 1992 to 'have regard to such aspects of government policy as the Secretary of State may direct'. I am inclined to categorise OFSTED, the Office for Standards in Education, which the Schools Act formally calls the Office of Her Majesty's Chief Inspector of Schools, as a commissariat, but the judgement may have to be revised in the light of how it works in practice. Certainly, the first holder of the post of HMCI for England has been quick to claim greater independence for his service than HMI under the old auspices (Sutherland 1992).

Professor Sutherland's letter to *The Independent*, cited above, was a response to two misunderstandings in that usually well-informed paper, asserting that HMI had been abolished. The mistake is, though, understandable. Responsibility for quality assurance in HE and FE has passed to the funding councils, and some of the old mystique of HMI has gone with the explicit duties set out in the Schools Act. The administrative responsibilities of OFSTED, however, are much greater than those of HMI hitherto: it has to make and maintain the register of those inspectors who are thereby qualified to lead inspectoral teams; it has to provide or commission training for all team members, including the lay inspectors; it lets the contracts for the periodic full inspections and superintends the processes and outcomes of inspection.

Table 1.2 lists the new magistracies and new commissariats.

The changing character of the LEA

Inspection vividly exemplifies the LEA's significant loss of power. Under s.14 of the Schools Act, an LEA may have a schools inspection service, which may tender for the periodic inspections, within the rules of OFSTED, but it must be self-financing and may operate only in the LEA's area (DFE 1992). Otherwise, the LEA has power, under s.15, to inspect a school it maintains, but only if:

(a) there is a need to know; and
(b) it is not reasonably practicable for the LEA to find out by some other means.

The authority's officer 'shall have at all reasonable times a right of entry to the premises of the school', but the former penalty for obstructing him or her has not survived amendment of the 1944 provisions. Obstructing HMI or a registered inspector, however, does incur liability to a fine on conviction.

There is a depressing catalogue of other LEA losses: the collective right to negotiate pay and the important other conditions of service with the unions; the polytechnics and other large HE colleges (with the symbolic abolition of the term 'public sector HE' (Secretary of State 1987)); mainstream FE colleges, including sixth form colleges, previously accounted by law as schools; the power to determine school staffing establishments; those schools which have successfully bid to opt out; control of the main in-service training budget (the specific grant aided expenditure being 'devolved' because it may not lawfully be 'delegated'); and — though it is arguable how much there was formerly to lose — general curricular oversight.

In the years of intensive legislation on education, there have also been other changes, outside but directly affecting the service, which have seriously limited the discretion of the LEA, notably the requirement to put more and more of the specific services to competitive tender, and, above all, the revision, replacement and then further replacement of the system of central government grant for local authority expenditure, with strict 'capping' to control overall spending levels. With a financial framework in which only some 15 per cent of local revenue is locally raised, and a legal system in which there is no power of general competence (the authority being broadly constrained within its statutory or common-law *vires*), discretion becomes a rare commodity.

Change and transition

The reader will already have appreciated that this book has been written while significant primary legislation was being debated in Parliament. We have tried to confine our description to the situation as at 31 December 1992, though we have anticipated much of the Education Act 1993 on the basis of the White Paper *Choice and Diversity* (Cmd 2021) and the Bill as presented first to the Commons in October 1992. The following chapters refer variously (and explicitly) to the White Paper, the Bill, and the expected Act. We have tried to make the citations in their most relevant forms — for example by reference to the White Paper where the policy background is being discussed, or to the broad provisions of the prospective Act. To the charge that we should have waited some months, there is a ready answer based on recent experience. It will be some time before the newest 'law of education' is fully in place and operational. Meanwhile all education authorities have to review their roles and functions, which can most sensibly be done against the background of the present and immediately foreseeable legal position; in the English and Welsh county areas, there is a running process of structural review; and Chapter 2 describes the likely prospects for the Scottish education authorities (and John Dobie also points to the similarities and differences in educational reforms north and south of the Border).

In a simple political chronology, there have been uncertainties over: whether the FHE and inspection proposals in the 1991 (Schools and FHE) Bills would reach the statute book before the 1992 election; if enacted, they might not have been implemented because of a change of government; there was intense speculation in the summer of 1992 about the contents of the White Paper; there was uncertainty about possible revision of those proposals that were then published, as the White Paper invited comment; the next stage of doubt preceded the Bill; and there was keen expectation of significant amendments, including especially those tabled by the Government. Finally — in the legislative process — there will have been speculation about the several implementation dates.

But these are now quite common features of a large public service high on the political agenda, and with a recent history of rapid legislation and rapid amendment. The uncertainties which would have obtained in any case can still apply: over the interpretation of the legislation in administrative practice and the judgements of the courts; and through the capacity of any large service to adapt, absorb and even ignore elements of radicalism, even when that is enshrined in Acts of Parliament.

Imponderables include the pace of the growth of the grant-maintained sector of schooling. The White Paper envisaged 'a new and evolutionary framework for the organisation of our schools' (paragraph 1.7). Paragraph 1.67 warned that, though the emphasis in that document was necessarily on new legislation, there were existing policies still being put in train, new responsibilities being exercised by governing bodies, and new parental initiatives (presumably a reference to balloting on grant-maintained status).

It is presently for speculation to what extent the new inspectoral arrangements will mean that HMI has been transmogrified. Consultations on a common funding formula for grant-maintained schools were launched before Christmas 1992, but as part of a developmental process; nevertheless, there are grounds for believing that the CFF will produce a tendency for convergence, so that ultimately all schools, including those still maintained by LEAs, will be funded in broadly similar ways.

What can be predicted with some confidence, though, is that funding levels will remain controversial — as will the other outcomes of an intensive programme of primary legislation.

References

Baker, Rt. Hon. K. (Secretary of State) (1987) Second Reading debate on Education Reform Bill *Hansard* 1 December, col. 771.

Busher, H. and Saran, R. (1992) *Teachers' Conditions of Employment* Kogan Page, chaps 2 and 3.

Council of Local Education Authorities (1979) Minute 5 of meeting of 15 January, adopting 'Student Awards: Report of a Working Party', December 1978.

DES (1981) *Education Act 1981* Circ. 8/81, 7 December, para. 9.

DES (1983) *Assessments and Statements of Special Educational Needs* Circ. 1/83, 31 January, paras 14, 15.

DES (1989) *Assessments and Statements of Special Educational Needs: Procedures within the Education, Health and Social Services* Circ. 22/89, 29 September, para. 30.

DES (1992) [title as DES 1989] Addendum to Circular 22/89, 10 March, p. 3.

DFE (1992) *Inspecting Schools: A Guide to the Inspection Provisions of the Education (Schools) Act 1992* draft circular 9 November, para. 51.

ESAC (1987) *Special Educational Needs: Implementation of the Education Act 1981* Third Report, Session 1986–87 (HoC 201-I).

ESAC (1990) *The Supply of Teachers for the 1990s* Second Report, Session 1989–90 (HoC 208-I), para. 26.

Forth, E. (Parliamentary Under Secretary of State) (1992) speech in Standing Committee E on Education Bill *Hansard* 8 December, col. 567.

GTC (England & Wales) (1992) *Proposals for a Statutory General Teaching Council for England and Wales.*

HM Government (1990) *The Government's Response to the 2nd Report from the Education, Science and Arts Committee: The Supply of Teachers for the 1990s* (Cm 1148), July 1990, p. 8.

Harris, N. (1992) *Complaints about Schooling* National Consumer Council, pp. 119–24.

Hodges, M.W. (Chairman) (1973) *School Transport* DES/HMSO.

Hooper, Baroness (1987) Written Answer *House of Lords Hansard* 17 December, col. 909.

House of Lords (1991) debate on Children with Special Educational Needs *House of Lords Hansard* 20 November, cols 938–74.

Howard, A. (1987) *RAB: The Life of R.A. Butler* Cape, pp 360–1.

Kerry, Sir M. (1986) 'Administrative law and judicial review' *Public Administration* **64**(2) p.172.

Labour Party (1992) *It's Time to Get Britain Working Again* Manifesto, p. 18.

Lawrence, I. (1992) *Power and Politics at the Department of Education and Science* Cassell.

Liberal Democrat Party (1992) *Changing Britain for Good* Manifesto, p. 31.

Liell, P. and Saunders, J. B. (1992) *The Law of Education* (9th edn revised) Butterworths.

Loughlin, M (1990)'Innnovative financing in local government: the limits of legal instrumentalism' *Public Law* Autumn, p. 372ff.

Loughlin, M. (1991) *Public Law* Winter, pp. 582–6.

Mackay, Lord (Lord Chancellor) (1989) Written Answer *House of Lords Hansard* 9 March, col 1692.

Morris, R. (1990) *Central and Local Control of Education After the Education Reform Act 1988* Longman.

Morris, M. and Griggs, C. (1988) *Education — The Wasted Years? 1973–1976* Falmer.

Morris, R. (1992) *Discretionary Awards* Report to Gulbenkian UK and Sir John Cass's Foundations, unpublished.

Patten, Rt. Hon. J. (Secretary of State) (1992) Second Reading debate on Education Bill *Hansard* 9 November, col. 633, 634.

Poole, K. (1988) *Education Law* Sweet and Maxwell, p. *v.*

Pyke, N (1992a) 'County had "no-statement" culture') *The Times Educational Supplement* 11 September.

Pyke, N. (1992b) 'Tory calls for extra special needs staff' *The Times Educational Supplement* 11 December.

Secretaries of State (1992) *Choice and Diversity* (Cm 2021) HMSO, para. 1.7.

Secretary of State (1987) *Higher Education: Meeting the Challenge* (Cm 114) HMSO, para. 4.2.

Simon, B. (1991) *Education and the Social Order 1940–1990* Lawrence and Wishart, chap. 11.

Stewart, J. (1992) *Accountability to the Public* European Policy Forum, p. 7.

Sutherland, S. (1992) 'School inspectors alive and well' letter to *The Guardian* 31 December, printed 4 January 1993.

Thatcher, Rt. Hon. M. (Prime Minister) (1987) quoted at Conservative Party Conference by Goodwin, S. and Pienaar, J. 'No slacking on reform, Thatcher promises' *The Independent* 10 October.

The Independent (1987) 'Boy in speech therapy fight to get treatment' 27 March.

Timmins, N. (1992) 'Unelected bodies creating 'Crisis of accountability" *The Independent* 30 December.

Warnock, M. (1982) 'Children with special educational needs in ordinary schools' *Journal of the College of Preceptors* **32** (3) p. 61.

Warnock, Baroness (1992) speech on Second Reading of Education (Amendment) Bill *House of Lords Hansard* 11 June, col. 1396.

Wintour, P. (1992) '"Magisterial elite" running services' *The Guardian* 30 December; and 2nd leader in same edition: — 'The Quangos Keep Coming'.

Young, H. (1989) *One of Us* (1st edn.) Macmillan, p. 521.

2 Scotland: 'Wha's like us?'

John Dobie

Introduction

In Chapter 1 to this edition of *Education and the law* reference has been made to the great changes which have taken place in the way the education service is organised and administered since the publication of the first edition in 1986. The part of the United Kingdom which lies to the north of Hadrian's Wall has been only partially shielded from the winds of change which continue to blow so strongly in England and Wales. The position can best be illustrated initially by referring to a recent exchange of correspondence following a meeting between representatives of the Education Committee of the Convention of Scottish Local Authorities (COSLA) and Lord James Douglas-Hamilton, the Minister for Education and Housing of the Scottish Office. The meeting, held on 19 August 1992, had been an opportunity to discuss recent developments and proposals in relation to national testing, school management, opted-out schools and rationalisation, the Parents' Charter and teachers' salaries arrangements. The following statement was issued by Councillor Elizabeth Maginnis, Convener of the Education Committee:

> 'After a period of rapid change to the legislation for schools which has caused serious disruption to the educational process, there is now a need to reach agreement on the way ahead for the education service and achieve wide ownership of that policy. The Minister himself has been laying stress recently on such words as consolidation, stability and partnership and COSLA pressed the Minister today to apply these principles to any further proposals for the education services. We also asked the Minister to call a halt on new legislation on education while current changes are absorbed and major changes to the curriculum framework successfully completed. Unfortunately, the Minister's response to the various points put to him by COSLA suggests that, in practice, he has little inclination to co-operate with education authorities.'

In response the Minister for his part indicated 'that there was a time for consultation, for decision and for calm and steady progress. Each was important and we must seek to consolidate on the basis of the changes made and to ensure that significant progress continues. I assured you that I would be listening to all those with an interest and role to play in securing improvements in the quality of education in schools in Scotland.'

The national framework

These perceptions of the impact of change in the education service in the late 1980s and early 1990s need to be set in the context of the separate education system which operates in Scotland. It is important to remember that while there are many parallels with the system south of the Border, Scottish education has its own legislation, and is in the main conducted separately under the provisions of Education (Scotland) Acts. This separate tradition stems from the first Act of importance which was passed in 1696. This provided that a school should be established in every parish that did not have one, with a secondary school in every town. A series of Acts through the years followed, and the main current legislation is set out in the Education (Scotland) Act 1980 (a consolidation of previous Acts) and as subsequently amended in certain respects by more recent Acts. The Education (Scotland) Act 1980, as amended, covers general requirements in relation to pupils, maintained schools of all categories, placing in schools, grant-aided and independent schools, and makes provision for the Secretary of State to present regulations to which authorities must conform in carrying out certain functions.

The more recent Acts, as detailed below, have in the main sought to establish a system which gives greater emphasis to parental rights and participation in the management of schools.

These recent acts include:

1 Education Scotland Act 1981
2 The Education (No.2) Act 1986
3 School Boards (Scotland) Act 1988
4 Self Governing Schools etc, (Scotland) Act 1989

This list of Acts when contrasted with England and Wales may seem relatively slim. However, when set against upwards of 40 regulation orders and an increasing tendency to issue 'mandatory guidelines', it illustrates that contrary to myth the Scots have not emerged unscathed.

This separate tradition is administered and supported on a national basis by the Scottish Office Education Department whose headquarters are located in Edinburgh. As the Secretary of State for Scotland has responsibility for all departments, a junior minister carries immediate responsibility for the education service.

Education authorities

Responsibility for the provision of school education in Scotland rests largely with 9 regional and 3 islands councils as education authorities. Education authorities are under a statutory duty to secure adequate and efficient provision of school education for their area. They also have a duty to ensure the provision of further education, and powers to provide nursery education. From 1 April 1993 their duty as regards further education will change: they will retain a duty in respect of community education and a power to provide further education.

In September 1991 the Government published the Parents' Charter in Scotland, and stated its intention to explore how school boards could be encouraged to develop their work. Against that background the administration of education at school level was addressed by a consultation paper 'School Management: The Way Ahead' issued by the Scottish Office Education Department in March 1992. That paper envisaged a substantial degree of devolution of the management of school administration and school budgets to school level. Decisions affecting schools would as far as possible be taken by the headteachers, with school boards having a guaranteed consultative role, within budgets assigned by the education authority. Subsequently, the Scottish Office Education Department has issued a consultative paper on the draft guidelines which education authorities should take into account in formulating a scheme for devolved management to schools. Education authorities had until February 1993 to comment on the draft guidelines. Thereafter, revised guidelines were to be issued at the end of March 1993 and education authorities will be required to put in place a scheme approved by the Secretary of State by 31 July 1993. The scheme must be fully in place to cover all schools by 1 April 1996.

In a consultative document on the reorganisation of local government in Scotland ('The Structure of Local Government in Scotland — Shaping the New Councils') it has been indicated that no action stemming from the Government's consideration of the issue of devolved management will remove from education authorities their statutory responsibility for ensuring the provision of education in their areas, and education authorities will continue to provide, or arrange for the provision of, a wide range of support services for schools, their staff and their pupils. However, it is important to recognise that the Government is also committed to the principle of self-governing schools in Scotland and has encouraged primary and secondary schools to apply for self-governing status. However, to-date, no education authority schools have so far been granted this status. In the four cases where moves in this direction have been made, all have been rejected mainly on the grounds that they have sought such status against a closure decision on grounds of viability. It is fair, therefore, to say that in the context of 2,946 education authority schools in Scotland the interest in opting-out is minuscule at the present time.

However, it will be apparent that the changing role of education authorities in further education, and under such devolved school management arrangements as may be determined, taken together with the potential developments flowing from the promotion of self-governing status for schools, are important background factors in any consideration of the place of education in the new local government structure.

As indicated earlier the Government's consultative paper on a new local government structure for Scotland is at the time of writing out to consultation. In essence single tier authorities will come into operation and education will need to find its place in a unitary system. The Government's proposals proffer four separate structures all of which, as presaged by the Prime Minister at the Conservative Party conference held in Brighton in the autumn of 1992, involve the break-up of Strathclyde Regional Council. In its consultative paper the Government describes its views about the place of Education in a uniform system. It states that under the present arrangements education authorities vary widely in size from Strathclyde, with a population of 2.3 million, to Orkney with a population of some 19,570. The Wheatley Commission, which made recommendations for the 1975 local government organisation in Scotland, expressed a view that an education authority serving less than 200,000 people would face difficulties in providing an acceptable standard of service. The Government suggests that this has not turned out to be the case in practice. In some instances the larger education authorities provide specialist services for the smaller on a repayment basis: and in other cases the small authorities look to colleges of education and similar institutions for consultancy services. Broadly speaking, it feels that the larger the number of authorities, the more need there will be for joint or consultancy arrangements: and in a system with few or no very large authorities it might be necessary for new specialised provision in certain areas to be undertaken by other agencies such as colleges of education, by the private sector or centrally.

The consultative paper then goes on to set out the Government's view about the advantages and disadvantages of the four separate systems as follows:

A 15 unit structure which would entail relatively little change from the present arrangements. By aligning education authority boundaries with those of health boards it would facilitate co-ordination in such areas as the provision of specialised services for pupils with special educational needs. In the Government's view in the larger authorities any present difficulties arising from remoteness of the authority from the population served might continue. These difficulties could be reduced by the combined effect of the proposed developments in school management and of divisional or area structures aimed at the decentralisation of decision making.

The second option would be a 24 unit structure. The Government believes that this would provide a workable structure with little increase in the number of smaller authorities. While the arrangements that would be required to move from the present structure to a structure of 24 units would necessarily be more complex than those entailed in a 14 unit structure, there is no reason to suppose that the arrangements or the final structure would give rise to major difficulties.

A 35 unit structure is also outlined for consideration. Under this possible structure, 12 of the proposed mainland authorities would be smaller than any of the present mainland authorities, and some degree of joint provision of specialised services might well be necessary. At this level, the smaller authorities might also find it difficult to undertake effective rationalisation of school provision, particularly since in some cases it might be necessary for authorities to take account of the position in neighbouring areas. At the same time, the option would have the advantage of giving each authority a clear local identity which some of the larger regions may at present lack.

Finally, the Government has identified a 51 unit structure. This structure would represent a radical change from the present arrangements with 37 of the 48 mainland authorities being smaller than the present smallest mainland authority. With this number of authorities, effective rationalisation of school provision would be very difficult in some — particularly urban areas. Substantial joint, and indeed central, provision of specialised services would also seem essential. Some of the small authorities might face difficulty in managing education effectively and economically.

Needless to say local government organisations (and their staff) are in ferment again as the pros and cons of the proposals are examined, costed and debated. Whatever the outcome a considerable period of disruption for the administration of the education service lies ahead for Scotland until 1996 (and possibly with effects beyond that time).

It is perhaps ironic that the 35 unit option, which cannot be ruled out, will broadly reflect the organisational pattern of *ad hoc* education authorities as existed in 1930.

Mr A.L. Young, former Director of Education of Aberdeenshire until 1975, described in a history of the Association of Directors of Education in Scotland, *The First Twenty Five Years*, the *ad hoc* education authorities as they had developed:

> The Education (Scotland) Act 1918 received the royal assent on 21 November 1918, ten days after the signing of the armistice that ended the Kaiser's war. The Act transferred the responsibility for the public schools of Scotland from 947 school boards and 39 secondary education committees to the education authorities of five burghs (Glasgow, Edinburgh, Dundee, Aberdeen and Leith) and 33 counties. A Boundaries Extension Act of 1920 incorporated Leith in the City of Edinburgh. Kinross shared a director with Clackmannan till 1930 and then combined with Perthshire, and Moray and Nairn also amalgamated in 1930, bringing the number of authorities to 35. Three counties have changed their names — Forfarshire has become Angus, Haddingtonshire has become East Lothian, and Linlithgowshire has become West Lothian.
>
> The new authorities were *ad hoc* bodies, elected to deal with education only. The first election of these authorities was held in the spring of 1919 and the system of proportional representation was used. Elections were held thereafter triennially until 1928. In 1930 (under the Local Government (Scotland) Act 1929) education became the responsibility of the County Councils and, in the case of the cities, of the Town Councils.

Retinens vestigia famae ?

School boards

In November 1988 Government legislation for the establishment of school boards in Scotland was approved. Prior to that time s.125(1) of the Local Government (Scotland) Act 1973 required an education authority to appoint bodies to discharge, subject to any directions given by the authority, 'such of the functions of management and supervision of educational establishments or groups of educational establishments under the control of the authority (including functions relating to attendance thereat) as the authority shall determine'. Thus school councils were established. The composition of school councils included representatives of parents, teachers and at least one person interested in the promotion of religious education. Other than these mandates, authorities were free to decide on the constitution, composition and functions of the councils. Following the passage of the School Boards (Scotland) Act 1988, boards for individual schools replaced school councils, which had operated for groups of schools on an area basis. There is now a parental majority on a board, whose membership also comprises co-opted members and teaching staff representatives. The regional/island councillor for the area may attend, but is not in membership and does not have a vote. Boards have some involvement in senior staff appointments, but their direct budgetary power is restricted to approval of capitation expenditure. The headteacher must refer to the board the capitation element of the budget, but is encouraged to discuss the whole resources and financial position with it. It has to be said that the development of school boards in Scotland has not been as enthusiastically received as the Government would have wished. Approximately 30 per cent of schools have failed to establish boards and many others have required by-elections in order to achieve the minimum number of members. As in the case of opting-out, there is no real evidence to show that Scottish parents wish to assume significant responsibilities in the day-to-day management of their schools.

As referred to earlier in the section on education authorities, the Government is now planning to extend the involvement of school boards in their approval of devolved school management schemes. These schemes are required to take into account guidelines issued by the Scottish Office Education Department. If the schemes are to be approved they must contain:

- responsibility for the school's budget to be devolved to the headteacher, with a specific consultative role for school boards;
- methods of budget allocation that are clearly set out and straightforward to understand;
- at a minimum, provision for devolved budgets covering staffing, furniture, fixtures and fittings, minor repairs and maintenance, supplies and services and energy costs;
- at the outset, decisions to be taken at school level on a minimum of 80 per cent of all expenditure identified as relating to the school;
- provision for funds to be carried over from one year to the next;
- the ability to transfer funds from one budget head to another;
- schools to be able to choose suppliers of services, for example, for minor repairs to property;
- phasing-in of the new arrangements between now and 1996.

Admissions

In the arrangements for admission to schools there are some distinctive features in Scottish legislation. The right of appeal to the sheriff is such a distinctive feature. The sheriff is a judge whose powers are approximately equivalent to those of a circuit court judge, although there is no exact equivalent in the English legal system.

Two sections of the 1981 Act amend the part of the 1980 Act which deals with children requiring special education. These amendments largely cover the sections of the 1980 Act which dealt with children with special educational needs. The Scottish legislation refers to the 'recording' of children, which is similar to the statement about children and, again, an appeal can be made to the sheriff against a placing decision.

Changes to schools

There are some points of difference in the establishment, discontinuance and alteration of schools by education authorities. The particular difference is referred to in s.22A–D of the 1980 Act inserted by section 6 of the 1981 Act whereby, by regulations made under the Act, the Secretary of State requires proposals to discontinue a school to be submitted to him only in prescribed cases. These include cases where alternative provision, especially in county areas, would mean an unreasonable travelling distance for pupils or where a proposal would mean that all or some of the pupils would no longer receive school education where adequate arrangements had been made for religious instruction.

Although in other cases an education authority has power to discontinue a school, the procedure to be followed in carrying out consultations is prescribed by the regulations.

In this respect there has been one major case of significance, when the father of a pupil at London Street Primary School, Edinburgh, petitioned for a judicial review of Lothian Regional Council's decisions in respect of proposals for that and two other schools. The Lord Ordinary in dismissing the petition said that:

> Education authorities are obliged by regulations to consult the parents of children at a school before making any decision to discontinue or relocate it, but there is no requirement that a set of proposals pertaining to several schools be treated as a package. Accordingly, the parents of pupils at one school which was to be discontinued did not have to be consulted about the possible relocation of another school to the site of the discontinued one. (*Shaw v Lothian Regional Council*, 26 August 1992)

Religion

There is no 'dual' voluntary system in Scotland. The Education (Scotland) Act 1918 provided for the transfer, on agreed terms, of voluntary schools (mainly Roman Catholic and Scottish

Episcopalian) to the state system. This means that in any case where the Secretary of State is satisfied, upon representations made to him by any church or denominational body acting on behalf of the parents of children belonging to the church or denominational body, and after inquiries are made, that a new school is required, it is lawful for an education authority to provide a school.

It is also lawful for those vested with the title of any school independently established after 1918 to which the relevant section of the Act of 1918 would have applied had the school been in existence on that date, with the consent of the Secretary of State, to transfer the school to an education authority, which is bound to accept the transfer upon terms as to price, rent or other consideration as may be agreed. There are now no Scottish Episcopalian (the equivalent of Church of England) maintained schools.

The Authority appoints staff, but Roman Catholic candidates must be approved by the church as to their religious beliefs. In recent times there has been a clarification of this arrangement whereby s.21(2) of the Education Act 1980 was amended by paragraph 8(7) of Schedule 10 of the Self Governing Schools etc. (Scotland) Act 1989. In the early 1980s the Secretary of State had held in the case of *Mrs Ruddy versus Tayside Regional Council* that *fresh approval was not required* when a member of staff was subsequently promoted and continued to teach in the same school. Following representations from the Roman Catholic hierarchy the new provisions in the 1989 Act changed that position so that approval was required in the case of any post irrespective of whether the candidate was internal or external. The wording of the Act now states that 'A teacher appointed to any post of any such school by the education authority ... shall require to be approved as regards his religious belief and character by representatives of the church or denominational body in whose interest the school has been conducted'. The words 'any post' make it clear that the Church has an unfettered right to exercise its power of veto so that any legal appeal would be unavailing. However, teachers are now entitled to have reasons for the Church's objection to be stated in writing.

Ss.8–10 of the 1980 Act deal with religious instruction and require that where by custom religious education has been given in schools under an education authority, it shall not be lawful for an authority to discontinue religious observance unless and until a resolution in favour of such discontinuance has been approved by the majority of the local government electors for an education area voting in a poll taken for this specific purpose. Parents may withdraw any pupil from instruction in religious subjects and from any religious observance in school if they so desire.

There is no 'conscience clause' in the Scottish legislation under which a teacher may opt out of religious observances in school and from giving religious instruction, although there is such a clause in England. Schools are not required to hold a daily act of corporate worship.

The making of a syllabus for religious education does not require elaborate arrangements to produce an agreed syllabus. The Scottish Consultative Council on the Curriculum, the principal advisory body of the Secretary of State on all matters pertaining to the school curriculum, guides development in religious education as in other areas.

School staff

Requirements relating to the employment of staff in primary schools are still founded in the Schools (Scotland) Code 1956 amended by the Schools General (Scotland) Regulations 1975. Guidance from the Secretary of State on the establishment of promoted and other posts is currently based on *draft* circulars issued by the Scottish Office Education Department in 1988 and by the Scottish Joint Negotiating Committee (Teaching Staff in School Education) from 1987 onwards.

Requirements relating to secondary school staff are again set out in the Regulations, but they have to be read along with guidance on the establishment of promoted posts. In 1988 the Scottish Office Education Department also suggested model staffing arrangements in draft circular form.

Salaries and conditions of service are negotiated in the Scottish Joint Negotiating Committee (Teaching Staff in School Education) set up under and in the terms of ss.91–97D of the 1980 Act. Decisions are intimated to every education authority by circular which have binding effect. The salaries and conditions of service of educational psychologists and advisers are also dealt with by this committee.

Arising from an agreement reached in the Scottish Joint Negotiating Committee (TSSE), the following provisions relating to working hours, class contact and class size are standard for teachers employed by Scottish education authorities. However, it is possible for education authorities to conclude local agreements to vary these provisions. Such local agreements are reported to and ratified by the Scottish Joint Negotiating Committee (TSSE).

The standard provisions are:

1 Normal working hours are $32^1/_2$ hours per week, exclusive of lunch breaks and intervals.

2 Teachers are required to attend school during the normal school day but there are flexible arrangements for the balance of time within normal working hours which is outside the normal school day. During this period essential non-teaching duties (for example, preparation, correction) are carried out, either on school premises or elsewhere at the teacher's discretion.

3 Teachers undertaking teaching duties during the period between the end of the school day and 6.30 pm ('twilight classes') are paid for these duties.

4 The amount of class contact time a teacher works must not exceed the limits imposed by the following:

Primary Teachers   A maximum of 25 hours' class contact each week during the normal working hours.

Secondary Teachers   A minimum of 200 minutes of non-class contact each week during normal school hours.

5 The maximum class size for time-tabled classes is as follows:

		Number of pupils Normal Maximum	Upper limit
Primary		33	39
Composite classes		a maximum of 25	
Secondary	Years 1–2	33	39
	Year 3	33	39
	Year 4	30	34
	Years 5–6	30	
Practical		20	

6 Guaranteed provision of cover after a teacher's third day of absence.

It will be recognised that there are three significant areas of existing arrangements in Scotland which do not exist in England and Wales, i.e.:

• maximum class size;
• definition of contact and non-contact time; and
• the guaranteed provision of cover after a teacher's third day of absence.

Recently a move by the employers to reinterpret the absence cover agreement was eventually frustrated by action taken by the teachers' unions in the courts.

The difference between Scotland and England and Wales in relation to the definition of teachers' time can be usefully illustrated as in Table 2.1.

Table 2.1

Scotland		Hours	England and Wales	Hours
Pupil Year	190 days	1045	'Directed Time'	1265
In-Service days	5 days	27.5	spread, reasonably, over 195 days at work with a teaching requirement of 190 days.	
Parents Meetings	up to 30 hrs	30		
Planned Activity Time	up to 50 hrs	50		
Total		**1152.5**	**Total**	**1265**

Note	Note
'It is recognised that the balance of the teacher's duties on and off the school premises requires additional working time beyond that specified above. It is neither possible nor desirable to specify this precisely. However for planning purposes and to prevent the imposition on teachers of excessive workloads authorities will adopt a 35 hour week'. [1365 hours]	A teacher shall, in addition to the above mentioned requirements, work such additional hours as may be needed to enable him/her to discharge effectively his/her professional duties, including, in particular, the marking of pupils' work, the writing of reports on pupils and the preparation of lessons, teaching material and teaching programmes. The amount of time required for this purpose beyond the 1265 hours shall not be defined by the employer but shall depend upon the work needed to discharge the teacher's duties.

It had become increasingly evident to the Management Side of the Scottish Joint Negotiating Committee (TSSE) that in terms of the future well-being of the education service there was a need to examine the structure and functions of teaching in the 1990s. Part of that examination was to be the search for agreement about the management and use of teacher time. Issues such as the use of planned activity time, staff development and appraisal, in-service days and absence cover arrangements were to be included as part of a review to use teacher time in a flexible and co-ordinated way. An opportunity presented itself following the April 1990 salaries settlement when a tripartite review group (education authorities, unions and the Scottish Office Education Department) was established to look at the structure and functions of teaching in the 1990s. Management objectives as part of this review included: the elimination of restrictive practices; the promotion of cost-effective staffing; the improvement of morale and industrial relations; increased pay levels to recruit and retain staff; the creation of appropriate incentives. The review group would be invited to look at the role of the teacher, the stresses of the job, the use of 'para-professionals', and the assessment of future career patterns.

The Management Side produced late in 1990 its views on the 1990s Review and released the documents for consultation to interested bodies in three parts. Part 1 dealt with general policy issues and was a final version of COSLA's views on the needs of the education service in the 1990s. Though there was not a consensus view achieved there was sufficient support from education authorities, Scottish Office Education Department and many non-teacher union bodies to allow the process to continue. The paper encompassed a range of issues related to changing social and economic factors and their impact on the education service.

Part 2 concentrated on the future role of the teacher. It was designed to take up many of the issues raised in Part 1 as they apply to the role of the teacher. It set the role of the teacher in terms of the need to provide a responsive and accountable service located in the context of changing demands. In this respect the challenges of budgetary constraints, demographic change, competition, decentralisation and empowerment, and the quest for quality were all identified. Reference was made to many of the reasons which led to industrial relations problems — pay issues, innovation overload, and the decline of professional autonomy. Part 2 addressed the need for attractive recruitment, retention and professional incentives to help to address these problems. Also addressed was the need to develop an appropriate career structure that would be flexible and encourage the good classroom practitioner. Part 2 concluded with a reference to managing the pace of change in a sensible way and referred to such matters as personal and professional development and the role of the para-professional.

Part 3 was a draft statement of principles underlying a new salary structure and conditions of service designed to meet flexibly the needs of the service in the 1990s and to lead to a new and valued role for the teacher.

From December 1990 until late in 1992 the teachers' unions took every opportunity to avoid negotiating on Part 3 particularly as it included reductions to the teachers' leave year and a 35 hour working week as opposed to a notional one. They held to their view that the review related to competitive salaries for the 1990s and indicated they were not prepared to trade conditions for pay. More recently, faced with the growing exasperation of the Management Side and the Scottish Office Education Department, and the fear that their statutory negotiating body might be replaced by an independent pay and conditions review body, the Staff Side have recently met the Management Side in a negotiating sub-committee. The prospects for progress, however, are less than bright and the likelihood of the Government either removing the statutory basis for the SJNC (TSSE)'s agreements or the creation of a pay and conditions review body looms larger.

The General Teaching Council for Scotland

In 1966 the General Teaching Council for Scotland was constituted in accordance with the provisions of the Teaching Council (Scotland) Act 1965. The functions of the Council are:

1 to keep under review standards of education, training and fitness to teach appropriate to persons entering the teaching profession and to make to the Secretary of State from time to time such recommendations with respect to these standards as they think fit, and to make recommendations on such other matters (in the same field) as they think fit, or as may be referred to them by the Secretary of State;
2 to consider and make recommendations to the Secretary of State on matters (other than remuneration and conditions of service) relating to the supply of teachers;
3 to be informed of the nature of instruction given in colleges of education and to undertake such other functions in relation to such colleges as may be assigned by the Secretary of State;
4 to establish and keep a register containing the names, addresses and such qualifications and other particulars as may be prescribed of persons who are entitled to be registered and who apply in the prescribed manner to be so registered; and

5 to determine whether in any particular case, under its disciplinary powers, registration is to be withdrawn or refused.

The effect is that all teachers employed in maintained schools in Scotland must be registered teachers. In order to be entitled to registration as a teacher by the Council an applicant must have secured a teaching qualification awarded by a Scottish College of Education under conditions prescribed by the relevant regulations. An applicant for exceptional admission to the register must satisfy the Council that the evidence of attainment he/she presents is equivalent to that required for the award of a teaching qualification under the relevant Scottish regulations.

As yet, lecturers in further education colleges need not be registered, but many are. Only graduates or the equivalent can qualify to teach in secondary schools. From 1986 primary school teacher training has consisted of either a four-year graduate course (BEdn) or a one-year postgraduate course.

Teacher training

Although voluntary bodies instituted teacher training at the beginning of the century the state has always been responsible for training. No local authority has ever provided a teacher training college. Prior to 1959, a national committee oversaw a number of provincial committees, but in 1959 each college achieved autonomy with its own governing body. Co-ordination was carried out by the Scottish Council for the Training of Teachers with a large input from the Scottish Education Department through the Inspectorate. Finance is made direct to the colleges by the Scottish Office Education Department and the constitution of the governing bodies allows for representation of the local authorities and the directorate of education. As in England and Wales the process of rationalisation of colleges of education is leading to greater co-operation, and in some cases mergers, with universities and other central institutions.

Examinations

All maintained secondary schools, and many independent and grant-aided schools (that is, independent schools receiving a grant from the Government) present candidates for the examinations arranged by the Scottish Examination Board. From 1888 until the institution of the Scottish Certificate of Education the examinations had been conducted and certificates awarded by the Scottish Education Department. In 1964, by virtue of powers granted to him under the

Education (Scotland) Act 1963, the Secretary of State published the Scottish Certificate of Education Examination Board Regulations 1963 which provided for the establishment of a board to take over the conduct of the examinations. There is, therefore, one board, the Scottish Examination Board. Changes in recent years have led to the introduction of courses leading to awards at standard grade, highers and the certificate of sixth year studies levels. Currently there has been published the findings of the Howie Committee which has been examining the nature of provision and examination arrangements for upper secondary schooling. The report, which is out to consultation, has provoked a wide-ranging debate on future directions for Scottish schooling. A prominent element in the debate has been the fear that the proposals for a two-year Scottish Certificate (ScotCert) for vocationally-oriented pupils and a three-year Scottish Baccalaureate (ScotBac) for the more academically able will create a two-tier system endemic to the Scottish egalitarian tradition.

At the same time COSLA is pressing ahead with discussions with the SEB and the Scottish Vocational Education Council about the possibility of merging to provide a single examination body. This development returns to merger proposals which were first made in the early 1980s.

Grants

Education authorities have powers under the Education Acts to grant bursaries (awards), but while regulations allow bursaries to be awarded in respect of full-time further education courses, they are not intended to apply to awards for major courses at universities, central institutions (including colleges of education) or other courses of similar standard. Students attending such courses apply to the central department, the Scottish Education Department, for a student's allowance. The level of awards for full-time further education courses are based on recommendations made annually by COSLA.

Conclusion

In Scotland, as in England, power is distributed among government, education authorities, teachers and other groups. While Scotland has its own legislation, some of the Acts cover, in general terms, the same provisions as in the equivalent Acts for England and Wales. Historically, Scotland has developed a unique system dating from the schools attached to mediaeval monasteries. In 1560 the leaders of the Reformed Church proposed a comprehensive system of education for all children capable of profiting by it, but it took 400 years to achieve the aim.

There is a strong central government machinery in Scotland in the Scottish Office Education Department and it tends to play a very positive interventionist role. Ian Flett, who wrote the Scottish chapter in the 1986 edition of this book, felt that 'the size of the country and the local authority structure — there is, for example, only one local authority association, the Convention of Scottish Local Authorities — has created a very close and fruitful partnership between the Scottish Office Education Department and the education authorities'.

This judgement may still be valid in that for various reasons the radical Conservative policies for educational reform so evident south of the Border have to some extent been tempered, but nevertheless a form of creeping Anglicization by way of Acts of Parliament, regulations and 'mandatory guidelines' has started to change the traditional arrangements in Scotland. In recent years it has become a standing feature at the annual conferences of the Association of Directors of Education in Scotland for the President of the Society of Education Officers to make envious noises about the arrangements for educational administration and provision in Scotland when contrasted with recent events in the South. However, such speeches may well need to be tempered as the twin forces of local government reorganisation in Scotland and a raft of changes emanating from Scottish Office Education Department policies merge in the period to 1996. Meantime, the Scots will continue to use one of their traditional sayings when toasting colleagues from the South:

> 'Here's tae us wha's like us?
> Damn few, and they're a' deid.'

3 The schools
Brian Unwin

In the period since 1985, there have been four major pieces of legislation dedicated to schooling — 1986, 1988, 1992 and 1993; two enactments relating to the teachers' pay and conditions — 1987 and 1991; and two, the Local Government Act 1988 and the Local Government and Housing Act that have had a direct effect on the organisation of the education service. These, taken together, have had, either directly or indirectly, a significant effect on the way in which schools are managed and those matters in which they have either complete or partial control.

It has been a period in which schools (governing bodies and staff) have had to adapt and respond rapidly. The overall effect has been to shift fundamentally the centre of gravity of power, not just between the LEA and individual schools, but also between the LEA and central government as a result of the increased powers taken by the Secretary of State. Whilst gaining autonomy in significant areas of activity, schools have increasingly had to refer to the centre. This is particularly true of the city technology colleges and the 'arts' colleges, where funding is centrally determined, and in the grant-maintained schools, where elements of funding, for example, capital funding, is centrally decided through the Funding Agency (England) and the Funding Council (Wales) which will intrude between this relation when the 10 per cent entry point (1993 Act) is triggered.

Independent schools, though not included in the legislation for the major aspects, have been affected on particular issues such as the prohibition of corporal punishment (1986 Act) in respect of pupils on the Assisted Places Scheme. They have been expected to consider the requirements of the National Curriculum and the consequent assessment requirements and also to publish information about the school and its results. The 1993 Act requires independent schools to tighten their employment controls and procedures for appointment and disciplinary procedures to prevent the appointment of unsuitable employees, both teachers and non-teachers.

All of these changes have established new statutory relationships, together with a re-framing of old and traditional relationships. Not all of these relationships are capable of precise definition and have had to be explored over the period of transition. The level of autonomy of individual schools, whether county or voluntary (aided or controlled) is to be enhanced still further by the process of incorporation set out in the 1993 Act, which will give governing bodies a legal entity, thus protecting governors from individual liability to an extent.

All of the active partners in education have over time come to terms with the new relationships and at what point they would individually identify the point of balance. There are significantly different views of the balance of advantage of the legislative changes.

From a school perspective the extent of change in the powers to decide crucial matters such as the allocation and distribution of finances, the appointment and dismissal of staff, the control of buildings and the repair and maintenance would be determined as much by the LEA's previous level of investment in such matters as by delegation of these powers to individual governing bodies and the theoretical and practical ability to vire funds that this gives.

A description of the detailed changes is the only basis on which a clear analysis may be made of the changes that have occurred and are occurring in the autonomy of individual institutions, irrespective of the technical/legal status.

The freedoms were and are circumscribed by the practical realities of resourcing levels. Certainly for governing bodies, headteachers, senior staff and LEA officers, the provision of legislation, particularly 1986 and 1988, have imposed a steep learning curve and required a significant development in working practices and relationships.

The new responsibilities of all governing bodies of maintained schools originate from the decision to delegate the control of the majority of resources allocated for the running of the school to the governing body. The process by which the Schemes of Delegation were to be established was set out in ERA ss.33–35 and ss.38–43 provided the main structures of the schemes. The details were set out in Circular 7/88 *Education Reform Act — Local Management of Schools*, and later refined in Circular 7/91 *Local Management of Schools — Further Guidance*. The structure of the schemes made it necessary for the LEA to identify and categorise all of its expenditure on the education service, i.e. monies to be delegated to schools either by formula or by other means. Exceptions, both mandatory and discretionary, were to be retained and controlled by the LEA. The remainder, i.e. the bulk of the resources, were delegated to schools. The excepted items should not account for more than 10 per cent of the LEA general schools budget. Over the time from the first year of the Schemes of Delegation, the proportion that is not delegated to schools has been reduced in some LEAs to less than 10 per cent and others to 15 per cent of the potential school, budget by the date required, 1 April 1993 (the 13 Inner London LEAs by 1 April 1995).

The effect of these very detailed schemes on schools has been very significant, not only in the way that school budgets are built by the LEA, but particularly the manner in which they are prioritised and managed at school level. For county and voluntary aided and controlled schools the disaggregation of the LEA budgets and the distribution of an increasing proportion of it by formula to schools created problems. Some schools were losers in the sense that under LMS they received less money, others received a larger budget than they were currently receiving from the LEA. Most schemes introduced transitional arrangements so that increases and decreases in budgetary shares were phased over three years. At the end of the transitional period schools had, by school management decisions, to get expenditure within the budgets determined by the schemes. Though some schools who would have suffered seriously were enabled, under the 1 per cent rule (introduced by Minister of State Angela Rumbold), to phase the reduction of the deficits over a longer period of years.

Though the arrangements for LMS were mandatory, a number of LEAs had, prior to LMS, in various schemes given schools considerable flexibility in managing their own budgets. Without doubt, the main areas of budgetary autonomy for schools were in prioritising and viring between budgetary heads, expenditure of materials and equipment, staffing (both teaching and non-teaching), and premises costs (rates, fuel, maintenance, minor works). It must be remembered that, because of the requirements of the Local Government Act 1988 in relation to competitive tendering, some contracts had already been made and governing bodies were bound by them (school meals, ground maintenance, building maintenance) for the rest of the term of the contract.

However, the ability to prioritise schools' needs within the budget share gave many schools freedom to spend in areas that had previously been controlled by the LEA and to vire spending from one head to another, and as the 1991 Circular (7/91) introduced the facility for cheque books for schools, direct purchasing became a possibility. Though the governing body was in control over its own budget, they had no control over the size of the budget and had to work within that allocation. Nor was it possible after the Scheme of Delegation had been approved for any school subject to it to receive any additional sums of money unless the circumstances could be said to qualify under the LEA's contingency funds. Practically, as the governing bodies had the freedom to spend and allocate within the arrangements of the Scheme they were also constrained by the limit to their funds. It was illegal to set a deficit budget, and any deficit that arose from deficiencies in the budgetary estimates or unforeseen circumstances would be set against the following year's budget.

In the main, whether schools started as winners or losers was dependent on the extent to which they had benefited from LEA schemes of positive discrimination which could not be continued, the nature of the age profile of the staff as to whether it was a gain on the average figure allocated as against the actual cost of staff salaries, and the fuel/insulation efficiency and state of the buildings.

To meet these new responsibilities, the governing body needed to consider how it would manage the situation and what information it would require from the LEA and its own senior staff, led by the headteacher. Budgetary control mechanisms needed to be changed or made more sophisticated, as in practice, most budgetary areas would, over time, be affected by the decisions of the governing body. Some schools had bursars or financial officers with particular financial and accountancy skills prior to 1988. The arrival of delegation accelerated the process of restructuring the non-teaching staff significantly. Electronic equipment was installed and most governing bodies established finance committees with clear remits under regulations 25 and 26 of The Education (School Government) Regulations 1989, SI 1503.

As the extent of the new responsibilities became clear, governing bodies together with the headteacher and the senior management team, considered how best to utilise senior staff time with the structures that were required to advise the governing body on the needs of the school and to facilitate the execution of the governing body's duty.

Personnel responsibilities

Arguably the most important effect of the responsibilities of governing bodies of county and controlled voluntary schools as a result of delegation was the acquisition of employment functions that extended their powers and responsibilities significantly. The first stages were achieved in the 1986 Act, but the major powers and responsibilities were achieved in the 1988 Act. As a result of the Education Reform Act 1988, staffing complements were determined by the governing body within the constraints of their budget.

(a) The Education (No.2) Act 1986

The 1986 Education Act restructured governing bodies (ss.3–10) by determining a new composition involving elected parent and teacher governors, the co-option of representatives of local commerce, industry and the community, and establishing the extent of their powers through new Articles and Instruments. Within this structure, their accountability to the LEA, parents and community was set out. In order to fulfil their responsibilities and duties they had to consider the change in the pattern of relationships, firstly, with the LEA on appointments. In this situation the LEA clearly was the employer (except in aided schools), but had a duty to work in partnership with the governors on headteacher appointments and to consult with governing bodies before exercising its employment responsibilities on whether to retain a post, to advertise or to redeploy existing staff.

For the appointment of headteacher (s.37), a joint panel of the LEA and the governing body with equal representation was established. This panel had to follow procedures that were laid down in detail, which included the requirement to advertise the post nationally. The deputy headteacher could be appointed by the headteacher procedure or as for other staff. The LEA had to set staff complements, but within these it was for the headteacher and the governors to decide the structure within the parameters established. These statutory requirements led to increased dialogue between individual governing bodies and the LEAs, which, as well as changing the substance of what was discussed and the introduction of the elected parents and teacher governors with co-opted governors, moved the focus of the discussion to the school as opposed to an LEA perspective, particularly in the matter of prioritisation of allocation of resources in relation to the school's needs.

The internal management of personnel issues was very much the headteacher's, but the decision on final sanctions such as dismissal were retained by the LEA after consulting the governing body, though voluntary aided schools were already the employers for that purpose.

(b) The Education Reform Act 1988

The Education Reform Act ss.44–47 established significant changes and the majority of these were set out in Schedule 3 to the Act. In short, whilst the CEO (or representative chosen for particular expertise, finance, personnel etc.) retained a right of presence and advice in some circumstances, the balance of power had changed decisively in favour of the governing bodies of those maintained county schools that were fully delegated (s.36). The governing body was now the 'relevant body' and had the responsibility for handling the contract, i.e. appointment, discipline, dismissal, grievance, promotion, competency, of all members of staff within the rules set out in School Government Regulations, within the national conditions of service (School Teachers' Pay and Conditions Document 1992) and any local agreements relevant to the situation. The particular split of responsibilities was set out by DES Circular 13/89 (Welsh Office 37/89). The LEA still formally managed the technical aspects of the contract and its issue and its termination if necessary. This relationship was not always fully understood in the early days of implementation, and in particular for sensitive matters such as dismissal through cause of redundancy, there were in some situations disjunction in the process, in particular, where LEA officers proffered advice that in effect was a directive old style by a paternalistic LEA. There were particular sensitivities in LEAs that had formal 'no-redundancy' policies with accompanying containment agreements. Some governing bodies led by governors with industrial and commercial backgrounds were much more rigorous in pursuing the employment responsibilities, not least in expressing 'loss of confidence' in senior staff.

The new duties and responsibilities of governing bodies in relation to dismissal (by cause of redundancy) mean that they have through their committees to arrange the consultation process, the determination of criteria, selection of individuals and the hearing of and the determination of appeals under Employment Acts 1975–1992. The acquisition of these duties highlights the importance of skills of judgement and analysis in making decisions that have to be defended in quasi-judicial, if not judicial hearings. The same is equally true in relation to the making of appointments and resolving grievances and matters of pay.

Through s.49 of the 1986 Act, the Secretary of State took reserve powers to introduce regulations to establish the appraisal of teachers, and in 1991, he activated this power and by SI 1991/1511 inserted appraisal into the conditions of service of headteachers and teachers, making the LEA the appraising body for county, voluntary controlled schools and voluntary aided schools. The governors should formally approve these arrangements. In grant maintained schools, however, the governing body was the appraising body. In schools where there were clear and consistent communications and where job descriptions had been carefully drawn up or modified to meet the new circumstances over time, appraisal has not only been successfully introduced but has been welcomed positively, an acknowledgement of the positive professional development opportunities. However, where there was lack of harmony, if not actual dissension, and where job specifications were vague (e.g. for a Head of chemistry), the introductory period could be much more bumpy and unpredictable.

On the matters of pay and conditions, in 1990 the governing bodies of county and voluntary schools were allowed to use the discretions previously exercised by the LEA in terms of placement on the standard scale, acceleration through the incremental scale, to exceed the proportion of individual incentive allowances to introduce a discretionary scale, and award inter-incremental allowances and determine the point on the spine for heads and deputies. The availability of these discretions produced the need for governing bodies to establish pay policies, including criteria for making the awards described above and to conduct an annual review of staff pay and to establish clearly the mechanisms whereby these discretions would be exercised.

The extent to which these discretions have been exercised is very variable. Some governing bodies have used some as temporary awards. Many bodies have been cautious because of the roll-over implications for the budget. In reality, the main constraint for most governing bodies has been the low levels of funding which enables them to maintain their existing position rather than extend incentives. In some parts of the country, initially, the entry points for recruitment (particularly in shortage subjects) were raised, though with the improvement in teacher supply, this may have slowed up. In some grant-maintained schools, the restructuring grant and the additional funding has led to more significant use.

Governing bodies, too, have found that they have needed advice both from the LEA and the headteacher because they needed to establish procedures to fulfil these duties. Equally, they have to be familiar with the School Government Regulations 1989 (SI 1503) and 1991 (SI 2854) to avoid breaching the rules. It was also clear that in order to meet their responsibilities, they would need to give executive powers (i.e. delegate by remit) to appropriate committees established under these regulations. For many governing bodies, this was an unfamiliar procedure and required both training and the establishment of trust. Explicit in the regulations was a firm distinction between the establishment of policy, which was a matter for the whole governing body, which they could not delegate, and the execution of policy which they could; the highlighting of the distinction between the governing body's duty of governance and the headteacher's responsibility to manage. It became apparent that the responsibilities of governing bodies were significantly increased by the Education Reform Act in matters other than staffing and finance and extended through the maintenance of building, health and safety and the letting of the building out of school time for potentially a wide range of activities.

For county and controlled schools, the Education Reform Act 1988 established, in effect, a landlord–tenant relationship between the governing body and the LEA in respect of buildings and grounds. The funds within the delegated budget were available for minor repairs and maintenance, including internal decoration and could include some minor works. The LEA would be responsible for structural matters and major repairs and DES Circular 7/88 (WO 36/88) set out a clear table of guidelines. Such a division could create grey areas that cause dispute, and the absence of sufficient funds both capital and current for building has, in some cases, exacerbated these disputes about responsibilities. Again, the governing bodies, after setting the parameters, have delegated the execution of their policy to the headteacher and senior staff.

The responsibility of the governing body for health and safety in respect of the building and for the employees is explained in DES Circular 7/88 (WO 36/88) and in DES Circular 13/89 (WO 37/89). It is a significant responsibility. Governing bodies have, in the main, adopted the LEA health and safety policies and as a consequence have reported deficiencies and breaches directly to the LEA through the headteacher. In law, for county and controlled schools, the LEA is the employer for health and safety purposes, whereas in aided and GM schools, CTCs, and independent schools, the governing body, as employer, is responsible. For maintained schools, the divided responsibility between governing body and LEA (together with the headteacher and individual teacher's particular responsibilities) raises issues of who is responsible where there is a significant difference of opinion between the parties which may only be determined in court. Governing bodies have acquired significant responsibilities in this area and the issue of the Management of Health and Safety Regulations 1992 (SI 2051) requires them to assess the risks, decide strategy and agree and implement procedures and then review their practice. The health and safety legislation and regulations emanating from the EEC have imposed a raft of regulations (Personal Protective Equipment at Work Regulations 1992; Manual Handling Operations Regulations 1992, Provision and Use of Work Equipment Regulations 1992, Health and Safety (Display Screen Equipment) Regulations 1992,) which increase year by year. A complex set of relationships between the LEA, the governing body and the staff needs to work effectively if their respective responsibilities under the Act and the subsequent regulations are to be met. Delegation has changed the balance within the relationship.

The landlord–tenant relationship has in some respects clarified some of the out-workings of s.42(a) and (b) of the 1986 Education Act, which gave governing bodies control of the premises of the school out of school hours for use by the community. The LEA can still direct the use of part of the school for youth and adult, provided that the extent of the building directed for use does not amount to control of the building. Indeed, where there was already extensive community provision, the LEA can also delegate the management of staff to the governors. Where the use of premises was directed by the LEA, that direction has to be accompanied by appropriate funding. The Act of 1993 should further clarify the effect of s.42 (see below).

As a result of the Further and Higher Education Act 1992, the decision on whether formally to register post-19 pupils at the school will be important, as funding for this activity, and in long term for adult and community activities, will come either from fee income or from the nearest FE college, via the Funding Council. DFE Circular 1/93, *The Further and Higher Education Act 1992*, makes it absolutely clear that governors may not use any of their LMS budget for such purposes. A new set of relationships for the governing body and headteacher to develop.

Governing bodies have needed to be mindful that if they sanctioned activities out of school hours that were not clearly educational, they would have to examine with the LEA whether the LEA insurance covered the activity. If that activity was not covered, the appropriate insurance and public employee liability had to be arranged and separately funded. In short, the legislation had extended governing bodies' powers and responsibilities, and in using these extensions to develop the use of the school and provide an extension to the range of activities and experiences to the community, they could be taking on even more responsibilities.

The provisions in the 1993 Act for incorporation of all county, voluntary and maintained special schools increases significantly the powers and responsibilities of all governing bodies but they will still, unless they are voluntary aided, be unable to enter into contracts of employment.

Schedule 12 of the 1993 Act sets out in detail the powers and responsibilities of governing bodies, and in so doing, redefines the control of premises for county schools, Education (No. 2) Act 1986 s.42 and the Education Act 1944 s.22 in respect of voluntary schools. Apart from the ability to own land and other property, or dispose of land and other property, the governing body may enter into other contracts, but not employment (unless a voluntary aided school), invest sums of money not immediately required and accept gifts, including land. A number of practical possibilities emerge, not least that the governing body may enter into commercial relationships with other bodies or companies for the specific use of the premises, an extension of community activities outside school hours. This would be a control agreement for all, or part of the school premises. Issues such as insurance, health and safety and planning permission would need to be carefully examined. Clearly, the governors have more freedom to utilise their building, but equally more detailed work to ensure the viability and relevance of the activities. How far schools will use these flexibilities, or have the resources to purchase land, is open to question.

The balance of advantage of having the additional powers through incorporation against losing the shield/protection of the LEA in respect of the final employment responsibilities, public liability is a fine one. Although governing bodies may arguably be better protected against liability, their responsibility will still be extensive and will be corporate, and they will be accountable to the Charity Commission for any trusts and have to exercise high standards of control and accountability.

Governing bodies of maintained county schools with delegated budgets have, since 1989, developed a new relationship with the LEA and the LEA, in return, has perforce had to change its relationships with governing bodies from being a directive organisation to a service organisation regarding a governing body as a client who uses the services of the LEA, financial, professional (educational), personnel and legal. Such 'cultural' changes have followed the legal changes rather than led them in the majority of authorities.

This development of the notion of clients' services is of crucial importance, as LEAs, in the provisions of the 1993 Act, can provide such services (other than through marginal capacity) only for a two year period, after which the LEA will, if it wishes to continue a relationship with GM schools, have to establish commercial type operations on a business basis on the pattern of school meals, ground maintenance etc. As the majority of schools become either more autonomous or completely autonomous, they will continue to need specialist professional services. Presently, the vast majority of that expertise (other than financial and accounting) is located in LEAs.

The individual schools (whether designated county, voluntary or grant maintained) will develop varying relationships with the Funding Councils which, as a result of the 1993 Act, will come into operation and distribute grants as soon as they are established; in England at the 10 per cent entry point (in Wales the Secretary of State for Wales assumes those powers until the Schools Funding Council for Wales is activated) and the councils will take those powers and responsibilities set out in Schedules 1 and 2 of the Act shared to the 75 per cent point with LEA and after that transferred fully to the council (planning in relation to school places, the establishment and alteration of schools). In the circumstance where the LEA does not voluntarily withdraw from its powers enabling the Funding Council to assume its ultimate functions early, the governing body will have to develop a relationship with both organisations, at least in the transitional period before the assumption of full powers by the Funding Councils. The professional staff of the school might well, on behalf of the governing body, be responding to information requests from the LEA, the Funding Council and the DFE. The requirement for accurate and rapid communication is paramount and has led to significant administrative reorganisation in schools and the provision of appropriate hardware and software.

Before the 1986 Act, curriculum matters and issues, though reported and discussed by governors were not normally a matter for decision. The actual curriculum decisions were made by the professionals. The 1986 Act required a number of decisions from governing bodies. In order to arrive at these decisions, there had to be informed discussion and debate on the nature of the curriculum to be taught in the school. The first decision was to decide the school's curriculum policy. The basis of these discussions would be the LEA's curriculum policy, which could be modified by the governing body after considering any representation by the chief officer of police and by the community. If there were disagreement or differences between the two policy documents, the headteacher was placed in the sensitive position of deciding when they diverged which to implement in school.

Another curriculum responsibility was to determine whether sex education should have a place in the school curriculum and also to approve the form that it was to take and to formulate these decisions into a policy. However, if the governors decided it was part of the school curriculum, parents could not require the removal of their children from that part of the curriculum as they could for religious education and the religious aspect of assembly.

By the time this arrangement had time to settle down, the provisions of the Education Reform Act 1988 had been enacted and were being phased in by statutory order. Apart from the requirements for worship and religious education, which though changed were already subject to statutory requirements, the National Curriculum and the mechanisms for its formulation and assessment (ss.1–15) were established in law. The Education Reform Act 1988 significantly altered the governing body's responsibility for the curriculum in that the National Curriculum was established and they had to ensure that it was put in place and the headteacher could determine the nature of non-statutory curriculum provisions. The full effects of the introduction of the National Curriculum into schools have not yet been fully experienced, not least because it is such a significant departure from previous practice. Experience has affected and is affecting schools differentially, depending on the nature of the balance of their curriculum provision prior to 1989. For those schools where there was a significant difference in the curriculum being offered in 1988 and that which would be needed in the years up to 1995, when full implementation of the orders was required, significant problems had to be solved over time. The basic problems centred on resources — staffing and materials, staff training, appropriate physical provision and teaching methodology. Making decisions in these key areas is made more difficult by the modifications to the original orders, modifications that have required different books, materials, staffing resources and methodologies.

A significant number of schools have had to make adjustments to the staffing profile (by subject expertise). The requirements for sciences, modern languages and technology led to the need to change the balance of expertise within the staff. The internal decisions on how to respond to the flexibilities in the arrangements for art, music and physical education at Key Stage Four have been an important consideration in arriving at the final balance of teaching expertise required to deliver the curriculum. In Wales, the particular requirement for Welsh as either core or as a foundation subject has added a further pressure. The difficulty of statutorily defining a curriculum has been, in part, illustrated by the variation in the original orders relating to English and technology and, to a lesser extent, other subject areas.

The nature of the balance of curriculum and that of the content and levels expressed in the statutory orders for each of the subjects has, for some schools, raised serious issues of space, its suitability and the availability of properly developed areas. The orders for science and for technology, in particular, led to difficulties for governing bodies and LEAs, in delivering their statutory duty.

As the assessment requirements at each of the Key Stages are implemented, pressures on space are created to hold the assessment and a pressure on the time of staff to conduct the assessments and mark them if required. Neither governing bodies nor headteachers have the power to vary the statutory requirements for assessment.

The relationship between the governing body and pupils and parents has been significantly changed by the legislation in respect of the provision of information. As a result of the 1986 Education Act, the governors are required to provide for parents an annual report (s.30) and hold an annual parents' meeting (s.31), the purpose of which is for the governing body to account for its stewardship for the previous year's activities. The original requirements for the content have been expanded considerably by subsequent legislation (1988 and 1992). The content ranges from financial information on a budget statement and an out-turn statement, through the schools public examination results (at the relevant stage, the Key Stage assessments), a report on last year's annual meeting's resolutions, if any, and what action had been taken, and to the most recent addition in 1992 of the attendance and truancy figures expressed in percentage terms, as required by regulation.

Similarly, the school prospectus, in its regulated form stems from the 1980 Education Act (Schedule 2 Information) which requires items of specific information to be included. This is a responsibility of the governing body, the execution of which is often delegated to the headteacher and senior staff. The numerous contents of this document have been added to by each of the major enactments which necessitate a yearly updating and which, in the climate of market forces bearing on admissions, are regarded by some to be key marketing factors.

The school, whether through the authority of the governing body or of the headteacher, has gained more autonomy in making initial decisions, though those decisions are subject to appeal or decision by an independent person or body. The 1986 Act established a detailed procedure to deal with pupil exclusions from school and involved the governing body (or a committee of the governing body) to deal with any representation by parents and also to make a decision to appeal against a determination by the LEA to return the pupil to school in a maintained school. Parents acquired the right, if they so wished, to appeal to an appeal panel of the LEA, established in the same way as the admissions appeal committee (Part 1 of Schedule 2 of the 1980 Act). The provision in the 1993 Education Act for the LEA to specify, after observing the rules, a named school in a School Attendance Order could breach the autonomy of a grant-maintained school in the matter of admissions, subject to the intervention of the Secretary of State.

In the discussion of the curriculum, the duty of the school to deliver the National Curriculum was explored. A concept central to the notion of National Curriculum is that of the entitlement of every child to experience the full curriculum, subject to the notion of difference in presentation but ultimately in the forms and nature of the instruments of the assessment process. It was logical, therefore, that the 1988 Act should require governing bodies and professionals to observe s.22 — the provision of information. Many circulars and accompanying regulations have been issued under these powers; a similar provision is made for grant-maintained schools under s.103. Under these arrangements, schools have to publish the school examination results in prescribed form both in the prospectus and in the annual report to parents. These requirements, as well as the requirements to report to parents individual pupil achievement, have been revised. The school attendance figures, together with the percentage of unauthorised and authorised absences, were added to the duty to publish information. The 1992 Schools Act, s.16, extended the categories of information to be published. In particular, the destinations of school leavers continuing in full or part-time education or employment, and such information as the Secretary of State considers relevant to assisting parents in choosing a school for their children; the authorisation for the comparative information and league tables of school performance must be published. s.22 of the ERA also places a duty on schools to have available to parents and to members of the public a range of information that has been published by the DFE, NCC or SEAC, CCW and Welsh Office ranging from the Statutory Instruments, through the formal circulars to the Assessment requirements and procedures. Additionally, the governing body must make available to parents and the public, copies of their main policy documents and minutes. This portfolio would include the policy on the curriculum, charging and remissions, complaints procedures, sex education, religious education, school worship, guidelines for conduct of the school, record keeping and disclosure, record of achievements, school sessions and times, disapplication of National Curriculum procedures and information for parents, minutes of the governing body and its committees (which would include the structure of the committees with remits and membership).

For members of staff of the school, the governing body would need to make known, at minimum, the nature of the policies that they have adopted in relation to making appointments; disciplinary, grievance, complaints procedures, the pay policy and the health and safety policy. As governing bodies have, in effect, the duty to handle and administer the contracts of those employees in the school, they also have to think more widely on the nature of their duties and to consider the importance of being 'good employers'; a concept that was new to most county schools, but was more familiar to voluntary-aided schools and became rapidly crucial to the governing bodies of those schools who followed the procedures set out in ERA ss.60–73 and achieved grant-maintained status as they then became the employer.

The accountability of the governing body and professional staff was again underlined by the introduction of a complaints procedure (s.23 of the ERA). The procedure was normally drawn up by the LEA and adopted by the governing body. The complaint could be made to either the LEA or the governing body. In either case, the LEA had a duty to monitor the progress of the complaint. It must be emphasised that complaints under this procedure relate exclusively to the delivery (or non-delivery) of aspects of the National Curriculum, other statutory provisions on the curriculum and the arrangements for religious worship. The complainant would set out to establish the unreasonableness of the schools' actions which were the subject of the complaint. The LEA, in the case of county, special and voluntary schools maintained by them, was made responsible for seeing that the complaint was followed through, i.e. an investigation had to take place and the results made known to the parent. Until this process was complete, the Secretary of State would refuse to move on a complaint under ss.68 or 99 of the 1944 Act. The process underlines the shift in the balance of duty and power between LEAs and schools, and the governing body and the headteacher in particular.

In similar vein, arrangements have been established for disapplication of the National Curriculum for groups of pupils at schools undertaking curriculum development (s.16 ERA); or under s.18, for pupils with statements of special educational needs; and under s.19 (temporary exceptions for individual pupils). For s.19 disapplications, the parent is entitled to all the information, which must also be given to the governing body and the LEA by all maintained schools. If the parent disagrees with the headteacher's decision, either to disapply certain parts of the National Curriculum, or there is a refusal by the headteacher to accept the parent's view that disapplication was appropriate, he or she can appeal to the governing body, who have the power to confirm the headteacher's decision or direct him or her to take appropriate action.

Circular 17/89 (School Records) explained in detail the Education Regulations 1989. That circular together with 5/92, 7/92 and most recently 14/92 *Report on Individual Pupils' Achievements* describe in meticulous detail what is required. Governors have a duty to ensure that records are kept for each and all of the registered pupils. The nature and format is up to the school, provided the requirement of the Record of Achievement and other format of the formal reporting within prescribed frequences is observed. There is a further duty to ensure access is available to parents to see their child's record (excluding exempt material) and for amendments and additions to be made. If the headteacher or authorised teacher refuses access to copy the facility, or to amend, then the governors have to hear that appeal from the parent. The arrangements made for disclosure must be formulated in a policy and be available for inspection as any other required policy.

The circumstances where the governing body, usually through a properly established committee, acts as an appeal body on the matter of a particular decision of the headteacher about a member of staff or pupil of the school, dictate the relationship between the headteacher and the governing body have to be fully understood, because as well as the processes being quasi-judicial (with further process beyond the governing body's decision and the decision of the LEA, where relevant, and the consequences of that) the working relationships in the school have to continue. For the governing body automatic support of the headteacher, and for the headteacher, mere expectation that the governing body will always be supportive do not necessarily assist each to fulfil their statutory duties. The development of a *modus vivendi* and understanding has proved to be essential.

The governing body's duty is related to governance, that is, setting policies and frameworks and delegating to the headteacher and the staff the execution of those policies and the management of the school on a day to day basis. This line is never clear, but intrusion too far by one or other party across the boundary becomes the subject of controversy and dispute. This is a crucial area and open consideration of the interface by governing bodies would assist in establishing the parameters of the discussion.

Not only is there a conceptual difference between management and governance, but the interface is also in part determined by the nature and character of the persons working together, which is perhaps best portrayed by stereotypes: the chairman of governors or other influential governor who has a regular presence and insists on involvement in detailed decisions that are properly matters for the professional staff; the headteacher who regards the governing body as unhelpful and unnecessary and broaches no argument. It is accepted that both are at extreme ends of the spectrum. They exist, though most situations are much more balanced and work out with mutual trust and respect.

The provision for the daily act of collective worship in maintained schools (ERA s.6) again underlines the relationship between the headteacher and the governors, for in a county school the headteacher decides, after consultation with the governing body, and in a voluntary school, the governing body decides after consultation with the headteacher. In practice, wise counsels usually produce a consensus based on practicalities. These matters, together with the procedure for disapplication of the requirements for Christian worship are made fairly clear in the 1993 Act. This is an area of school activities where conviction and conflict of values are not always necessarily or easily reconcilable with the requirements of the legislation.

5.9 of the 1992 Schools Act established the arrangements for inspections of schools, and the basic framework is set out in Schedule 2, Part I. Regulations and circulars set out the governing body's duties to arrange a meeting between the registered inspector and the parents of pupils registered at the school at a time and place likely to be convenient to as many parents as possible. They may not, however, attend that meeting unless as a parent. The staff must facilitate fully the inspection by making the premises and full documentation available. The report itself must conform to reporting on the areas set out in the guidelines and in the specification agreed.

When the report has been written and delivered, the governing body have two important duties. Firstly, related to the publication and distribution of the report, there are duties to ensure that parents of every registered pupil receive a copy of the summary report, to make reasonable arrangements for the full report and the summary of the report to be available for inspection by any member of the public and local employers and to provide a copy of those documents to any one who asks, charging within the costing levels set out in the regulations. In Wales, prospective parents (i.e. parents considering applying for their child's admission to that school) may, according to *The Parent's Charter*, ask for a copy of the full report.

Secondly, and arguably much more important, there is a duty to consider the report and its findings as a matter of urgency. For within 40 working days of the receipt of the report they have to have formulated an action plan that addresses the findings and ensure that the points of the action plan are clearly laid out, as is the identification of the person(s) responsible for taking action within a specific timetable. They also have to show the criteria for assessing the success or failure of the actions taken to meet the report's findings.

Once the governing body have completed their action plan, they must, within five days, send it to all parents, all staff employed at the school, OFSTED (for an LEA school) or the Secretary of State (for a GM School), and to those who appoint foundation governors, if any.

For all governing bodies, this raises important aspects of their relationship with the head and the staff and also might require them to examine their own accountability. It is an important issue as to whether the action taken implies blame or responsibility for the areas of deficiency. This could be particularly important when the registered inspector's report is negative and either implicitly or explicitly puts the school in the 'at risk' category as defined in the relevant section of the 1993 Education Act with the possibility of an education association looming. The period between the report and the production of the governing body's and LEA's comment and agenda for action will be particularly difficult and will be crucial to the decision as to whether the Secretary of State will establish an education association as set out in the Act. In effect, an education association is a governing body with similar but more extensive powers selected and appointed by the Secretary of State. The association will take the school through to either GM status or oblivion. It is an open question as to whether an educational association will have that special expertise, charisma, power or resources to turn round a school with problems that appear to be intractable after years of conscientious work by the LEA, the governing body and senior staff.

By the end of 1993 the distinction between the duties and responsibilities of governing bodies of county schools, voluntary-aided schools and grant-maintained schools will be much narrower than between different sorts of schools at the end of 1989, and arguably there will be even less difference once funding councils come into play and if a common unit of resourcing for schools is introduced. The actual outcome will depend on whether, as a matter of policy, the Government wishes a convergence in the level of finances.

The key differences all stem from the full incorporation of the governing body of grant-maintained school and in the ability of that body to issue contracts of employment, funded from their budget presently determined by the DFE, and in due course by the funding council. Being the employer entails the formulation and issue of the contract, payroll responsibilities (National Insurance, superannuation etc.), the establishment of disciplinary, grievance, competency procedures and their proper use in relevant situations, the training and staff development functions, appointment of new staff, complying with the relevant aspects of employment law, and answering for any mistakes either to an industrial tribunal or court of law. There are also questions of the ownership of the buildings and land of the school and their charitable status, which gives particular financial advantages. The funding of minor works and repairs and maintenance is the governors' responsibility, and capital grants, for buildings are directly funded by the DFE. The responsibility for insurance, employer public liability, building grounds, visitors etc. are vested in the governing body. In effect, it is responsible, with the exception of capital grants, for prioritising the expenditure across the whole range of school activities and needs, including the requirement to determine the National Curriculum. For all of these responsibilities, the governing body is held totally accountable.

An aided school is also the employer, but its funding is provided by the LEA, which is also responsible for funding the internal maintenance. Buildings are normally owned by the foundation, trust, diocesan or other religious groups, with an 85 per cent contribution from the DFE for capital projects, and a 15 per cent contribution from the governing body, or trust etc. However, the 1993 Act makes provision for this 15 per cent to be provided from public funds in particular circumstances. The funding for staff, materials, and other resources, is calculated in exactly the same manner as for county schools.

Both aided and county schools work within the same budgetary framework and enjoy similar freedoms to vire and manage their budgets. They are not, however, completely independent and have, in varying degrees, the diocesan or trust bodies and/or the LEA between them and final responsibility in limited areas. No school funded from the public purse has the power to determine the levels of its own budget and can raise revenue/income only at the margins.

In all categories of schools, the powers and responsibilities of the governing bodies have grown significantly, though they do not have the power to discipline their own membership. However, the powers of the Secretary of State, 1988 and 1993, and the LEA, 1993, have been extended to allow for the appointment of additional governors to the body.

Such an extension of power has, over the period, by regulation, contract and custom and practice, led to a change in both the structured relationship between the governing body and the headteacher (and indeed the rest of the staff). The distinctions between governance, conduct and management, though clear in conceptual terms, have practical difficulties of interpretation at institutional level. The personal relationship between the headteacher and the governing body has become more critical. Governing bodies vary considerably in the extent to which they delegate responsibilities to the headteacher. Schedule 3 of the Education Reform Act enables governing bodies to delegate to the head teacher all appointments other than those of the headteacher and deputy headteacher. Interpretation varies considerably from only senior appointments requiring the presence of governors to complex tiers of committees, depending on the seniority of the post.

As a governing body concentrates on its policy and government responsibilities, the role and function of senior staff are advisory, and they are busy drafting both for the full governing body and for the committees with executive powers established under regulations. The increased workload for governing bodies has required them to trust small groups in committee to exercise the powers of their whole body, and, equally, the mutuality of trust has to be present between the governing body and the head teacher to carry out the delegated duties as well as the duties under contract. This trust is dependent on the quality of information that is provided by the professional staff for the governing body, and upon which they base their policy decisions.

Over the period 1986 to the present, schools and governing bodies have accommodated, remarkably successfully, to the plethora of new requirements. They have adjusted their relationship with the LEA and internally adapted their own precious time to accommodate the new workload and additional significant financial and policy issues. In the main, governors have been appreciative of the efforts of the staff of the school in coping with the increase in the information requirements, both in what is required for parents in relation to the prospectus and in reporting of achievement and in statistical returns to LEAs and central government. Governors and headteachers have relished the ability to vire monies from one budgetary heading, to another though at the same time have felt constrained by overall levels of resourcing. They have welcomed the ability to prioritise their spending to match the specific and particular needs of their school. They have been much less appreciative of the vacillation about the final provisions for the National Curriculum in each of the key stages, with English and technology causing great concern, and about the publication of league tables for National Curriculum assessments at the four key stages and the publication of examination results.

As the year 1993 progresses, the headteachers and governing bodies together will be confronting the inspection of schools arranged by OFSTED as a result of the 1992 Act, and decisions on community education in schools as affected by s.12 of the Further Education and Higher Education Act 1992 (implying significantly different relationships with further education colleges). The implementation dates of the provisions of the 1993 Act will also be keenly awaited.

4 Voluntary schools
Neil Gill

Pre-1944

The story of how a national public education system developed in this country over the last two hundred years is well documented elsewhere (e.g. Burgess 1958, Cruickshank 1963, Curtis 1967, Parry 1971, Hurt 1972). Looking back one can pick out the main threads and features of that story quite easily, and it is interesting to note how the influence of religion, in particular the interplay between religious and political groupings, has conditioned that story. By the 1840s struggles between the Church of England interest, as represented by the National Society, and the interest of 'Dissent', as represented by the British and Foreign Schools Society, had hardened. The former could still claim to represent the majority of the nation but non-conformists were a large and influential minority. The political parties were influenced by this grouping, the Tories generally being supporters of the Church and the Whigs of Dissent. Both Churchmen and Dissenters alike however agreed that religion was an essential part of education, the secularists being at that time quite a small group.

The majority of schools was in the hands of the National Society throughout the early part of the nineteenth century. This did not cause a great deal of difficulty in the large towns which had national schools and undenominational schools existing side by side. It was otherwise in the country villages, where as a rule the only available school was the national school, in which religious instruction was based on the catechism. Church teaching was often insisted upon as a condition of pupils being admitted to the schools. 'I cannot take one step in educating a child who has not either received, or is not, if of such an age as to admit of previous teaching, in a definite course of preparation for Holy Baptism' said Archdeacon Denison on one occasion, 'and in the latter case I should not admit the child into the school until Holy Baptism had been received (Curtis 1967, p. 237–8)

One of the early decisions of the Committee of Council set up to determine how grants should be distributed was to insist that all building grants should involve the right of inspection. The contention which this evoked with the National Society resulted in the Concordat of 1840 which Kay-Shuttleworth negotiated and which might now be thought to constitute a significant precedent for church schools, as will be seen later. Under this Concordat the Archbishop of the Province had the right of nominating persons as inspectors of church schools; duplicate copies of the inspectors' reports were to be sent to the Archbishop and the diocesan bishop.

Possibly an even more significant development in the light of hindsight were the proposals in Sir James Graham's Factory Bill a few years later, that new schools should be built partly through Treasury grants and partly through loans, and should be maintained by fees and through the local poor rate. In fact Graham's Factory Act of 1844 abandoned the idea of aiding the provision of schools in the face of vehement non-conformist opposition — an interesting illustration of how religious controversy arguably postponed the hope of establishing universal elementary education in this country for a generation.

Religious controversy was still an important factor surrounding the implementation of Forster's Elementary Education Act 1870 when in due course that appeared on the statute book, marking as it did the beginnings of the 'dual system' that exists to the present time, although significantly modified. For example, the opposition of Dixon's non-conformist-inspired League of Education was so strong in Birmingham that some non-conformists refused to pay the education rate on the grounds that part of it was going to support denominational teaching. The League started a campaign for purely secular instruction in 1872; this policy did not receive wholehearted support in the face of a strong move for non-sectarian religious teaching. There was in consequence a serious division in the Government which was arguably a factor in its defeat in the election of 1874.

Most of the new voluntary schools established after 1870 were Church of England schools, with the Roman Catholics, although a much smaller body, being equally enthusiastic to provide extra school accommodation in those years. The churches in fact provided about the same number of places as the boards set up under the Forster Act were able to, even with rate aid. At the end of the nineteenth century, three-fifths of the available places in elementary schools in this country were in Church of England schools. The first half of this century however saw an almost equally dramatic decrease in the number of such schools so that in 1939 the Church had only 8,478 schools out of a total of 22,000. Nonetheless the growth of council schools should not minimise the importance of the contribution made by the religious denominations, in particular the Church of England and the National Society.

After 1902 council schools were generally referred to as provided schools, in contrast to church schools which were known as non-provided schools.

The 1944 Act

Perhaps the biggest single problem which the voluntary schools have faced in this century has been the growing expense of providing and running the school and the simultaneous decline in the amount of money available to all denominations to meet that expense. Increasingly therefore the state and the local authorities have had to supplement the efforts of denominations, including Roman Catholics, who had become a much more significant factor in the provision of education in this country and for whom it was very much a matter of faith that any child of Roman Catholic parents should be able to be educated in a Roman Catholic school. One of the major aims of the 1944 Education Act, which put new burdens on the denominations, was the regulation of the relationship between the voluntary schools and the state and in particular the LEAs. It has tended to be forgotten that the Roman Catholic community was not particularly happy about the 1944 settlement, which was accepted because there was nothing better on offer at the time. However, the intention was to seek to have the financial arrangements improved in favour of denominational schools, and in this respect signal successes have been registered. There was, for example, the device of the controlled school, which enabled denominations other than the Roman Catholics (who were not prepared to adopt this option) to unload onto LEAs the whole financial burden of maintaining a school in exchange for a loss of freedom for the voluntary body which still however owned the premises; in fact about one-third of all non-RC voluntary schools are now controlled schools. Apart from this, one can see what a relatively much easier situation even aided schools have now in terms of the maintenance expenses and their share of the capital expenditure on schools. However, as will be seen later in this chapter, the difficulties which the Church of England and the Roman Catholic church have experienced in recent years in discharging even these reduced levels of responsibility may well be very significant for the future of aided schools.

In terms of structure the current system of voluntary schools is essentially that established by the 1944 Act, which in its turn continued the earlier dual system in a modified form. The voluntary schools fall into three categories: special agreement, aided and controlled. The smallest class consists of the special agreement schools sanctioned by the Act of 1936. Although that Act set a deadline for proposals in respect of about five hundred voluntary senior public elementary schools which was not generally met, the Third Schedule of the 1944 Act made provision for a revival of those proposals, as a result of which about one hundred and fifty secondary schools were set up and were given the name special agreement schools. At that time there were financial advantages associated with such schools but these have largely disappeared and although it would still be technically possible for proposers to seek to establish a new special agreement school there would be no purpose in doing so now in view of the distinct advantages involved in establishing an aided school.

If the governors or managers of a voluntary school were both able and willing to contribute half the cost of improvements or alterations to the school buildings to bring them up to the standard required by the Building Regulations of the time, the 1944 Act provided that they could apply for aided status. If this was granted, the school retained its right to provide denominational religious instruction according to the trust deed, and the appointment of the teachers would be made by the governors or managers. If the governors or managers were unable or unwilling to contribute 50 per cent of the cost, the LEA was empowered to take over the maintenance of the school as a controlled school. (The contribution of VA school governors has been reduced three times since 1944 to its present level of 15 per cent because of difficulties experienced by voluntary bodies in securing the necessary resources.) In such a case two-thirds of the governors or managers were appointed by the authority and the religious instruction was based on an agreed syllabus.

The compromise which resulted in the establishment of these three kinds of voluntary school was the result of widespread consultation with the religious denominations during the period; such compromise is what is meant by a modified 'dual system', and it is worth amplifying this point a little in view of the possible ending of that system with which we are now faced. From one point of view, the retention of a modified 'dual system' in 1944 marked the recognition by the state of the part the religious denominations had played in education in the past and the connection they had with it and continue to have. On the other hand, it has saddled voluntary schools with a heavy burden. Few voluntary schools in 1944 conformed to the standards laid down by the Building Regulations;

the majority have had to be rebuilt or drastically altered, often at great expense to the providing bodies. The difficulties implicit in this situation still continue as will be seen later in this chapter.

Powers and responsibilities

There are important differences of powers and responsibilities amongst the four categories of maintained school; i.e. county, voluntary controlled, special agreement and voluntary aided. These complexities are explained in various sections of the 1944 Act, and other rights and responsibilities are also defined in subsequent Acts, especially in the 1946 Act and its First Schedule. An important companion to the 1944 Act was a booklet originally written in 1946 by Alexander and Barraclough which quickly became an indispensable working document and which after four editions was re-written and expanded under the shorter title *County and Voluntary Schools*. The eighth edition, still with that title, was prepared under the aegis of the Society of Education Officers in 1992 and it codified in considerable detail the range of duties, obligations, powers, financial responsibilities and relationships relevant both to county schools and in separate chapters with the three types of voluntary schools. Detailed reference should therefore be made to what is still in most respects the most authoritative document on this matter, although significant changes have been foreshadowed in the White Paper and Education Bill of 1992, as will be seen later.

Most existing voluntary schools are either Church of England or Roman Catholic, with a certain number of Jewish schools largely concentrated in particular areas. Some of the older foundations, many of which are grammar or former grammar schools, have lost the links they may have had with the Church and are now non-denominational. The essential reasons for the greater autonomy of voluntary schools remains to safeguard their distinctive character, denominational or otherwise, and to recognise their degree of financial independence. It is important to understand the present and historical nature of these schools in order to appreciate the significance of the possible changes with which the education system is faced today and the place of voluntary schools in those changes. Accordingly, the following four sections of this chapter highlight the salient features of the schools, broadly following the headings and selecting commentary in the previous edition of this book (pages 58–73).

The school premises

Historically issues relating to the premises of voluntary schools have generated more problems than issues relating to other aspects of voluntary schools. The term 'school premises' is the all-embracing term to describe the combination of site, playing fields — whether integral with or detached from it — and all the buildings, but not a teacher's house, except in particular circumstances defined in the 1944 Act. The term is broken down into four elements, which are of special importance in understanding the different responsibilities of the LEA and voluntary school governors or trustees. These elements are defined as follows:

School buildings

Any building or part of the school premises except those parts of the building excluded by the Education Act 1946 because they are required *only* (a) as a caretaker's dwelling, (b) for use in connection with the playing fields, (c) for providing facilities to enable medical and dental inspection and treatment to be carried out, and (d) for use in providing milk, meals or other refreshments for pupils attending the school.

Other buildings

Those parts of the school premises excluded from the definition of school buildings as defined above.

School grounds

The playground, school garden and surrounds, roads, paths, boundary walls and fences on the school site.

Playing fields

This is self-explanatory.

There are complex arrangements for provision, alterations, upkeep, conveyance, ownership and disposal relating to the four types of school, which are the subject of very detailed exposition in *County and Voluntary Schools*, and what follows is simply a brief résumé of the issues involved. These complexities have an important bearing on the implications for voluntary schools acquiring grant-maintained status as will be mentioned later.

Capital expenditure

County schools

The position in relation to county schools is uncomplicated: the LEA is responsible for providing the entire school premises, their subsequent upkeep and any necessary alterations or improvements. It owns them and may dispose of them when they are closed. It must of course publish its intention to establish new schools, as well as to cease to maintain them, and in certain circumstances to enlarge them.

Controlled schools

The position here is not straightforward and varies according to the circumstances in which the provision of new buildings or extensions to existing ones occurs. Capital expenditure on controlled schools may be incurred for one of the four following reasons:

(i) the alteration of the premises of an existing school;
(ii) the transfer of an existing school to a new site;
(iii) the significant enlargement of an existing school;
(iv) the establishment of a new controlled school in new premises provided by the LEA.

The salient requirements of the Education Acts in each of these four cases may be summarised as follows.

(i) *Alteration of the premises of an existing school*
The LEA is responsible for the whole of the expenditure incurred on alterations, which are not significant enlargements of any part of the school premises, including the provision of furniture and equipment, and for their subsequent upkeep. It must convey its interest in any addition to the site to the trustees of the school but the legitimate interests of the authority are protected, under section 14 of the 1944 Act and the First Schedule of the 1946 Act, if the governors discontinue the school or if the premises are sold. The playing fields remain the property of the authority.

(ii) *Transfer of an existing school to a new site*
The financial responsibility of the LEA and the requirement to convey its interest to the trustees is exactly the same as in (i). The new factor in this particular situation is that, having provided the new site and buildings, which become the property of the trustees, the authority becomes entitled,

through the provision of the First Schedule to the 1946 Act, to part or to the whole of the sale proceeds of the old school premises, if they are disposed of.

(iii) *Significant enlargement of an existing school*

The Secretary of State must be satisfied that there is a need for such an enlargement, and that either it is required wholly or mainly to provide accommodation for pupils who would have been accommodated in another voluntary school if that school had not ceased to be available, or that it will ensure better provision of primary or secondary education at the premises to be enlarged, or that it will ensure there are sufficient suitable primary or secondary schools in an area, or for all these reasons. The LEA and the governors of the controlled school must each apply to the Secretary of State for his approval to meet the cost of significantly enlarging a controlled school, and unless both parties have applied to him he cannot direct the LEA to meet the cost of significantly enlarging a controlled school. The authority is not obliged to convey to the trustees its interest in any addition to the existing site or in buildings on it that are from time to time part of the school premises, but in certain circumstances it may be to its advantage to do so. This would be the case, for example, if the new extension subsequently enabled the old premises to be disposed of so that their sale value would accrue to the authority, or part of the proceeds could be used to meet the cost of the new site and buildings if the proceeds exceed that cost. As in (i) and (ii) the playing fields remain the property of the authority.

(iv) *Establishment of a new controlled school in new premises*

A new controlled school may be established in new premises where it is impossible significantly to enlarge an existing controlled school and it is necessary to provide accommodation for pupils who would have been accommodated in another voluntary school if it had not been discontinued. In such circumstances the authority may pay for the whole of the building work approved by the Secretary of State and the new premises remain its property, as of course do the playing fields. Additionally, if the new controlled school is to be a middle school, it may be so established for pupils for a substantial proportion of whom accommodation would have been provided in some other voluntary school if that other school had not been discontinued or had not ceased to be available, and in this case, too, the authority may carry out the work for which it pays.

Aided schools

The complexity of the issues relating to aided school premises arises both from capital expenditure that may be incurred on them and their subsequent upkeep. Capital expenditure at aided schools may be incurred for one of the four following reasons:

(i)   the alteration or significant enlargement of the premises of an existing school;
(ii) the transfer of an existing school to a new site;
(iii) the substitution of a new school for one or more existing voluntary schools;
(iv) the establishment of a new school.

In all four cases capital expenditure on furniture and equipment is the responsibility of the LEA. The salient requirements of the Education Acts in respect of capital expenditure on building or construction work may be summarised as follows.

(i) *Alteration or significant enlargement of an existing school*
The governors are responsible for the capital expenditure on alterations to or the significant enlargement of the buildings of an existing school and, for all approved work, receive a contribution of 85 per cent of the cost from the DFE. For an alteration that is not a significant enlargement, the LEA is responsible for any other capital expenditure on any addition to the existing site or other buildings (as defined above), on school grounds and playing fields and boundary walls and fences. For a significant enlargement the governors are responsible for capital expenditure on any addition to the existing site. The authority must convey its interest in any addition to the site to the trustees of the school and in any buildings that are to form a part of the school premises but its legitimate interests are protected if the school is discontinued. Any playing fields remain the property of the authority.

(ii) *Transfer of an existing school to a new site*
If an existing aided school has to be transferred to a new site because it is not possible to alter the premises on the existing site to bring them to prescribed statutory standard, the LEA must meet the cost of the new site as well as that of the school grounds, of any road charges and of other buildings. It must convey its interest in the site and other buildings to the trustees but its legitimate interests are protected if the school is discontinued. The playing fields are the authority's

responsibility and remain its property. The governors must provide the new buildings and will normally receive a grant of 85 per cent of the cost, though the Secretary of State will take into account any sums that may accrue to the governors or trustees from the sale of the existing site and buildings. Paragraph 7 of the First Schedule to the 1946 Education Act also empowers the Secretary of State to direct that a payment should be made to the LEA from the proceeds of the sale of any land vacated, after considering the terms of any trust in which the land is held.

(iii) *Substitution of a new aided school for one or more existing voluntary schools*

Substitution does not arise if a voluntary school is merely transferred to a new site so that the premises may conform to the prescribed standards. Substitution arises if the new provision is to be greater than that required for the pupils from the voluntary school that is to be discontinued. Substitution for two or more existing voluntary schools arises if the new provision is to be equal to or greater than that required for the pupils from the voluntary schools that are to be discontinued.

In these circumstances the new site, the school grounds, any road charges and the school buildings must be provided by the governors and an 85 per cent grant is payable by the Secretary of State again, as in (ii), after any proceeds from the sale of existing premises are taken into account. The LEA's responsibility for providing other buildings and its requirement to transfer them to the trustees is unaltered and its legitimate interests are similarly protected if the school closes. Its responsibility for and ownership of playing fields are also the same as before.

(iv) *Establishment of a new aided school*

The financial responsibilities in this case are divided between the LEA and the governors in exactly the same way as in (iii) above and the governors may claim 85 per cent of the cost of the approved work for which they are responsible from the DES.

Special agreement schools

Capital expenditure on the premises of special agreement schools is in practice limited, because of the grant facilities now available for aided schools, to the following two situations:

(i) the alteration of the premises of an existing schools;
(ii) the significant enlargement of the premises of an existing school.

The financial arrangements, the division of responsibility between governors and LEA and the responsibility for the provision of furniture and equipment are in all respects the same as those outlined above in relation to alterations or significant enlargements at aided schools.

Responsibility for upkeep and repairs in aided and special agreement schools

In county and controlled schools the responsibility for upkeep and repairs of buildings, school grounds and playing fields is that of the LEA as 'landlord', although schemes of local management introduced under the Education Reform Act may provide for shared responsibility. In aided and special agreement schools it is divided between the LEA and the governors, and the complexities of this division of responsibility are illustrated in the detailed schedule on pages 166–168 of the eighth edition of *County and Voluntary Schools* referred to earlier.

The division of financial responsibility for repairs is not straightforward, and it is because there is no statutory definition of what constitutes 'repairs to the interior' of school buildings that there is a need for that specific guidance contained in the schedule and drawing in *County and Voluntary Schools*. Even that, however, cannot wholly eliminate areas of uncertainty and in the last resort any irreconcilable differences between the LEA and individual school governors would need to be settled by the courts.

Perhaps one of the most intractable difficulties that from time to time arises between the two parties concerns 'consequential damage'. This may involve, for example, damage to a hall floor or school decorations as a result of neglect in maintaining the roof, which is the responsibility of the governors. The wrangle that can arise in this kind of situation may stem from the fact that although it is the governors' responsibility to maintain the roof in good order, the LEA has no legal power to require them to fulfil it, so that if the authority is caused to incur expenditure through the negligence of the governors, an arbiter may be needed to settle the dispute. This will initially be the Secretary of State but in the last resort it may need to be the courts. Disputes of this kind are rare and are normally resolved amicably between the LEA and school governors, but the potential for difficulty is inherent in the lack of legal definition of the division of responsibility.

Perhaps the most significant example of 'consequential damage', which did not arise from neglect by either partner, was that caused by the use of high alumina cement (HAC) in the mid-1970s. Substantial expenditure was incurred both by LEAs and governors in making premises safe and these major works were the subject of prolonged discussion with the DES, as it then was. Legally, however, the Education Acts make no provision for altering the normal division of responsibility between LEA and governors solely because of the causes of the work involved. It follows, therefore, that work due to HAC or other structural defects must be treated no differently from other repairs, and the division of responsibility should follow the normal principles.

Establishment, discontinuance and alteration of voluntary schools

The legal requirements for all voluntary schools — controlled, aided and special agreement — in respect of proposals to establish any school to be maintained by an LEA as a voluntary school, or to make a significant change of character or significant enlargement of an existing voluntary school, are identical and are defined in s.13 of the 1980 Act. This specified that any persons making such proposals must consult with the LEA and publish their proposals in such a manner as may be required by the Secretary of State and submit to him a copy of the published proposals. The same two month period for objections must elapse, as in the case of proposals made by an LEA, but in the case of voluntary schools they must be submitted direct to the Secretary of State. He may then reject the proposals, approve them without modification or, after consultation with the persons by whom they were made and the LEA by whom the school is, or is to be, maintained, approve them with such modifications as he may think desirable.

S.13 of the 1980 Act is not the section that defines the powers of governors of voluntary schools to publish proposals to discontinue existing schools. This power is primarily vested in LEAs, in s.12 of the Act, though of course voluntary school governors may submit their objections to the authority's published proposals in accordance with s.12(3). s.14 of the 1944 Act, however, which, as was explained above, remains unaltered, gives the governors of voluntary schools certain carefully defined and very restricted powers to declare their intention of discontinuing existing voluntary schools. It is obviously essential that proposals to take out of use any places in voluntary schools, which are an integral part of a local authority's maintained school provision and help it to fulfil its statutory obligations in accordance with s.8 of the 1944 Act, should only be made after consultation with the authority and with its full knowledge.

S.14 therefore requires the governors of any voluntary school who propose to discontinue any such school to serve both on the Secretary of State and the LEA at least two years' notice of their intention to do so. If, however, expenditure other than in connection with repairs has been incurred on the premises, either by the Secretary of State or by the LEA, the governors may only issue such notice with the specific approval of the former who, if he grants it, may impose specific requirements relating to repayment of such expenditure and the possible continuing need for the use of the buildings by the local authority for any purpose connected with education. The objects of this section are to avoid difficulties which might arise if voluntary school governors were to seek to discontinue a school without giving the LEA reasonable opportunity to provide alternative accommodation and, where such arrangements have been made, to prevent a change of mind on the part of the governors. It must be said, however, that this section of the 1944 Act has rarely been invoked and a decision to publish proposals to discontinue a voluntary school is normally the outcome of consultation between the LEA and individual school governors, resulting in their publication by the former in accordance with s.12 of the 1980 Act.

The Education (No.2) Act 1986

Composition and functions of governing bodies

These are set out respectively of course in the Instruments and Articles of Government. The 1986 Act made significant revisions in both these areas. The principal feature of these revisions was to reduce the power and influence of the LEA. Even though the statutory responsibility for making Instruments and Articles of Government for voluntary schools was placed upon LEAs they had to secure the agreement of voluntary school governing bodies in doing so.

Part 2 of the 1986 Act sets out the composition of governing bodies for various sizes of school. Even in a controlled school the number of foundation governors, along with parent/teacher and co-opted governors, was increased *vis-à-vis* the number of LEA governors. In the case of aided and special agreement schools specific provision was included for the number of foundation governors to outnumber all other categories of governor by two or three, dependent on the size of the governing body. Part 3 of the 1986 Act, dealing with the organisation and functions of schools and governing bodies, gave the responsibility to the governors of county controlled and special agreement schools for determining the aims of the secular curriculum in a school, albeit having considered the policy of the LEA as to the secular curriculum. S.19 specifically provides for the content of the secular curriculum for a voluntary-aided school to be under the control of the governing body, with a requirement for that governing body to 'have regard' to the policy of the LEA as expressed in the LEA's own curriculum statement.

Ss.22–28 of the 1986 Act dealing with discipline, provided for the setting up of complex systems of exclusion and reinstatement of pupils, including an appeal process, which have often proved cumbersome to implement and which have imposed particular obligations upon governing bodies of voluntary aided and special agreement schools.

The Education Reform Act 1988

The Education Reform Act did not make any particularly distinctive impact upon voluntary schools separate from that which it made on all schools through its provisions on the curriculum, pupil admissions and new financial and staffing systems. Two particular points may be highlighted, however. S.30 amended the appropriate section of the 1980 Act and added a new sub-section (6) to that section which required that the LEA 'if so requested by the governors of an aided or special agreement school maintained by the authority may make arrangements with the governors in respect of the admission of pupils to the school for preserving the character of the school; and the terms of any such arrangements, shall, in default of agreement between the authority and the governors, be determined by the Secretary of State'. The effect of this section, due in no small measure to pressure from the Roman Catholics, is to enable the governors of the voluntary schools concerned to refuse admission to pupils not professing the faith of the foundation, even though the school may not be admitting up to its standard number for admissions.

S.45 prescribed the arrangements for the appointment and dismissal of teaching and non-teaching staff in an aided school with a delegated budget. The power to appoint and to dismiss now lies entirely with the governing body, who continue to be the employers of staff at aided schools; the LEA's previous powers in relation to staffing appointments no longer apply. Aided schools are however able to agree with the LEA arrangements giving the Chief Education Officer advisory rights in relation to the appointment or dismissal of staff.

The general effect of the Education Reform Act was to reinforce the position of voluntary schools within the educational system and to underpin the success with which the churches had dealt during the seventies and eighties with challenges both from without and within on such issues as crypto-selection, multiculturalism and race. In consequence the re-assertion as a first priority of the value of schools with a religious ethos, and allied to this the priority of religious education, has been strengthened. Voluntary schools have been able to invoke the fact that the majority of them are well supported locally, well behaved educationally and make a full contribution to the enlargement of parental choice.

In the publication *Signposts and Homecomings* (1981) the Roman Catholic Church reaffirmed that the purpose of RC schools was to serve the RC population, and whilst in some areas this population happened to be largely white, the schools could often point out that they included children of many national origins, especially from Europe.

Perhaps more heartsearching re-examination took place within the Church of England, not surprisingly given the double role that it has seen its schools as having: serving those who practise the faith and also the whole local community of children. This re-examination arguably started with the 1970 Durham report but the key document is probably the National Society's *Future in Partnership* (1984). In this, concern was expressed that scope for individual school governing bodies to act unilaterally in ways that sometimes ignored local sensibilities was on the increase, and frank warnings were given that voluntary schools which 'misused' their status would get no support from the Church. In this context the suggestion emerged for getting church schools together through mediation by diocesan boards agreeing matters like admissions in common. A group of 20 headteachers meeting at Allington Castle in 1981 signed an 'agreement' noting the need to share more experience with local county schools and implying that they were prepared to surrender a certain degree of autonomy to further a negotiated local approach with boards and authorities. This did not however engender wide support, and disagreement continued over what approach should be adopted on particular contentious practices. For example, the London Board's 1984 guidelines admitted that there was continuing disagreement on the processes of interviewing prospective pupils and their parents, with some church schools insisting on it and others insisting on giving it up. The National Society has sought to express a consensus view, especially in its booklet *A Shared Vision* (1992).

Retrospectively it does not seem surprising that in the years immediately following the Allington statement no consensus, however desirable, should have emerged. There were two major and complementary difficulties. On the one hand governors were clearly unwilling to surrender any of their powers to diocesan boards if they had little confidence in those boards, consisting as many of them did for the most part of lay people and operating with a minimum secretariat. It was argued that these were hardly adequate structures to maintain current responsibilities, let alone a future, when provision both numerically and financially should reflect the Church's proper regard for its schools. On the other hand dioceses themselves saw little point in enhancing the quality of their boards or in providing more, better qualified and more highly paid officers to administer voluntary schools so long as the boards' role remained merely advisory. It had been clear for many years that except in respect of financial support as, for example, helping governing bodies with their 15 per cent liabilities, diocesan boards of education had no real powers over any one of 'their' schools, but could merely make recommendations to the governors which would be accepted only if they related to uncontroversial and relatively unimportant issues. This critical issue, that governors and headteachers would not surrender prized autonomy to the boards as then structured and staffed, whilst boards had little incentive to restructure their machinery and improve the quality of their staffing unless there was a real job for them to do, has now taken on a new and most interesting significance in the light of the three most recent developments: the Diocesan Boards of Education Measure 1991, the Education (Schools) Act 1992, and the Government's White Paper, *Choice and Diversity*, with its consequential Education Bill, both published later in the same year.

The DBE Measure 1991

This measure, which replaced the Diocesan Education Committees Measure of 1955, provided for the establishment in every diocese of a diocesan board of education responsible to the diocesan synod. It required each diocesan bishop, after consultation with the board, to appoint a diocesan director of education to act as secretary of the board.

S.3 identified certain transactions before entering into which the governing body of any church school and the trustees of any church educational endowment must obtain the advice or consent of the board. Such transactions included the discontinuance of the school, any change in the status, size or character of the school, any significant enlargement of premises, any disposal of the premises, or any amalgamation with another school. S.3(2) stipulated that the governing body of any aided or special agreement school should not enter into arrangements in connection with any alteration or repair of the premises towards which grant was paid by the Secretary of State or for which the prior approval of the Secretary of State was required, without obtaining the written consent of the diocesan board.

S.3(4) required that if the governors of a voluntary school resolved at the statutory first meeting to hold a ballot of parents on the question of whether grant-maintained status should be sought for the school it should obtain the advice of the relevant diocesan board and have regard to that advice before confirming that decision by a further resolution of the second statutory meeting. S.5 required that the statement submitted under the 1988 Act to support a proposal for the acquisition of grant-maintained status for a Church of England voluntary school shall include an account of the advice given by the board and provide confirmation that the governing body of the school has had regard to that advice or, if it has departed from it, the reasons for so doing.

Later sections give diocesan boards powers to issue directions to governing bodies of aided church schools in certain circumstances: s.7 where the board is satisfied that the governing body of a school is discharging its functions in relation to any matter affecting the status, continuance, size or character of the school or to any significant enlargement of its premises in a manner which is not in the best interests of that school or of church schools generally; s.8, where the board is satisfied that the trustees of any church educational endowment held wholly for a church school are discharging their functions in relation to the endowment in such a manner that the endowment is not being applied in the best interests of the school or that the trustees of any such endowment have failed to discharge their functions in relation to that endowment.

S.9 strengthens the powers of the diocesan director of education in providing an entitlement for him/her to attend any proceedings of the governing body of an aided school for the purpose of giving advice to that governing body where the chief education officer of the local education authority concerned is also so entitled by virtue of s.45(6) of the Education Reform Act. (Schedule 15 of the Education Bill 1992 makes certain amendments to the DBE Measure, reflecting the fact that all the provisions relating to grant-maintained status are to be re-enacted in the new bill.)

The Schools Act 1992

The Education (Schools) Act 1992 was a short but quite controversial piece of legislation, the original Bill being modified in certain important respects as it progressed through the various committee stages of the procedure. Certain aspects seem to be of some interest for voluntary schools.

S.9 prescribes the duty of the newly created post of HM Chief Inspector to secure that all schools are inspected at certain prescribed intervals by a registered inspector. Subsection 4 specifies the general duties of registered inspectors and the teams they will be leading to report on, *inter alia*, 'the spiritual, moral, social and cultural development of pupils at the school'. The inspection of denominational education under these arrangements is specifically excluded under sub-section 6. However, s.13, applying to any voluntary and any grant-maintained school in which denominational education is given ('denominational education' being defined as religious education otherwise than in accordance with an agreed syllabus) provides for an inspection under this section to be conducted by a person chosen by the foundation governors in the case of a controlled school and the governing body in any other case. The general duty of a person chosen, who need not be a registered inspector, shall be to report on the quality of the denominational religious education provided at the school.

This has given rise to the possibility of informal partnerships in the future between independent inspectors and diocesan education teams in the carrying out of inspections of voluntary schools. The financial implications of expanding the professional staff of the diocese, whether Anglican or Roman Catholic, are daunting to bodies already operating under very severe financial constraints in many cases. However, the additional costs are thought by some to be inevitable if the Church is to be prepared to support its schools in a changed situation. The churches obviously hope that the inspection teams set up under both ss.9 and 13 will reflect the expertise currently held amongst HMI and LEAs, but it is almost inevitable that there will be some places in the country where inspection teams independent of both the diocese and the local authority will win contracts for the inspection of church schools. There is some disquiet amongst Roman Catholics about the idea of such teams making assessments of moral and spiritual education in Catholic schools, and in these circumstances it is seen as important to ensure that sufficiently good relationships exist for the churches in general to be confident that the teams will carry out a professionally competent job in their inspection of church schools.

The White Paper 1992 *Choice and Diversity* and the Education Bill 1992

The Education White Paper *Choice and Diversity: A New Framework for Schools* (Cmd 2021, July 1992) has some important implications for voluntary schools. The Education Bill, published on 30 October 1992, contained most of the White Paper proposals, and both documents are considered together in this section, reference being made to any significant points of difference.

Chapter 6, paragraphs 9 and 10 of the White Paper explicitly set out the importance which the Government continues to attach to the dual system of county and voluntary schools stemming from the 1944 Education Act and the religious settlement which underpins it. The Government believes that 'the contribution of voluntary schools provided by the churches and others cannot be over-estimated', and it points in justification of this view to the schools' popularity with parents and to the role they play in enhancing choice and providing 'powerful reinforcement of the spiritual and moral dimension of education which is of great importance to children'. Consequently, the Government wishes to see the role of the churches and other voluntary bodies in education preserved and enhanced and in particular to play a positive part in the further development of grant-maintained schools. Paragraph 6.10 re-affirms the provisions of the Education Reform Act that the governors of ex-voluntary-aided GM schools will not be liable for the 15 per cent contribution to capital and external repair costs, and guarantees the position of the foundation through the device of the foundation governors having a majority on the governing body, thereby protecting the established trusts, character and ethos of the school.

Chapter 4, on the role of voluntary bodies in setting up new grant-maintained schools in response to local demand, proposes that until the 75 per cent 'exit point' is reached or until the Secretary of State has agreed to the LEA's request to be relieved of its duty to provide sufficient schools, voluntary bodies will continue to be able to propose the establishment of new LEA-maintained voluntary schools. In addition, and this is a new power, contained in clause 206 of the Bill, once the 10 per cent 'entry point' is reached voluntary bodies will be able to propose the establishment of new GM schools; in these circumstances, the voluntary bodies would have to provide 15 per cent of any new capital costs but once the school was established it would be funded as to both recurrent and capital expenditure on the same basis as other grant-maintained schools.

Interestingly, clause 205 of the Bill extends the powers of LEAs in respect of voluntary schools by enabling them to propose significant changes in character or enlargement of such schools. It is understood however that the Government is prepared to amend this clause so that LEA's powers are not extended in this way, although the Secretary of State will be given such powers.

The White Paper thus brings to a head the issue that has been simmering for some years as to whether religious bodies other than the Christian and Jewish ones that already provide voluntary schools should set up their own schools. Views on this issue have been expressed on a cross-political party basis, and it does seem likely that the first grant-maintained Muslim schools could be expected in inner city areas such as Bradford and Tower Hamlets where local councils have had difficulty in providing places to keep pace with the increase in the number of children. Before such schools receive approval to 'opt into' the State system, it is expected that the proposers will have to convince the Secretary of State for Education that they will teach the National Curriculum and that they will not create surplus school places.

The extent to which the Government intends to open this particular door to non-Christian voluntary bodies is unclear. A spokesman for the Adam Smith Institute who has campaigned privately for some years for legislation to allow such groups to set up schools, believes new state-maintained schools could be set up fairly quickly. At a conference of the Muslim Education Co-ordinating Council UK, as reported by Geraldine Hackett (1992), a number of Muslim organisations agreed that applications should be made for state funding, and a warning was given that secular education was producing an under-class of Muslims who were under-achieving whilst at the same time Muslim private schools were on the verge of collapse because of the impact of the recession on the Muslim community. However, there does seem to be division among Muslim parents about Muslim schools. Research published in 1992 by the Cambridge University Department of Education (ESRC 1992) has found that some Muslim parents have reservations about such schools, partly because of educational standards, partly because of the strictness of the regime and partly because of the fear that their children would be isolated from the mainstream community.

These proposals of the White Paper may also affect providing bodies on what might be called the fringe of mainstream Christianity. The Christian Schools Campaign, representing about 70–80 small schools, some of which take children from 5 to 16 and which tend to be linked to local evangelical churches, have expressed interest in the possibilities. The problem for such schools may be the narrowness of the education they provide.

Within the Department for Education the current prediction is that the number of voluntary schools to secure approval is likely to be limited whilst there remain significant numbers of surplus places throughout the country. Many of the approximately two hundred small religious schools that are thought to wish to take advantage of these proposals exist in sub-standard buildings and if they are to enter the maintained system the Government will need to be committed to providing the additional 85 per cent capital resources to bring the schools up to standard, unless the money is taken from the allocations for existing county and voluntary schools.

Chapter 11, of the White Paper entitled 'Tackling failing schools' refers in paragraph 14 to the discussions which the Government is having with the churches as to how to tackle voluntary aided schools that are 'failing'. The Government has not involved LEAs in these discussions, and this seem rather strange in view of the fact that, other than in respect of RE and collective worship, diocesan bodies have not historically had any responsibility for assuring quality in voluntary schools except in partnership with LEAs. This again raises important issues concerning future powers of diocesan boards of education; the Church of England has urged that the churches should be strongly represented on any education associations set up under clause 194 of the Bill to 'secure . . . the elimination of any deficiencies' in a church school.

Two other proposals in the White Paper seem to illustrate the special favour with which voluntary schools are viewed by the current Government. Chapter 10 proposes, in the interests of promoting much greater diversity and specialisation by schools, particularly technology, an expansion of the Technology Schools Initiative which will develop a network of specialist technology schools with City Technology Colleges at its centre. Any existing VA school will be able to apply to become a Technology College whilst retaining its VA status; the school would be able to seek funding from the Secretary of State and private sponsors, following a procedure similar to that of GM schools becoming GM Technology Colleges, and the foundation governors of the VA school will remain in the majority. Chapter 12, entitled 'Opportunities for small schools', proposes that small primary schools, particularly in rural areas, will be able to opt together for GM status as a 'cluster' of schools; as a special privilege voluntary-aided and special agreement schools will have the further option, described in 12.7, of applying for 'associate membership' of clusters, thereby retaining their own governing bodies but taking advantage of the economies of scale and closer co-operation which the cluster arrangements are intended to offer.

The Education Bill also makes certain provisions of importance for church schools not all of which were foreshadowed in the White Paper. Clauses 211, 212 and schedule 11 provide for the incorporation of governing bodies of county, voluntary and maintained special schools. The Department's reasoning for this change is to protect governors from individual liability (a reason not readily understandable in view of the recent tightening up on liability of company trust and charity law), but the way in which this concept of corporate status has been unexpectedly introduced into the Bill is surprising and is likely to have consequences which will be quite significant. The implications for church schools bristle with uncertainties and it seems relevant to identify several main issues which will need to be resolved.

(i) Sub-section 211(4) may lead to the same confusion about trust property as arises with grant-maintained schools because it provides that land is attributable to a governing body if 'it was held by or on behalf of any persons as members or former members of the governing body'. Governors may argue that school premises are held by the trustees on their behalf. What will be the position where the trustees are holding funds which have in fact been raised by the governing body or land acquired with funds raised by the governing body?

(ii) Paragraph 10 of the Schedule provides that where the governing body of a voluntary school is dissolved because the school is discontinued, all land and other property which immediately before the date of dissolution was the property of the governing body and all rights and liabilities of the governing body shall be transferred to and vested in the trustees of the school. How would for example the incumbent and church warden trustees of a voluntary-aided school be able to deal with all this together with the even more alarming provisions about rights and liabilities? Any such rights or liabilities acquired or incurred for the purpose of the school pass to the trustees. Does this mean that the trustees will be liable on contracts entered into by the governing body which they have no funds to fulfil?

Clause 229 provides for the instrument of government of any aided secondary school to name one or two sponsors and for there to be up to four governors appointed by the sponsor(s).

Although a somewhat bald reference was made to this provision in the White Paper the Bill does little to fill in important details such as the financial arrangements, the suitability of particular persons to sponsor a school, how the sponsorship may continue over many years if not for the lifetime of the school. Other clauses empower LEAs, foreshadowed in the White Paper, to assist the governors of aided and special agreement schools with their 15 per cent contribution to certain building maintenance and capital costs. Whilst in some circumstances this might be beneficial both to LEAs and to voluntary school governors, the very existence of this power might put pressure on LEAs to exercise it even though the LEAs might be unwilling to do so. The clauses of course mark a further erosion of the principle of local contribution.

Conclusions on the 1992 proposals

Taken as a whole, the implications of the proposals for voluntary schools in the White Paper and the Bill may be seen as pointing to an opportunity for the churches to discover an enhanced sense of significance and mission for their schools. In January 1991 there were approximately 1.6 million pupils being educated in voluntary church schools in England and Wales; out of nearly 23,000 maintained schools, just under 7,400 were church schools, with the Church of England (4,903) and the Roman Catholic (2,220) providing by far the majority. As has been seen, the Church of England has been traditionally more cautious about emphasising the specifically religious or Anglican character of schools because of its long tradition of serving both the local community and members of the faith. Some Anglican schools, particularly those in inner city areas, now have a majority of Muslim pupils, and many Muslim parents feel that a church school will provide better discipline and a more 'moral' education than a county school. However tensions do arise and at a Church of England controlled school in Berkshire, with 98 per cent Asian pupils, a thousand parents and members of the Asian community recently signed a petition accusing the teachers of racism and complaining that their culture was being devalued. They were angered by the governors' failure to appoint a Muslim headteacher, and they wanted equal representation on the governing body.

Whilst Roman Catholic schools have traditionally been thought to be much closer to their Church, a report in the first half of 1992 from the Arundel and Brighton Diocese showed that Catholic schools were admitting an ever-increasing proportion of non-Catholic pupils; in secondary schools it was reported that 29 per cent of pupils were non-Catholics. In July of 1992 Cardinal Basil Hume, the

Archbishop of Westminster, told a conference that he did not believe Roman Catholics could justify all the effort and expense involved in preserving and running Catholic schools unless all immediately concerned — governors, teaching staff, parents and pupils — embraced wholeheartedly the ideals of Catholic education and strove to realise those in the day-to-day conduct of the school.

As mentioned earlier the debate has been fuelled by the demand of Muslims and others for their own voluntary-aided schools; the Secretary of State has been told by the High Court to look again at the Government's refusal to grant VA status to the Islamia primary school in Brent. The Director of the Anglican Southwark Diocese has urged that in appropriate circumstances VA schools might seek grant-maintained status as the best means of securing their future, arguing also that the diocese must be prepared for GM schools to turn to the board for more support and help once they no longer have ties with the local authority. This view was not fully endorsed by the Southwark Diocesan Schools Committee and the General Synod Board of Education in its official response to the consultation process expressed significant reservations on the issue of grant-maintained status. Others within the Church are even less optimistic, pointing out that as many dioceses currently have neither the staff nor the resources to bolster church schools, there is a danger if large numbers of voluntary schools opt out that the basic principle underlying the dual system itself will be critically undermined, and the degree of independence historically from central government which church schools currently enjoy will be compromised. The future role for many church schools therefore looks somewhat unclear although possibly quite exciting.

RE and collective worship

In view of the current controversies about religious education and worship in all maintained schools, county or voluntary, it might be worth reminding ourselves briefly of the relevant provisions contained in the 1944 Act which have determined this area of work for nearly fifty years. 'Religious instruction', as it was called, and worship were made obligatory in every maintained school. Parents retained their right to withdraw the child and no teacher was compelled to give religious instruction. The Act prescribed that every school day should begin with collective worship attended by all the pupils, but such worship should not be distinctive of any particular denomination. The religious instruction was to be based on the agreed syllabus that had been adopted by the LEA using the cumbersome and involved machinery prescribed in the Fifth Schedule. Interestingly enough the first agreed syllabus had been adopted in Cambridgeshire as early as 1924. Other authorities had followed suit with the result that a number of agreed syllabuses were available in 1944. They were however little more than outlines and it soon became evident that teachers wanted more detailed guidance with regard to teaching method, illustration and background information. To meet these needs most authorities went on to revise their syllabuses and added to their contents.

In the years following 1944 the agreed syllabuses produced in this way concentrated on presenting fundamentals of the Christian religion. Even at the time, doubts were expressed whether the syllabus approved by all the denominations, as it had to be in accordance with the terms of the Fifth Schedule, could give doctrinal teaching which was sufficiently definite to be useful, although many agreed syllabuses subsequently produced seemed to illustrate that the body of doctrine about which there was dispute was comparatively small when compared with the bulk of Christian belief common to all denominations. Many Anglican dioceses prepared their own syllabuses to be used in conjunction with an agreed syllabus providing the supplementary instruction deemed to be necessary.

The changes introduced by the Education Reform Act in the areas of religious education and collective worship were important. s.11 requires every LEA to constitute a Standing Advisory Council on Religious Education (SACRE) to advise the Authority on matters connected with religious worship in county schools and religious education in accordance with an agreed syllabus. The section provides for the constitution of the SACRE, the appointment of members, voting, review of agreed syllabus and the SACRE's annual report.

S.2 provides that in addition to the national curriculum as described in that section and s.3, every maintained school shall secure that its curriculum includes provision for religious education for all registered pupils at the school. s.8 stipulates that the duty to provide religious education for all registered pupils at a maintained school should be subject to exceptions or to special arrangements. Sub-section 2 of this section provides that religious education in the basic curriculum is to be of the kind required by such of the provisions of ss.26 to 28 of the 1944 Act and 84 to 86 of the ERA as applied to the school. Sub-section 3 provides that any agreed syllabus of religious education must reflect the fact that the religious traditions of Great Britain are 'in the main Christian', whilst taking account of the teaching and practices of the other principal religions represented in the Kingdom.

S.6 requires that all pupils in maintained school should take part in an act of collective worship normally on the school premises on each school day. This may be a single act of worship for all pupils or separate acts of worship for different religious groups. These provisions supersede the provisions as to collective worship in s.25 of the 1944 Act. S.7 concerned special provisions as to collective worship in county schools. The section was introduced by the Bishop of London on a third reading in the House of Lords; it has important implications and reflected a quite widespread desire to have the place of Christianity explicitly recognised in the law on religious education. Sub-section 1 says that the collective worship required in county schools 'shall be wholly or mainly of broadly Christian character' which means that the collective worship 'reflects the broad traditions of Christian belief without being distinctive of any particular Christian denomination'. Sub-section 3 says that it is not necessary for every act of collective worship to comply with sub-section 1 if, 'taking any school term as a whole, most . . . such acts which take place in the school do comply with that sub-section'. Sub-section 4 introduces flexibility in respect of the 'relevant considerations' set out in sub-section 5, namely (a) any circumstances relating to the family backgrounds of the pupils concerned which are relevant for determining the character of the collective worship which is appropriate in their case; and (b) their ages and aptitudes. Sub-section 6 provides that under s.12 a SACRE may exempt from the requirements of sub-section 1 any county school or any class or description of pupils at a county school.

The way in which the provisions of sub-section 6 are triggered is for the head teacher of a county school to make an application to a SACRE, after consultation with the governing body of the school, for a determination. s.12, sub-section 5, provides for a review, in specified circumstances, of any such determination that the requirement for Christian collective worship should not apply.

S.84, 85 and 86 adapt in respect of grant-maintained schools which were respectively former county schools, controlled school and aided or special agreement school the provisions as to collective worship and religious education of the Education Reform Act. s.87 details the effects upon the required provision for religious education in a grant-maintained school which receives approval from the Secretary of State for making a significant change in the religious character of that school.

Implications for religious education and worship in the 1992 White Paper and Education Bill

Chapter 8 of the White Paper, entitled 'Spiritual and moral development', refers to the importance that the Government wishes to continue to exercise in the school's role of promoting pupils' spiritual moral development through its teaching and pastoral care. LEAs that have not already done so will be required to review their agreed syllabuses for religious education, GM schools will be able to use any agreed syllabus adopted since the Education Reform Act 1988, and the constitution of agreed syllabus conferences and SACREs will be amended to allow for separate committees for GM schools if 75 per cent of either primary or secondary pupils in the LEA are in GM schools. Grant-maintained schools which were formerly aided or special agreement schools will be required to advise the SACRE in any case where they are required to teach the agreed syllabus at the request of parents by virtue of s.86(3) of the Education Reform Act. Additionally, the White Paper proposes to provide former county grant-maintained schools with the same powers as county schools to seek a determination from the local SACRE under s.12 of the ERA, lifting the requirement that worship should be broadly Christian for the whole school or for specified groups of pupils at the school, and providing that where a determination is already in force with the school when it becomes grant-maintained, that determination will remain in force until such time as it is reviewed.

Whilst the relevant clause in the Education Bill is an improvement on the arcane wording of the former provisions in the 1988 Act, what is perhaps the main criticism still remains. Because of the negative formulation of the clause it does not say what shall be put in place of the Christian worship if a determination is made although it hints at a possible solution with the words 'the . . . worship . . . shall not be distinctive of any particular Christian or other religious *denomination*, but this shall not be taken as preventing that worship from being distinctive of any particular *faith*'. The weaknesses implicit in the vague wording 'wholly or mainly of a broadly Christian character', present in the 1988 Act remain, and will doubtless continue to be a source of contention in some schools.

A special consultation paper amplifying the proposals of Chapter 8 of the White Paper was issued in the Summer of 1992. Arguably there is a basic anomaly at the heart of the proposals in that there is a clear assumption that LEAs will have a continuing future function in respect of the operation of the SACREs. However there is no explanation in the proposed legislation as to the procedures by which, if a large number of schools acquire grant-maintained status, the LEA would have the resources or indeed the will to manage local arrangements required of them in respect of RE and collective worship.

References

Burgess, H.J. (1958) *Enterprise in Education* 'The Story of the Work of the Established Church in the Education of the People prior to 1870' National Society and SPCK.

Cruickshank, M. (1963) *Church and State in English Education, 1870 to Present Day* Macmillan.

Curtis, S.J. (1967) *History of Education in Great Britain* University Tutorial Press.

ESRC (1992) project on 'Muslim Pupils in British Schools' Cambridge University Department of Education.

Hackett, G. (1992) *The Times Educational Supplement* 7 August.

Hurt, J (1972): *Education in Evolution — Church, State, Society and Popular Education 1800–1870* Paladin.

National Society (1984) *A Future in Partnership.*

National Society (1992) *A Shared Vision.*

Parry, J.P. (1971) *The Provision of Education in England and Wales* Allen and Unwin.

5 Quality assurance in education

Graham Platts

> Quality assurance: All those planned and systematic actions necessary to provide adequate confidence that a product or service will satisfy given requirements for quality. (British Standards Institution BS 5750)

Ensuring the best possible educational opportunities for all pupils and students has always been the first priority for those working within the state system, and the many achievements of the last century or so bear ample witness to this fact. Historically, however, 'quality' in education has tended to be seen in terms of the resources and other support available to the *providers* and to the effectiveness with which these have been deployed through our schools and colleges. The accent, therefore, has been on *what* is delivered rather than *how well* it has been received. A significant development, particularly since the late 1980s, has been an acknowledgement that the *consumers* of educational services may have different expectations of what quality in education should represent. 'Ensuring' has therefore given ground to the necessity of 'assuring' parents and others that the services provided are not only of the best quality, but that they take into account the aspirations and needs of those whose taxes fund the education system and who share in the teaching/learning process.

The British Standards Institution's definition of quality systems (BS 5750) has been widely influential in education as well as in the spheres of manufacturing and service industries. The 'confidence that a product or service will satisfy given requirements for quality' depends on the existence of a quality policy, a quality management and a quality system as well as quality control. In educational terms — recognising the complexity of the service as well as the diversity of expectations it is required to meet — this can be taken to mean:

- setting the targets — reaching agreement about what is to be taught and what should be expected of pupils and students as they progress through the system;

- managing the process — creating a management structure capable of meeting the requirements of the wider community and of providing complementary support on 'technical' matters or beyond the boundaries of the individual institution's jurisdiction;
- establishing accountabilities — clarifying particular responsibilities for maintaining quality within the system;
- evaluating the outcomes — determining the measures by which the service's effectiveness is identified, for the purposes of internal quality management and external quality assurance.

Some pieces of this quality assurance jigsaw in education have been in place individually or together at various times in the past: it is the present contention that in the 1990s, for the first time, the legislation has brought them together.

Primary and secondary education

The maintenance of high standards in the public education service has been at the heart of the political and legislative vision in England and Wales for most of the last one hundred and fifty years. In 1840, when a national system of elementary schools was still only in its infancy, the first inspectors were appointed 'to furnish accurate information as to the discipline, management, and methods of instruction pursued' and to ascertain 'at the periodical visits of inspection, what improvements in the apparatus and internal arrangement of schools, in school management and discipline, and in the methods of teaching, have been sanctioned by the most extensive experience'. (Maclure 1986, pp. 48–51) Inspection, however, was 'not intended as a means of exercising control, but of affording assistance; that it is not to be regarded as operating for the restraint of local efforts, but for their encouragement.' Thus did HMI operate until recent times.

The inspectors were directly assisted by central government until the 1920s, when national regulation of the secondary school curricula (and the inspection of timetables) was relinquished and general oversight of schools handed to local councils. During the inter-war years the councils had considerable discretion to vary the local curriculum, at a time when particular objectives or standards were not prescribed by regulation. It was believed for many years that the 'encouragement' of individual schools would be secured by association with the examination boards controlling the syllabuses which in turn were under the influence of the Secondary Schools Examination Council (formed in 1917). A broad form of national consensus thus prevailed and largely determined what was taught as well as the proper expectations of pupils' educational attainments.

The 1944 Education Act required local education authorities to carry out duties under the 'control and direction' of the newly-created Minister of Education. 'High standards' remained a central concern, but were identified in terms of the LEA's duty to secure that '*efficient* education (my italics) shall be available to meet the needs of the population of their area', and broad aims for the secular curriculum were defined: 'the spiritual, moral, mental and physical development of the community' (s.7). Thus the first step was taken in modern times to identify the core of quality education provision.

The 1944 Act also set out responsibilities for the school curriculum (s.23, later repealed) which found clearer expression in the subsequent model articles of government for schools:

> The Local Education Authority shall determine the general educational character of the school and its place in the local educational system. Subject thereto the governors shall have the general direction of the conduct and curriculum of the school . . . the headmaster shall control the internal organisation, management and discipline of the school . . .

The Act did not, however, deal with the school curriculum in detail, though it did provide for the inspection of schools (as well as HE and FE colleges) by HMI and LEAs. An assumption clearly existed that the *quality* of the secular curriculum would be recognised without the need to define precisely the nation's expectations of its education service.

Curricular matters were largely, if not exclusively, determined by the headteacher and the teaching staff, through the formation of the Curriculum Study Group in 1962 followed in 1964 by its successor, the Schools Council for Curriculum and Examinations gave status and impetus to the wider endeavour. Governors were generally reluctant to intervene where professional expertise was thought to be the proper basis for decision-making about what should be taught, while the examination boards, it was felt, still represented the best source of information about the school's 'standards'. LEAs in the post-war period generally did not assume a vigorous leadership role in relation to the curriculum and in 1977 when the Department of Education and Science asked them to describe systematically their arrangements for the school curriculum in their area (Circular 14/77), it was revealed how little they knew about schools' work and how few local curriculum policies existed at that time.

The 1950s and 1960s, then, saw much curriculum innovation and the development of educational practice, particularly in response to the emerging consensus that all children should be able to derive maximum benefit from the local authority system. This view was soon to lead to the reorganisation of many schools along comprehensive lines and to the widespread understanding that both curriculum content and teaching style had to change if the new system was to succeed. However, while some argued the merits of allowing schools to innovate freely in response to the evolving educational needs of their communities, others saw major disadvantages in the legislative uncertainty about who precisely had responsibility for the curriculum and maintaining educational standards in schools. It was clear that the absence of strict accountabilities had resulted in a wide variety of practices between schools and a marked diversity in educational quality. These concerns were exemplified by particular cases which resounded loudly from the headlines of local newspapers, notably involving Risinghill Secondary School and William Tyndale Junior School (both in London), that seemed to highlight the worst excesses of institutional autonomy and the indifference of 'remote' LEAs.

The notion of 'educational efficiency', therefore, gave way to a concern for 'school effectiveness' and the late 1970s and 1980s saw an extended period of government action, one main purpose of which was to address directly (and repeatedly) the question of 'quality' by raising standards in all schools. With hindsight it is possible to see clearly the strategy unfolding systematically through the Education Acts of 1980, 1986, 1988 and 1992. Educational quality in the state system would be assured by:

1 appointing parents, teachers and members of the local community to governing bodies alongside representatives of the LEA, so that those with a direct interest in the school's continuing effectiveness have oversight of its work and development;

2 strengthening the powers of governing bodies and specifying their precise responsibilities and duties, so that decisions about the school's management and future progress are taken locally;

3 requiring the public disclosure of information about the school and its achievements, so that the governing body may be accountable to parents and others for the education provided in the community;

4 re-defining the respective functions of the Secretary of State, LEAs, school governing bodies and headteachers, so that the curriculum of each school meets the requirements of the law;

5 setting out precisely the content of the curriculum to be taught by all maintained schools with pupils aged between 5 and 16 years as well as the arrangements for regular assessment, so that there are consistent national expectations of the education to be provided and clear levels of pupil attainment;

6 prescribing school development priorities to be supported by education and training grants, so that progress towards the best educational standards in schools is targeted and controlled;

7 determining the means by which schools are to be inspected periodically, so that their effectiveness is confirmed and/or their failings are highlighted for correction.

The Government itself would add to this list the creation of grant-maintained schools and city technology colleges (not to mention technology schools and city colleges for the technology of the arts) to make a direct contribution to educational range in the local authority system following the legislation of the 1980s. New and different types of school clearly add to the diversity of educational provision within an area, and therefore to the quality of opportunity overall for parents and pupils; we must wait and see whether a change of school-type in itself necessarily leads to enhanced educational quality for the school's pupils. Indeed, some may think that the emphasis on institutional autonomy in the Education Act 1993 will in fact begin to undermine that network of relationships developed so methodically in the 1980s for the purpose of quality assurance in education.

The various contributors to the education system (central government, LEAs, governing bodies, teachers, parents and Her Majesty's Chief Inspectors of Schools) now find themselves engaged, for the most part, in a collective endeavour to ensure quality schooling for all pupils in the maintained sector. The signs are that such collaboration will not last indefinitely and may not last much longer. For the foreseeable future, however, the roles and responsibilities, powers and duties of each party are clear and it is to this theme that we shall now turn.

Central government

For most of this century central government has not intervened directly in the detailed prescription or implementation of the school curriculum, choosing instead to allow LEAs to exercise general oversight of their schools and to entrust HMI with the task of identifying good and bad educational practice where this existed. Nevertheless, politicians came under increasing pressure from the

1960s to take some direct responsibility for local authority education and the work of individual schools. This pressure arose from the public's growing expectations of the system, changes in the country's economic structure and employers' requirements of new recruits, the well publicised failures of individual schools, a series of informed criticisms about the service published as 'Black Papers' and the widely perceived fact that for too long the Government had remained non-interventionist in an area of state activity which was too important to leave to unfettered local discretion. In short, educational quality was *not* being assured.

The 'Great Debate' was launched in 1976. Public discussion of education, it was said, had been hijacked by 'the professionals' so that others' legitimate concerns about standards and priorities in the school curriculum went unrecognised. The argument was fuelled by a confidential memorandum from the Department of Education and Science (now the Department for Education) *School Education in England — Problems and Initiatives* that was leaked to the press at the time and which, among other things, argued that the DES should be permitted to give 'a firmer lead'.

The debate culminated in the publication by the DES of a 'Green Paper', *Education in Schools — A Consultative Document* (1977), which summarised the outcomes of the discussions and outlined future intentions. The paper had much to say about the curriculum and directed various criticisms at primary and secondary schools, as the following extracts show:

> In some classes, or even some [primary] schools, the use of the child-centred approach has deteriorated into lack of order and application.
>
> There has been considerable criticism on the grounds that the [secondary] curriculum has become overloaded and that essential educational objectives may have been put at risk.
>
> The offer of options and the freedom to choose do lead some boys and girls to abandon certain areas of study at an early age. This is questionable in a society like ours where the rapidity of change puts a premium on the sound acquisition of certain basic skills . . .
>
> Variations in the approach to the curriculum in different schools can penalise a child simply because he has moved from one area to another.

Among the issues for the future were:

> Teachers should be able to identify with some precision the levels of achievement represented by a pupil's work.
>
> Teachers in successive classes or schools need to agree about what is to be learned.
>
> It is reasonable to expect that children moving from a primary school in

one part of the country to another elsewhere will find much that is familiar in kind if not in detail.

It is clear that the time has come to try to establish generally accepted principles for the composition of the secondary curriculum for all pupils. (Maclure 1986, pp. 394–400)

It is clear that Mr Callaghan's speech had much to do with perceptions of education in the 1980s, though it should be noted that teachers' shortcomings (rather than those of the LEA) were identified at that time as the root of the problem and their potential for solving the problems had to be at the centre of the drive for school improvement. While it would be up to the local education authorities, therefore, to co-ordinate the curriculum and its development in their own areas, there was still concern to allow the exercise of 'proper professional freedom' to meet the requirements of local circumstances and local interests, but in the years following the emphasis on others' contribution to the raising of standards increased.

Alongside continuing work by HMI on *Good Teachers*, and *The Initial Training of Teachers*, the government was also turning its attention to institutional improvement, *Better Schools* and *Quality in Schools: Evaluation and Appraisal*. The DES published *A Framework for the School Curriculum* in 1980 and LEAs were required (after 1981) to publish particulars of the curriculum of each of their schools. HMI later began the publication of its *Curriculum Matters* series which made an important contribution to the process of developing general agreement about curricular aims and objectives. Education legislation in the 1980s gave significant impetus to these trends of prescription in the curriculum and diversity of responsibility for its proper implementation.

The National Curriculum

The Education Reform Act 1988 went much further than ever before in placing the school curriculum on the statute book. Building on Butler's aims in 1944 (s.7) it defined the 'balanced and broadly based curriculum' as one which:

(a) promotes the spiritual, moral, cultural, mental and physical development of pupils at the school and of society; and
(b) prepares such pupils for the opportunities, responsibilities and experiences of adult life.
(s.1)

These ends could only be met by providing a 'National

Curriculum' in all maintained schools, comprising mathematics, English and science, and Welsh in Welsh-speaking schools (the 'core' subjects), as well as history, geography, technology, music, art and physical education, with a modern foreign language during the last five years of compulsory education and Welsh in non-Welsh-speaking schools in Wales (the 'foundation' subjects). Religious education would also be taught within the broader 'basic curriculum'. More than this, each of the National Curriculum subjects should be organised so as to relate to the progress of pupils through the system in terms of four 'key stages' (for pupils aged 5–7, 8–11, 12–14 and 15–16). They would, moreover, specify:

(a) the knowledge, skills and understanding which pupils of different abilities and maturities are expected to have by the end of each key stage (the attainment targets);

(b) the matters, skills and processes which are required to be taught to pupils of different abilities and maturities during each key stage (the programmes of study); and

(c) the arrangements for assessing pupils at or near the end of each key stage for the purpose of ascertaining what they have achieved in relation to the attainment targets for that stage. (ss.2–3)

Separate arrangements were confirmed for religious education which would require the adoption of an agreed syllabus prepared or endorsed by a local standing advisory council on religious education and a standing conference, developing the principles for religious education defined in the 1944 Education Act and based on the model originally developed by Henry Morris in Cambridgeshire before the war. The principle of daily collective worship was also restated.

Educational quality could be assured if each school knew precisely *what* it should teach and *how* its pupils should be assessed. This definition, representing a minimum standard of quality, would then provide parents and others with either the reassurance that their school was performing effectively or good reason to think otherwise. Almost inevitably there were misgivings in some quarters about the statutory requirement to teach a National Curriculum and the legislation on religious education and collective worship generated particular controversy at Westminster. There was considerable difficulty about the type of collective worship that schools should be required to provide and this is reflected in the final form of words which determined that such events should be 'wholly or mainly of a broadly Christian character'. The Act went on to define what was meant by this statement:

collective worship is of a broadly Christian character if it reflects the broad tradition of Christian belief without being distinctive of any particular denomination . . . Every act of collective worship . . . need not comply . . . provided that, taking any school term as a whole, most such acts which take place in the school do comply . . .

Such complexity contributes little to quality assurance in schools, and it is also possible to be critical of legislation which requires sixth-form students at school who are aged eighteen years or more to attend collective worship compulsorily unless their parents withdraw them.

To assist with the development of the National Curriculum and the detailed arrangements for pupil assessment, the Act brought into being two bodies corporate, the National Curriculum Council (or the Curriculum Council for Wales) and the School Examinations and Assessment Council. NCC and SEAC set to work briskly, but it soon became clear just how difficult the job would be, difficulties which, to some extent, were compounded by having different Councils dealing separately with issues of curriculum and assessment. This was in marked contrast to the experience of teachers who had the subsequent task of integrating as closely as possible the teaching and assessment arrangements in the classroom. The amalgamation of the Councils into a single new body, the School Curriculum and Assessment Authority (SCAA), foreshadowed in the 1992 White Paper *Choice and Diversity: A New Framework for Schools* (Cmd 2021) and the 1992 Education Bill, is expected to increase the coherence of their work, but only after the enormous apparatus of the National Curriculum which its predecessors had devised had been largely digested by schools.

Professional development and teacher training

The government recognised two other strategies that would have to be developed if quality assurance was to be a realistic goal and the National Curriculum as successful as most people in the education service hoped. Its impact on schools would be felt by every teacher and its requirements demanded a substantial cultural shift from their professional experiences. The National Curriculum needed to be supported by a programme of in-service training for a significant proportion of the workforce so that its aims and objectives were implemented as efficiently and effectively as possible.

This was done by building on two existing pieces of legislation. First, the Education (Grants and Awards) Act 1984 which enabled the Secretary of State to pay education support grants to local education authorities for specified curriculum-related activities which were to be 'encouraged'; secondly his power to pay training grants for teacher in-service training under s.50 of the Education (No. 2) Act 1986. By 1991 these had been rationalised under a new scheme, the Grants for Education Support and Training (GEST), in order to support more directly the introduction of the National Curriculum and the Local Management of Schools. In 1992/3 £228 million was allocated for the GEST programme which, with the addition of on-going expenditure from the previous year, supported a total of £377 million.

GEST expenditure would also be monitored and evaluated by the DES/DFE, largely on the basis of information supplied by LEAs in relation to their objectives which were outlined in the initial bid for particular grant-supported activities. Other means were also employed, such as the use of electronic data interchange (EDI) which assisted both LEAs and the DFE to develop compatible computer systems holding data relating to teachers. The development of the basic curriculum in schools would be monitored and evaluated on the evidence of information (from HMI findings and schools'/LEAs' performance in assessments) that 'expenditure allocations have facilitated the smooth implementation of the new requirements' (draft DES Circular July 1991, para. 110). Monitoring and evaluation, however, chiefly comprised the use of quantitative performance indicators, an approach which only indirectly focused on issues of quality assurance in the development of the National Curriculum.

The second strategy involved the reorganisation of initial teacher training. In order to circumvent the difficulty that most teacher-trainers had no direct experience themselves of teaching the National Curriculum and to acknowledge the widely-held view that 'on-the-job' training should displace an over-emphasis on 'pedagogic theory', the DFE issued Circular 9/92 (35/92 from the Welsh Office) on *Initial Teacher Training (Secondary Phase)* in June 1992. 'Quality assurance' in teacher supply would now be a matter for schools to determine as partners of higher education institutions, at least in relation to the secondary PGCE. The Council for the Accreditation of Teacher Education (CATE, created in 1984) would have general oversight of the arrangements and advise the Secretaries of State for Education, Wales and Northern Ireland on whether particular HE institutions should be accredited to offer courses of initial teacher training leading to qualified teacher status. The institutions, for their part, were required to enter into partnership with those individual secondary (including middle) schools, sixth form and tertiary colleges that wished to take on a teacher-training role. The partnership would specify the joint training arrangements and it was expected that individual full-time student teachers would spend a minimum of twenty-four weeks in school during the PGCE year. By September 1994 all secondary PGCE courses in England and Wales would operate along these lines.

The proposals, when first aired in the previous January, met with an astonished response. It was by no means certain that schools would regard the major contribution to initial teacher training as their responsibility, particularly in a fast-emerging education market-place where the accent was on retaining the confidence of parents on the strength of the quality teaching provided and ensuring that the resources were available in the school to deploy to this end. The LEAs, too, had misgivings that many of the teachers in their employment were being hijacked for another purpose and that they had no formal means of participating in the new arrangements to safeguard their interests.

The practicality of the circular was also questioned. In response, attention was focused on the existing PGCE courses run by the Universities of Oxford and Sussex which were seen as models of participation between schools and higher education. They proved that the requirements of the Circular could be successfully implemented in other institutions. The magnitude of such a change, however, was easy to underestimate, as the HMI report *School-based Initial Teacher Training in England and Wales* (1991) indicated. First, it showed that most one-year secondary PGCE students spent between 75 and 94 days in school, and, at the other end of the scale, that only one course at that time provided between 115 and 124 days 'on the job' teaching practice. The target from 1994 would be a minimum of 120 days, so that all HE institutions would be affected and many would have to plan for a 50 per cent increase or more in the time spent in school during the PGCE year. HMI also pointed out that in 1990 7,193 student-teachers had been recruited to PGCE secondary courses in England and Wales. With pupil rolls in secondary schools now generally on the increase, the demand for newly-qualified teachers in September 1995 is unlikely to be less, so that every maintained secondary and middle-deemed secondary school in the country (including grant-maintained schools), as well as all independent secondary schools, would have to train, on average, one or two teachers if the overall target is to be met. In reality not all are likely to want this responsibility or be regarded as suitable providers of training and HE institutions will be looking to establish cost-effective arrangements. The early signs are that participating schools will find themselves training cohorts of perhaps twelve student teachers, always in the knowledge that some recruits to teacher training fail to complete the course while others disappear afterwards for various reasons into the 'pool of inactive teachers'!

The Government has therefore done what the DES urged in 1977 and taken 'a firm lead'. It has stated clearly (as far as the complexities of the National Curriculum allow) and precisely what schools should teach; it has identified priorities and committed resources in support of a large-scale and continuing programme of in-service training for teachers; and it has embarked on a major reform of initial teacher training which may yet affect all new entrants to the profession, including those in the primary phase. Brief mention should also be made of the discussion paper produced by Alexander, Rose and Woodhead (1992) (the 'three wise men'), which was widely regarded as a significant contribution to the identification of effectiveness in primary teaching and the professional priorities of teachers. The onus is now on the other parties concerned with quality assurance in schools to ensure that their complementary duties and responsibilities are carried out.

The local education authorities

The effect of education legislation in the 1980s has been to require that LEAs now step back from direct involvement in schools' decision-making and, with their reduced powers, take a broader view of the service locally. At the same time, there has been a continuous running commentary in the national media about the future of LEAs which has conveyed an over-riding impression that they no longer have any role in educational quality assurance. This has been reinforced by the slow but steady growth of the grant-maintained sector, the loss of sixth-form and tertiary colleges to the Further Education Funding Council from April 1993 and major developments in school inspection arrangements. The overall effect of these changes has been smaller education departments, in some cases hardly capable of sustaining an adequate number of staff to monitor and evaluate schools' effectiveness. The emergence in England and Wales of Funding Agencies for Schools (FAS) and the education associations to help tackle 'failing' schools also appear to call into question the continued participation of LEAs in the assurance of educational quality.

On the other hand, it is likely to be the LEA which in most instances for the foreseeable future continues to be the main provider (and maintainer) of school buildings: ensuring the best possible conditions, as it were, for effective teaching and learning. It is still unclear how quickly the FAS will become established to share this responsibility, but its role will be limited and the Secretary of State has said quite explicitly in *Choice and Diversity* that it will have no powers to maintain its own inspectorate (para. 3.13). The LEA retains an active interest in its schools' curricula and in those employed to teach it, as well as in the needs of all pupils and their parents' expectations of the local education service. LEAs, indeed, retain substantial responsibilities for the monitoring and evaluation of effective education in their area and, by implication, within the broader community for quality assurance through the local democratic processes.

The curriculum

The LEA's role in quality assurance begins with its duty, as respects each of its maintained schools, to exercise its functions — particularly relating to religious education, religious worship and the National Curriculum — with a view to securing that the school satisfies the requirements of the Education Reform Act 1988 (Chapter 1). Compliance with such a duty would seem to entail, as far as possible, the regular monitoring of schools' curriculum planning (the careful annual scrutiny of their timetables and examination courses at least) and periodic checking to ensure that what is happening in the classroom matches the school's stated intentions. Larger authorities which retain a strong team of advisers and inspectors will clearly be best placed to comply, but others are unlikely to have the resources even to 'contract out' such work on a part-time basis. These LEAs will need to develop strategies (and a number already have) to carry out their duty and the employment of advisers, inspectors or advisory teams within neighbouring authorities is already emerging as one practical solution to the problem.

LEAs also have a duty under the Education (No. 2) Act 1986 to determine and keep under review their policy in relation to the secular curriculum for all maintained (including special) schools, and to publish a written statement of that policy for all governing bodies and headteachers (s.17). It is sometimes forgotten that most schools offer a range of learning experiences rather broader than the 'basic curriculum' of the 1988 Act, so the LEA should ensure that within the totality of the school's provision an appropriate range of experiences is maintained and that the different components are held in proper balance. Once again, it is difficult to see how this can be done without employing (or having regular access to) a permanent full-time staff of advisers and inspectors charged with monitoring and evaluating children's actual learning programmes continuously.

The LEA must establish (s.11) a standing advisory council on religious education (SACRE) which is charged with important responsibilities relating to the character of collective worship in schools. The council is also a useful forum for advising the LEA about the form and content of RE which is to be taught by the county and controlled schools within its area. The final arrangements for the local agreed syllabus for RE, however, must be the recommendation of a standing conference before the LEA gives its approval. Such arrangements ensure that the syllabus has benefited from professional and lay influences outside the world of education, but do not necessarily mean that agreement about what religious education should be taught has been reached without vigorous discussion!

Authorities' curriculum policies should include reference to sex education in schools. S.46 of the 1986 Act requires that where sex education is given to any registered pupil in a maintained school 'it is given in such a manner as to encourage those pupils to have due regard to moral considerations and the value of family life'. The LEA's policy should clearly not depart from these principles — whatever else it may say — and the same duty is placed on governing bodies, which must agree and publish their own sex education policy for the school, as well as on headteachers who put the policy into practice. If sex education is not to be taught in a particular school, the governing body is required to declare that that is its policy. A similar duty falls to governing bodies and headteachers to ensure that political issues within the school curriculum are dealt with in a balanced way: partisan political views, for example, are not to be expressed (ss.44–45). The LEA has the duty to monitor such matters within its maintained schools.

Finally, it should be noted that local education authorities' 'policing' of the curriculum extends to making sure that examination courses offered by schools have been approved by SEAC and in future by the SCAA. One intention of this would be to minimise the likelihood of major discrepancies and inconsistencies arising between syllabuses and programmes of study at Key Stages 3 and 4, but resolving the question of curriculum emphasis in the last two years of compulsory schooling remains one of the great intractable problems with which the NCC and SEAC have struggled.

The teaching staff

Assuring educational quality must take account of the professional needs of those staff who are to deliver the curriculum and the LEA continues to have a duty to provide, with its schools, a framework of opportunities for in-service training and professional development under the annual GEST programme. In 1993/94, more than 75 per cent of this programme relates directly to developments arising from the Education Reform Act 1988, and about one–third of the total funds are to be devolved to schools either to support improvements in school management or related to the National Curriculum and pupil assessment. Those statistics indicate the relatively narrow scope available to LEAs and schools to exercise local discretion in the use of grants for education support and training, and demonstrates the Government's commitment to the principle of devolving decision-making — in the words of a former Deputy Secretary at the DES 'as close as possible to the point where the decisions bite' (Stuart 1992).

Devolving GEST funds has much to commend it, requiring the earlier comprehensive planning of course programmes and participation, greater responsiveness to consumers' actual needs rather than those deriving from others' perceptions, and a 'competitive edge' of quality on the part of LEA trainers so as to retain future business with local schools. Somewhat counter-balancing this has been the increase in bureaucracy which has also been devolved, particularly relating to schools' financial accountability for GEST funds in their budgets. Since the funding arrangements presuppose that grants will be used in full, any under-spending by a school will entail loss; 'surplus' monies may not be used for other purposes. Prudent management of GEST funds, however, should lead to increased quality in staff development, even if the devolved sums to the very smallest schools provide little or no flexibility of opportunity for those teachers.

LEAs have also played a significant role in recent years in supporting their schools by the employment (and recruitment) of teachers. Many schools continue to seek the advice of LEA staff when making appointments and the Chief Education Officer is still empowered to advise shortlisting and interviewing panels about the appointment of a headteacher (s.37, Education (No. 2) Act 1986 or, as more usually applicable as schools receive fully delegated budgets, para. 3 of Schedule 3 of the 1988 Act). The local education authority remains the employer of most teachers and therefore also bears some responsibility along with the school for ensuring that children are able to benefit from the proper range and quality of expertise among its teaching staff. In the late 1980s teacher recruitment became a matter of considerable difficulty in many parts of south-east England (in particular) and elsewhere, largely as a result of tighter control over the number of available teacher training places in the early 1980s. Schools in the more remote parts of England and Wales had to compete particularly vigorously to attract teachers and LEAs made a significant contribution to ameliorating this problem (supported by

GEST funding) by strategic recruitment to 'pools', by maintaining active brokerage arrangements between those seeking a teaching post and schools with a vacancy, and by enabling 'inactive' teachers to return to the classroom as effective practitioners in the new professional climate.

Teacher appraisal proved to be one of the key innovations of the 1980s, particularly following the decision of the Secretary of State, John MacGregor in 1989 to postpone the introduction of a national scheme to avoid overloading the education system at that time of major reform. In fact, appraisal had been one of the initiatives developed by a number of LEAs with some success which later came to be enshrined within the accepted canon of good educational practice. S.49 of the 1986 Act had indicated that regulations may be made 'requiring local education authorities . . . to secure that the performance of teachers . . . is regularly appraised' and these eventually appeared in 1991. The LEA was identified as 'the appraising body' responsible for all aspects of appraisal set out in the regulations.

The regulations were also concerned with headteacher appraisal which involves LEA staff more closely than teacher appraisal in schools. It was, indeed, a recommendation that in the case of headteachers one of the two appraisers should normally be an officer or adviser of the LEA. Emphasis was placed on the need for the appraisers to become as familiar as possible with the appraisee headteacher's school and its policies prior to the appraisal interview as a means of ensuring that the outcomes have a positive bearing on the future management of the school. Many headteachers elected to be appraised sooner rather than later (it was required in regulations that all teachers complete at least the first year of the appraisal cycle during the school year 1994/95) so that they would be able to bring to bear their own experiences in the implementation of their school's appraisal scheme. The urgency appears to reflect the commitment of both the DFE and the education service to a process that will surely be seen to make a significant contribution to quality in schools.

Pupils' 'entitlement' and parents' expectations

The National Curriculum is intended for the large majority (if not all) pupils aged 5–16 and, accordingly, its levels of attainment cover a wide spread of achievement appropriate for children of very different abilities. Teachers and parents alike, therefore, are invited to regard the National Curriculum as every pupil's 'entitlement', and measures exist to ensure that pupils outside the mainstream of schools' curriculum provision are not unduly disadvantaged in view of their special educational needs or for any other reason. These measures represent important aspects of quality assurance for the LEA at the margins of individual schools' influence over the effective education of young people.

Local education authorities have a duty under the Education Act 1981 to 'have regard to the need for securing that special educational provision is made for pupils who have special educational needs' and to secure that any child for whom they maintain a statement is educated in an ordinary school, subject to certain conditions. The Education Reform Act 1988 acknowledges that allowance ought to be made for some pupils' special educational needs and provides for the requirements of the National Curriculum to be disapplied or modified in individual cases (s.17). The Act makes clear, however, that exception from some or all of the National Curriculum should be only temporary wherever possible, usually for a period not exceeding six months, and that any disapplication of, or modification to, the National Curriculum would still have to observe the general requirements in respect of a broad and balanced curriculum and religious education and collective worship. LEAs have responsibility for the making or amendment of formal statutory assessments under s.5 of the 1981 Act and must consider whether in individual cases any action is required by them when a school makes a special direction to except a pupil temporarily from the National Curriculum.

The headteacher has a duty to inform the LEA and the school's governing body where a pupil is excluded from school for more than five days in any one term, or if the exclusion means that the pupil would be unable to take a public examination. This enables the LEA and the governing body to consider promptly whether or not it should intervene to reinstate the pupil. In the case of a permanent exclusion, the LEA (after consultation with the governing body) must inform the parents if it has been decided that the pupil is not to be reinstated. The parents then have a right of appeal against this decision. Here again, the LEA must arbitrate or be accountable in particular circumstances where it is felt that an individual pupil should not be denied access to the proper range of educational opportunities at school.

Under s.36 of the Education Act 1944, parents have a right to educate their children 'otherwise than at school' and a small, but significant, number do exercise this right. The only legal requirement (and measure of quality) is that this should be 'efficient full-time education' suitable to the age, ability and aptitude of the child in question. Hitherto, the LEA has had power to monitor the parents' alternative arrangements in particular cases and, typically, it has taken steps to satisfy itself that these are satisfactory before the child may be withdrawn from school. Clause 174 of the 1992 Education Bill requires the LEA to revoke a school attendance order unless the parents' arrangements are considered unsatisfactory. The LEA is also to be under a duty (hitherto, it has exercised a power) itself to provide education otherwise than at school. It will be interesting to see what contribution these responsibilities will make to the LEA's wider role in educational quality assurance and how effectively the duty will be met.

The LEA is also required (s.8 Education Act 1980) to publish information about its schools which would enable parents to make an informed decision when seeking a place at a school for their child. This requirement was substantially extended by the requirements under s.22 of the Education Reform Act 1988 and subsequent regulations. In the event of a complaint that the school or the LEA was failing in its duties towards the National Curriculum, LEAs were required (s.23) to establish local arrangements to deal (formally, if necessary) with curriculum-related complaints. The Parents' Charter also encouraged the establishment of formal arrangements to deal with other types of complaint and some LEAs have sought to pursue this.

It seems that the LEA can expect for the future to remain the arbiter in those instances where the concern of a parent (or other person) about a school cannot be resolved locally by informal means, as well as the upholder of pupils' and parents' other rights and entitlements in relation to the provision of education. Ensuring that schools comply with their wide-ranging responsibilities, however, represents a quite considerable task for the LEA and monitoring individual aspects of a school's work is usually better done in the context of a broader evaluation of institutional quality. It is therefore clear that most LEAs will wish to see these duties form the core (whenever possible) of a continuing monitoring and evaluation process, separate from the more or less formal or periodic inspection arrangements for which others have responsibility. Quality within the service and the assurance of this on behalf of the 'consumers' would be secured by developing and maintaining a responsive system in which the LEA's role was clearly understood. On the other hand, some LEAs are already finding that this role is beyond their current resources and see no likelihood of circumstances changing within the foreseeable future.

Governing bodies

School governing bodies have responsibility for setting the conditions in which effective teaching and learning can take place, and for assuring themselves (not to mention parents and others) that these conditions are being maintained in practice. In broad terms this means establishing guidelines for the general conduct of the school, (including pupil discipline) approving the school development and budget plans, overseeing staff appointments and deciding on a range of school policies. The governing body therefore has an important quality assurance role in terms of its function within the hierarchy of education management, as well as a monitoring responsibility on behalf of parents and other members of the community.

The local arm of a national system

Governing bodies of maintained schools enjoy a 'structural' relationship with their LEA which is in some ways similar to the LEA's relationship with central government. Just as the LEA has the duty to exercise its functions to ensure that its schools meet the curriculum requirements, so too does the governing body have this same duty in the case of its own school (Education Reform Act 1988, s.1). It must ensure that the National Curriculum is implemented, that religious education and daily collective worship are provided in an agreed manner (ss.6 and 10) and that each of the core and foundation subjects are taught for a reasonable time during each key stage so that the programmes of study are met and children can reach the prescribed attainment targets. It also has a duty alongside the LEA to exercise its functions with a view to securing that no course of study is provided for pupils of compulsory school age unless the qualification to which it leads has been approved by the Secretary of State or by a designated body (s.5).

Guarding against political indoctrination on the school's premises is a more overt 'policing' role, and in one light the governing body is clearly perceived as local guardian of the law as far as its school is concerned. It is also accountable for any failure on the part of the school to discharge its proper functions, and arrangements exist (Education Reform Act 1988, s.23) to require it to answer formal complaints about the curriculum where there is alleged to have been such a failure. The governing body of any voluntary or grant-maintained school providing denominational education must also secure that this is inspected at such intervals as the Secretary of State may prescribe, and it will be the duty of the person conducting the inspection to report accordingly (s.13 Education (Schools) Act 1992).

It is not difficult to understand the rationale for such a role but easy to underestimate the difficulty it represents in practice. Such expectations challenge the natural inclination of most lay governors not to (cross-)question 'the professionals' and some headteachers may feel uneasy at the prospect of governors adopting a more purposeful role within the school. The result can be an undermining of the confidence and trust that needs to exist between governors and staff if the school is to work for the best interests of pupils. One of the underlying purposes of governor training (hitherto mostly provided by the LEA) has been to assist in the amelioration of any unnecessary deference or suspicion in this relationship, but that is not to suggest that the tensions no longer exist.

The arbiter of local discretion

There are occasions when the governing body is expected to act within guidelines but exercise discretion in reaching its agreed position. For example, the LEA's duty to state its policy in relation to the secular curriculum (Education (No.2) Act 1986 s.17) is matched by the duty placed on the governing body by its articles of government to consider that policy when making its own written statement about the aims of the secular curriculum for the school (s.18). The governing body's policy on sex education is an explicit example of this working in practice. DES Circular 5/89 (*The Education Reform Act 1988: The School Curriculum and Assessment*) reminded LEAs to review their statements of curriculum policy 'in good time' to enable governing bodies to review their own curriculum aims and any modifications to the LEA's curriculum policy in anticipation of the introduction of the National Curriculum from Autumn 1989.

It follows from this that the governing body must then oversee the implementation of its policies by the staff. This implies a close monitoring of the school from day to day and — if quality is to be assured — a capability to evaluate what is happening in the classroom. Once again, this is a high-level demand of many governing bodies, most of whose members will have neither the time nor the experience to enter into a close and sustained professional relationship with the school. In practice, the governing body's responsibility to use its best endeavours to meet any special educational needs of individual pupils may mean no more than ensuring that such a demand on the school's resources is adequately recognised in the annual development and budget plans. However, for such policy decisions to be effective it is widely acknowledged that governors need to understand at first hand the issues involved in providing for such pupils.

The agent for promoting the school

The governing body is also required to promote the school's achievements and answer criticisms of its performance. To facilitate this, it must provide information to parents as required under the regulations based on s.8 of the 1980 Act, s.22 of the 1988 Act, and s.16 of the 1992 Education Act, much of this within the school prospectus. These refer to general matters of ethos and practice, the school's curriculum and syllabuses, the aggregated educational achievements of pupils at the school (as measured by National Curriculum assessment and testing as well as by external examination results) and a range of specified school policies. There is, in addition, a requirement to maintain for each registered pupil a record containing information about the pupil's educational progress and attainments at the end of each key stage which can be made available for the parent's scrutiny on request. More detailed regulations have also been issued in connection with the formal reporting to parents of their child's progress at school. All of these information systems are directly under the jurisdiction of the governing body.

The governing body must prepare its own annual report about the school in the previous twelve months, circulate this to all parents and then convene a meeting at which issues of interest or concern can be raised (whether or not these are included in the governors' report) and, if appropriate, further action sought. The governing body thereby makes itself directly accountable to parents for its decisions and the actions of the school. At this level in the quality assurance arrangements, however, there is a problem, for relatively few parents attend these meetings, calling into question an important assumption on which the system has been designed. Nevertheless, governors have now been drawn into the work of their school to the extent that local decision-making has been increased, no doubt to the benefit of quality assurance.

The headteacher and staff

The headteacher and staff are at the heart of quality assurance in schools. Not only are they collectively responsible for the determination and organisation of the secular curriculum for their school, they must also ensure that these minimum requirements are translated into the best possible educational opportunities for all pupils and students. This involves setting and maintaining the conditions in which effective teaching and learning can flourish as well as discharging a range of duties connected with the school's accountability to its community.

The school curriculum

The Education Reform Act 1988 places the headteacher in a line of responsibility extending from the Secretary of State through the local education authority and the governing body, having operational responsibility, day-to-day, for ensuring that the curricular and other legal requirements are met in practice:

- to provide a balanced and broadly based curriculum (s.1);
- to provide the 'basic curriculum' comprising religious education and the National Curriculum for pupils, as required (ss.2–3);
- to secure that all pupils in attendance at the school take part in the daily act of collective worship (ss.6–7, 10);
- to make application for any variation of the requirements on collective worship for the school (s.12);
- to direct that the provisions of the National Curriculum shall not apply, or shall be modified, for a particular pupil for a specified period of time (s.19);
- to provide either generally or to such persons as may be prescribed, such information relating to the school as may be required in the form and manner stipulated (s.22).

In effect, the headteacher must do as central government bids, but to this one should add other duties deriving from ss.17–19 of the Education (No.2) Act 1986 which recognise a broader sphere of influence on the school's operation:

- to make available in response to any reasonable request, the LEA's and the governing body's policy statement relating to the secular curriculum (replaced by Regulation 5 (5) of The Education (School Curriculum and Related Information) Regulations 1989);
- to ensure that the school's sex education curriculum is compatible with the governing body's policy, that so far as the school's curriculum relates to other matters it is compatible with the LEA's policy, and that it is compatible with the enactments relating to education (including, in particular, those relating to children with special educational needs);
- to have regard to any representation about the curriculum made by a member of the community or by the chief officer of police.

A list such as this somewhat disguises the complexity of these duties in practice, particularly at a time when the headteacher has had to reconcile the demands of the local authority, the governing body, the DFE, NCC and SEAC, not to mention parents and others, as well as those of the staff and pupils if the school is to continue moving forward according to plan. The streamlining of the National Curriculum for primary schools might be welcomed by many, but would nevertheless mean further radical change and a new educational system for teachers throughout England and Wales to assimilate. Large schools which can share 'innovation overload' have already shown their aptitude for taking new developments in their stride; smaller schools will continue to be stretched and increasingly open to the criticism of the 'three wise men' that 'it is unreasonable to expect that two or three teachers can be expert in ten subjects to the depth now required' (Alexander, Rose and Woodhead 1992, para. 79).

The conditions for effective teaching and learning

In support of this curriculum provision the headteacher has a duty under s.22 of the 1986 Act to determine the measures to be taken with a view to promoting among pupils self-discipline and the proper regard for authority, to encourage good behaviour on the part of pupils and to secure that their standard of behaviour is acceptable. Pupils may be excluded — implicitly to safeguard curriculum quality overall — though the headteacher must take the proper steps in doing so (ss.23–25) and may risk a 'fine' if this strategy is to be employed in future. More positively, certain other recent initiatives have added to the headteacher's armoury for quality assurance in the school, particularly the advent of teacher appraisal and of the school development plan.

Teacher appraisal has enabled teachers to set new professional targets for themselves, thereby (in theory) increasing their motivation and effectiveness. Even more has been expected of teacher appraisal outside schools. DFE Administrative Memorandum 2/92 confirmed that with the abolition of statutory probation for newly-qualified teachers from September 1992 the school's appraisal scheme would extend to NQTs. Successive Secretaries of State have also argued consistently for a link between the outcomes of teacher appraisal and performance-related pay, a link which has been almost universally resisted by those who fear that the potential benefits it could have for the school would be undermined by the uncertain advantages it might bring to the individual teacher. At the centre of this dilemma is the headteacher who is faced with making an expanding system work in the best interests of all parties.

The annual school development plan has its origins mainly in two parallel initiatives launched in the late 1980's. DES Circular 7/88 *Education Reform Act: Local Management of Schools* described the responsibilities of LEAs, governing bodies and headteachers under LMS, including the requirement for schools to develop and carry out a management plan. It was expected that this would 'need to take account of the full range of their responsibilities for the management of schools, including those on the curriculum' (paragraph 21). Shortly afterwards, in the DES Circulars on the 1989–90 ESG and LEATGS schemes, it was announced that, in the light of the major changes anticipated at that time, schools should prepare a National Curriculum Development Plan as the basis for the use of ESG resources to assist the implementation of the National Curriculum. The school development plan envisages the integration of these activities and it must now be approved formally each year by the governing body. In practice the budget and development plans are often separate documents, but they are nevertheless now more often consistent than not and represent a marked advance in schools' effective forward planning and of increasing usefulness to headteachers who are often both the prime mover of the planning process as well as the overseer of the plan's implementation.

The headteacher's accountabilities

The school development planning process has become one aspect of schools' accountability to their governing bodies. The headteacher is accountable in other ways and must:

- provide the governing body or (as the case may be) the LEA with such reports in connection with the discharge of his functions as may be required;
- provide parents with data about pupils' progress and performance in tests and examinations, as specified;
- publish annually a range of specified information about the school and its functioning.

The recording and reporting of pupils' progress and publication of other information about the school have been areas of significant development in recent years and are a consistent theme through the Education Acts of 1980, 1986, 1988 and 1992. A list of the various Statutory Instruments gives a flavour of the range and scope of this information to be provided as well as the demands that compliance will make of schools:

– Education (School Information) Regulations 1981 (Schedule 2)

- Education (School Curriculum and Related Information) Regulations 1989
- Education (School Records) Regulations 1989
- Education (Individual Pupils' Achievements) (Information) Regulations 1990
- Education (Information on School Examination Results) (England) Regulations 1991
- Education (Pupils' Attendance Records) Regulations 1991
- Education (School Curriculum and Related Information) (Wales) Regulations 1991
- Education (School Performance Information) (England) Regulations 1992.

Educational quality would be assured for parents (or at least most of them), it is believed, if they are informed about what the school *should* be doing, *aimed* to do and had *achieved* in relation to pupils' test and examination performance. Parents could then be relied upon to stand up for their children's best interests.

Parents and others

Parents have certain responsibilities to ensure that children receive the best possible educational opportunities. Under s.36 of the 1944 Act they must secure that each child of compulsory school age receives efficient full-time education suitable to his age, ability and aptitude, as well as to any special educational needs the child may have, either by regular attendance at school or otherwise. The LEA has a duty to monitor this and to take any necessary steps required for its enforcement. Since this Act was framed, however, parents have come to be seen less as potentially unwilling participants in a system whose compliance may require coercion.

It has been an assumption of recent education legislation that parents are a body of people continuously monitoring their school's work, capable of identifying quality provision (or lapses from expected standards) and willing to engage vigorously whenever necessary in the pursuit of the school's improvement. Implicitly, it is no longer sufficient to be merely a conscientious parent: the theory requires that one should have regard for the best interests of all children and act in support of these broader objectives. In this way, school quality can be assured, it is said, because parents' expectations and priorities have primacy over the 'professional agenda'.

Under the government's 'Parent's Charter' parents have rights 'to know' about their child's school (see DES Circular 7/92 *The Parent's*

Charter: Publication of Information about School Performance in 1992) and are encouraged:

- to have high expectations of schools' pupil progress reporting systems;
- to expect detailed information about schools' aims and performance from both the school itself and the LEA;
- to attend the annual meeting to discuss current issues after receiving the governing body's annual report;
- to complain to the school, as they feel necessary, about matters relating to the curriculum or its implementation.

The first national league tables of examination results were published in November 1992, with individual schools in each LEA ranked by the proportion of pupils obtaining five or more GCSE grades A–C. It is expected that these tables will include all independent schools in 1993, and similar league tables are promised listing all schools ranked by their National Curriculum assessment results. In addition, the Secretary of State has made it known that he wants others to take a complementary responsibility for quality control in schools. Examination boards have been under pressure to penalise candidates with poor spelling and universities have been told that they should make clear to schools the standards of spelling and grammar they expect from school leavers. Guidance on the new marking criteria for GCSE coursework is expected to be available in Spring 1993. (John Patten, Secretary of State at the Department for Education, in a speech at the annual conference of the Committee of Vice-Chancellors and Principals, 1992.)

Parents have an implicit policing role in the monitoring of schools' work (particularly in grant-maintained schools) and there is a view in some quarters that such 'parent power' alone would be sufficient as an instrument of evaluation to make unnecessary the continued existence of other external agents of quality assurance. This view holds that parents' concerns must and will be alleviated by the school itself taking appropriate remedial action in the event of any lapse from the highest standards of effectiveness, arguing that schools are always capable of providing the remedy from locally available resources. It will be important to see how grant-maintained schools fare in such a climate, particularly where the advice and other support services of the local authority are unavailable to them.

Her Majesty's Chief Inspectors of Schools

The new HMCI for England and the HMCI for Wales were the creation of the Education (Schools) Act 1992, on the one hand emerging from the long tradition of HMI working within the education system but on the other representing a significant break with that tradition. Although one of their functions is to advise the Secretary of State about standards in schools individually and collectively, HMCI have come to be much more closely identified with the new national regime of school inspections which will report on each of the 24,000 and more maintained and 'independent' schools in England and Wales every four years. (Independent schools are defined as those approved by the Secretary of State as suitable for children with statements of special educational needs, as well as grant-maintained schools, city technology colleges and city colleges for the technology of the arts: Education (Schools) Act 1992, s.9.) Their responsibility for inspecting within higher and further education has mostly transferred to the new Higher Education Funding Council or to the Further Education Funding Council. The role of advising about the detail of the pre-16 and post-16 curriculum in theory and practice has shifted to the NCC, SEAC and elsewhere. These changes have resulted in a smaller inspectorate and a significant reorganisation of their work, in particular the establishing of territorial monitoring teams to replace the assigned district inspectors for LEAs and to the creation of OFSTED (the Office for Standards in Education) separate from the DFE.

The powers and duties of HMCI

Under ss.2 and 6 of the 1992 Act, each HMCI has a duty to inform the relevant Secretary of State about:

- the quality of education provided by schools in England and Wales;
- the educational standards achieved in those schools;
- whether the financial resources are managed efficiently;
- the spiritual, moral, social and cultural development of pupils.

In order to do this, HMCI have the power to cause any school in England (s.3) or Wales (s.7) to be inspected. They also have the specific duties to establish and maintain a register of inspectors who will carry out this work, to keep under review the system of inspecting schools and to promote 'efficiency in the conduct and reporting of inspections ... by encouraging competition in the provision of services by registered inspectors'. Procedures for the registration of inspectors as well as the circumstances in which they may be removed from the register are laid down (ss.10–11), and a right of appeal established in the event of such a removal (s.12).

Schedule 2 of the Act anticipates a number of the practical issues.

Before each inspection, HMCI will invite tenders for the work from at least two registered inspectors who are 'at arm's length from each other'. It will be the registered inspectors' task to identify the inspection team (comprising other inspectors who have satisfactorily completed a course of training approved by the Chief Inspector) which must include at least one 'lay' member, defined as a person 'without personal experience in the management of any school or the provision of education in any school (otherwise than as a governor or in any other voluntary capacity)'. It is further stipulated that no member of the inspection team shall have had any connection with the school which might raise reasonable doubts about his or her ability to act impartially during the inspection. Before the inspection takes place, parents will have an opportunity to meet the registered inspector leading the inspection to hear what is to happen and will be able to make their own contribution to the inspectors' subsequent deliberations. After the inspection, parents will receive a summary of the inspection report's findings. The full report will lead to the preparation of an 'action plan' describing the steps which the governing body (for schools with delegated responsibilities) or the LEA (for other maintained schools) proposes to take (and when) in response to particular issues identified in the report. This action plan will also be available for consultation by members of the public.

The inspection arrangements in practice

It is intended that the new inspection arrangements will be introduced for secondary schools in September 1993 and for primary schools in September 1994. As with other recent initiatives in education this presents a demanding timescale for preparing to implement the Act. The process of training inspectors was launched in Autumn 1992 so that within two years HMCI would be able to set about the inspection of around 6,000 schools annually. In the meantime, LEAs, along with other organisations and individuals, must decide how they are to operate their inspection system, in particular the number of inspectors required to form an effective team which will appear competitive in terms of quality and cost against others tendering for the work.

Significant assistance in preparing for the new arrangements has been given by the publication by HMCI in England of the framework for the inspection of schools (HMCI 1992), a substantial and detailed manual of guidance about the requirements for inspections and the inspection schedule. For the first time, a comprehensive statement has been issued nationally stating what constitutes 'good' educational practice in the eyes of HMI when they visit schools and this will be an important bench-mark for the future. It is therefore now a matter of public record that schools should be aiming for a range of specified targets to support their claims to be providing quality education. Everyone knows what the expected standards are and, with the inspection report as a periodic focus on the school's actual operation, parents and others will be better placed than ever before to assess its effectiveness.

The new inspection arrangements are a radical departure, as such they have raised a large number of difficult legal questions. During the passage of the Bill there was concern that the 1992 Act would repeal s.77 (3) of the 1944 Act which conferred on LEAs an explicit right to inspect their own schools. Now it seems that LEAs may only carry out 'an inspection' to secure information which it is not reasonably practicable for them to obtain in any other manner as part of the exercise of their functions. They will clearly have to be especially circumspect in future about such inspections, for example when a school appears to be faltering, and may need to be prepared for any proposed visits to be challenged. In these circumstances it might be necessary to invoke their wider powers under s.8 of the 1944 Act and the implied duty of every public authority to do all it does as well as possible.

The barring of those who have previously offered significant, direct advice from the inspection of that school may also cause difficulty. LEAs and management consultants alike could argue that the providing of advice to schools so as to maintain or improve educational standards should not debar them from the subsequent inspection of those schools. Moreover, it is argued, there are benefits from having a system of inspection and advice which operates on consistent principles. How closely associated could an individual be with a school, if at all, before a legal challenge to his or her participation in its inspection is upheld? Would such a challenge mean that the registered inspector and others would have to re-tender, or possibly lose the business automatically? Smaller LEAs are finding it increasingly difficult to maintain separate teams of inspectors and advisers, and are also likely to be caught out by the determination of other LEAs to tender competitively for inspections outside their area. It is now emerging that the registered inspector leading the inspection team takes personal responsibility not only for handling the contract and the finances arising therefrom, but will also be named on the inspection report and therefore be the person against whom any action arising from the report will be taken. Some registered inspectors may find that quality assurance becomes for them an expensive liability!

Follow-up action

In the event of all the previous mechanisms for quality control failing and HMCI identifies a particular school as in serious difficulties, failing or 'at risk', the 1993 Education Act prescribes further steps to be taken to remedy the situation. First, the governing body's action plan will outline the steps to be taken and, in the case of county and voluntary schools, to this the LEA will add a supporting commentary. If this brings about no improvement, the Secretary of State has the power (possibly acting through the LEA) to nominate two additional governors at the school to alter the balance within the governing body. Or, he may replace some or all of the first governors of a county school, making clear in the case of a voluntary school that the foundation governors' appointing authority might need to take similar action. Alternatively, the Secretary of State can appoint an education association to take over the management of an 'at risk' school or group of schools, entrusting its development to the stewardship of a small group (typically 6) of part-time governors who are experienced in effective school management. In the last resort the Secretary of State may institute procedures to close a failing school.

It is clear that there now exists a comprehensive system for quality assurance in primary and secondary education that goes beyond the maintenance of quality, day to day, and which has sought to anticipate all possible eventualities that could arise in practice. While such a system remains in place or is available, it is difficult to imagine the failings of an individual school going unrecognised, unreported and unattended.

Further and higher education

'Quality' in further education has hitherto been a responsibility shared among HMI, the LEA and the institution itself. The 1944 Act (s.41) established the LEA as the 'provider' of further education as it was of schools and gave similar powers to carry out inspections (s.77). The Secretary of State was also charged with the duty of instigating the regular inspection of individual establishments by HMI who, in turn, developed their 'professional leader' role on the strength of much accumulated experience of good practice. LEAs and HMI have both continued to play these roles into the 1990s, but their activities are now curtailed: LEAs by the removal of the colleges from their purview (from April 1993) and HMI by the radical restructuring of the inspectorate in 1992.

The higher education colleges and polytechnics were also subject to LEA and HMI inspection until the 1988 Act brought them under the wing of the Polytechnics and Colleges Funding Council (s.128). The PCFC had the power to undertake other activities considered necessary in the exercise of its functions (s.132) and some work was initiated relating to educational 'quality' within its sector, for example to identify performance indicators. Across the HE binary line the universities were also formulating an approach to quality assurance, though the tradition of institutional autonomy deriving from their statutes and charters did not lead to easy or immediate agreement as to what should be undertaken throughout the sector.

The Further and Higher Education Act 1992 marks a distinct break with the past, not just in relation to the structure of tertiary phase education management but also in terms of increased expectations for institutional quality assurance. The government's White Paper which preceded the Act, *Education and Training for the 21st Century* (May 1991) spelled out its commitment to systems of ensuring quality as well as the framework of roles and responsibilities within which quality would be assured 'post-16'. Individual institutions have the primary responsibility for quality control, with examining and/or other external validating bodies responsible for guaranteeing the quality of the qualifications offered. The Further Education Funding Council (FEFC) and the Higher Education Funding Council (HEFC) are empowered to ensure that quality systems in general form a satisfactory basis for the funding provided to institutions for which they have responsibility. The Training and Enterprise Councils (TECs) are able to exercise influence in areas of further education in which they have an interest, and the FEFC for Wales (but not its equivalent in England) may ask the HMCI (for Wales) to assess the quality of education provided by any of its FE institutions. Let us turn to these emerging roles and responsibilities in practice.

Quality control in FE and HE

If individual institutions are to be responsible for quality control, the problem is '*Quis custodiet ipsos custodes?*' In response, managers in FE have usually turned to externally determined quality assurance systems, notably the British Standards Institution's BS 5750, 'Total Quality Management' (a management methodology widely practised in America and Japan) and 'Investors in People' promoted by the Employment Department (formerly the Manpower Services Commission).

British Standard 5750, introduced in 1987, is a series of standards on quality systems that can be used for the purposes of internal quality management and external quality assurance. Although primarily conceived as a system for ensuring quality in manufacturing and service industries, its emphasis on 'the needs of the user' struck a chord with FE colleges in the late 1980s. This led to the production of draft guidelines, *Guidance notes for the application of BS 5750 Part 2/ISO 29002 to education and training* and, subsequently, to an understanding that whether the product or output of an educational establishment is seen as the 'value added to the student' or 'the programme delivered', the resulting system addresses exactly the same factors (Sallis *et al.* 1992). A college which is awarded the BS 5750 registration mark has implemented and adheres to a management system adjudged to represent quality, defined as 'fitness for purpose', actual practice conforming to specification.

British Standard 5750 has been described as 'the essential heart of total quality management' which is more to do with the process and management of *change* in pursuit of continued quality improvement. TQM starts from the principle that the commitment to quality must be based on the interests, needs, requirements and expectations of customers (that is, students) and that such a commitment must be characteristic of every individual's contribution to the 'provider's' corporate culture. A major challenge for the system within an educational context, however, is that TQM depends upon practice and outcomes rather than external inspection or assessment by a third party. This requires a close working relationship and involvement not only between the college and its students, but also with all other individuals and organisations having an interest in the quality of education provided and the learning achieved. Whether such a comprehensive network can be maintained to support total quality is no doubt a matter of judgement in individual circumstances. (For a more detailed discussion of BS 5750 and TQM, see *Quality Matters: Business and Industry Quality Models and Further Education*, Further Education Unit Bulletin, August 1991.)

Training and Enterprise Councils have been keen to promote BS 5750, TQM and also 'Investors in People', a more recent National Standard which places the emphasis on managers' commitment to develop all employees as the primary strategy for the achievement of organisational objectives. Such an emphasis will clearly commend itself to any organisation whose effectiveness depends largely upon sustained and successful inter-personal transactions, including education and training. The TECs, indeed, are closely identified with 'Investors in People', offering advice to those who wish to work towards the National Standard, for, in common with the other methodologies, this, too, is a process rather than a product which organisations develop to suit their own requirements for quality in the light of their clients' needs.

The universities have developed a different approach to quality assurance, identifying this with the internal monitoring of academic standards for which they have responsibility under their charters and statutes. In 1990 the Committee of Vice-Chancellors and Principals (CVCP) set up the Academic Audit Unit (AAU) based at Birmingham University which has monitored and commented on the structures and mechanisms by which the institutions themselves assure the quality of the educational programmes they offer. The AAU's management board (with representatives from industry and commerce) which reported to the Council of the CVCP and its consultative committee to take account of outside views relating to quality assurance in the universities. Its directorate arranged for senior academics to be seconded and trained as part-time 'academic auditors' to work in a team of (usually) three examining how a university monitors the quality of its courses, its teaching and its academic staff.

Visits to the university have also been made by the auditors for three days every three years to carry out interviews with staff and students. A report was then made to the university which the CVCP has said should be published and there appears to be growing support for this view. The government, for one, needs to be persuaded that the universities (old and new) are capable of examining themselves rigorously and responding positively to any areas of concern identified. It is certainly expected that the publicity arising from a critical report would produce rapid improvement! Since 1992 the AAU has been subsumed within a new organisation, the Higher Education Quality Council (HEQC) which has established a successor body, the Division of Quality Audit. A Division of Quality Enhancement has also been created to assist and support institutions in their efforts to improve quality. This is expected to develop the process of self- and peer-evaluation that characterise the approach of the CVCP to quality assurance in higher education.

In recent years there have been determined efforts to establish staff appraisal systems in further and higher education, though any such initiative needs to form part of the conditions of service of individual members of staff and be developed with the recognised lecturers' unions locally. (The national agreement on FE staff appraisal is set out in paragraph 28 and Appendix X of the Silver Book, *Salaries and Conditions of Service for Lecturers in Further Education*). It has also often been thought necessary to develop a context for appraisal through a process of reviewing the institution, the department or some other organisational unit. This allows the professional development of individuals to take place within a broader framework of planning and progression. Experience so far, however, suggests that there is still some way to go before a lecturers' appraisal scheme developed by individual institutions for their staff achieves a level of status and rigour capable of making any significant contribution to quality assurance post-16 in England and Wales. Furthermore, the new arrangements for setting staffs' conditions of service by and for the incorporated governing bodies of a multitude of institutions will militate against the kind of national scheme envisaged in the Silver Book.

External quality assessment

External quality assessment will mainly be the responsibility of the FEFC and HEFC within their respective sectors. The FEFC is required to secure that provision is made for assessing the quality of education provided in its institutions and to establish a Quality Assessment Committee to advise the Council in the discharge of its duty (Further and Higher Education Act 1992 s.9). Most members of the committee will not be council members and will have successful experience of further education. The HEFC is similarly charged with the duty of securing that provision is made for assessing the quality of education provided by individual institutions and for establishing its own Quality Assessment Committee to undertake this function (s.70).

The FEFC is now developing its approach to quality assessment along the lines established by HMI in assessing education provision in both further education and sixth form colleges. As the White Paper indicated, HMI will continue to have a role for the immediate future in advising about educational quality in the FE sector, but the FEFC will eventually take over this responsibility, so a period of transitional arrangements is to be expected. The approach of HMI is based on a cycle of short inspections of colleges, supplemented by more regular, shorter visits, leading to the establishment of a database of relevant information and findings. The procedures will focus on the college as a whole, (including its aims, the extent to which these have been achieved and the management structure) the range and scope of courses as well as their appropriateness in the light of local needs, the student profile, the standards of learning achieved and the college's resources. HMI have also issued — as they have for school inspections — criteria used in making their evaluations of institutional and educational effectiveness, indicating that one focus will be the quality control arrangements employed for self-appraisal of performance. It is important to note that in future both schools and colleges will be assessed against published criteria, a marked development on past arrangements which have sometimes left institutions uncertain about the precise significance of inspectors' judgements for their forward-planning.

The universities have traditionally placed less reliance on external quality assessment, but the HEFC would be able to carry forward the work of the PCFC which was active in developing a system of quality controls in the late 1980s within the other arm of higher education. It should be noted that the PCFC has been supported in this work by other organisations, including the Council for National Academic Awards. Ways were devised of monitoring teaching quality which has been one of three criteria for awarding contracts to polytechnics and colleges of higher education under a system of competitive tendering for courses. Bids to run courses have been evaluated according to student demand, price and quality. Serious consideration has also been given to the possibility of seeking opinion from second-year students about the courses in operation. The PCFC sector has overseen the development of performance indicators in higher education as a mechanism for evaluating institutional objectives, though mostly for the purpose of aiding management decisions rather than for monitoring the quality of teaching and learning. The Further Education Unit at the DES has also pioneered work in this area which the FEFC may now take up.

Quality assurance post-16 remains a relatively complex network of activities. There is a developing tradition in further education on which the FEFC is able to build, but the shape of things to come under the new Funding Council has yet to emerge clearly. Even before the implementation of the Further and Higher Education Act there was a view in some quarters that post-16 and adult education is best described as 'an interesting cacophony rather than a seamless robe' which could bring about the reincarnation of LEAs to introduce a certain order (Kenyon 1992). There is then the parallel development of the HEFC and the HEQC and it remains to be seen which approach is more influential for quality assurance across the HE binary line now that the Government has achieved its rationalisation of higher education.

Conclusion

From the above, it should be clear that whereas a very comprehensive model for quality assurance (involving central government, LEAs, governing bodies, headteachers, parents and HMCI) exists within the primary and secondary phases of education, nothing strictly comparable exists across further and higher education. The government has, however, attempted to achieve a somewhat more consistent structure of education post-16 and this may pave the way for a greater consistency of practices for quality assurance. The tradition of, and concern for, institutional autonomy, on the other hand, seems likely to militate against the emergence of a single model for quality assurance, at least in the short term, and there would no doubt be some major tensions to case in the process. It is, though, reasonable to expect a number of developments to continue on various fronts while the issue of 'quality' remains a preoccupation within and outside the education service, and for new developments to emerge which have a bearing on this issue. One notices, for example, the new partnership evolving between FE and HE over franchising arrangements. Where one party contracts the other to provide the whole or part of a course, the franchiser has a direct interest in ensuring quality control of the franchisee's 'product'. (Warner 1992).

It is less easy to be confident that the trend of developments in the pre-16 sector will be towards an enhancement of quality assurance overall. As envisaged by the Education Reform Act, the quality assurance model for education pre-16 is already under threat. The concern arises from various quarters, including possible future education funding arrangements. With tighter limits on public spending there is likely to be less money available to LEAs to support their continuous monitoring and evaluation activities. The growth of the grant-maintained sector means a further reduced central budget, with a similar outcome. The new inspection arrangements are very demanding of finance and professional time, yet their impact on a particular school will be felt only once every four years at best. For these and other reasons there is now a danger that the vision for quality assurance in schools may be seriously compromised. On the other hand, as we move through the 1990s, there are signs of a change of heart about self-regulation, one of the central policy principles for many people in the previous decade and enshrined within much of the recent education legislation. In the wake of international financial and city scandals, the Chief Executive of the Prudential is reported to have called into question the ability of institutions to regulate themselves and raised a fresh debate on the matter (Newmarch 1992). Perhaps education will again feel the effects of a new current in national political life as we move towards the millennium.

References

Alexander, P., Rose, J. and Woodhead, C. (1992) *Curriculum Organisation and Classroom Practice in Primary Schools* DES.

HMCI (1992) *The Handbook for the Inspection of Schools* Office for Standards in Education, Elizabeth House, London.

Kenyon, B. (1992) *Education* 6 November, p.371.

Maclure, J. Stuart (Ed.) (1986) 'Minutes of the Committee of Council on Education, 1840–1: I — Instructions to Inspectors of Schools' in *Educational Documents: England and Wales, 1816 to the present day* (5th edn) Methuen.

Newmarch, M. (1992) *The Independent* 8 November.

Sallis, E. *et al.* (1992) *Total Quality Management* Coombe Lodge Report **23**(1), p.88.

Stuart, N. (1992) 'Lecture to the 18th BEMAS Annual Conference' in Ranson, S. *The Role of Local Government in Education: assuring quality and accountability* Longman, pp.11–12.

Warner, D. (1992) 'Classless study?' *Education*, 23 October, p.330–1.

6 The LEA, grant-maintained schools and the Funding Agency for Schools

Kathleen Higgins

'Before the Education Act 1980, schools were, in many cases, merely administrative units of the LEA.' (*Choice and Diversity*, para. 1.18)

Whatever the basis of this assertion, the last decade saw significant changes in the relationship between local authorities and schools culminating in the 1988 Education Reform Act and the creation of grant-maintained schools.

A key thrust of the legislation was the development of the autonomous school in the context of an increasingly prescribed national framework. The Taylor Report *A New Partnership for our Schools* (1977) set the tone with its emphasis on changes in composition and empowerment of governing bodies; aspects of its recommendations were enshrined in the 1980 Education Act. For some schools, this meant that for the first time they had their own governing bodies in LEAs where previously a sub-committee of the Education Committee had acted as governing body of a group of schools.

Local authority influence was further reduced with the 1986 Education (No.2) Act with the removal of the majority of the local authority representatives on the governing body. At the same time governing bodies were given the authority to appoint staff below the level of deputy headteacher and new responsibilities were given to governors for such areas of the curriculum as political education and sex education.

It was the 1988 Education Reform Act which gave governors of mainstream schools responsibility for school management under local management of schools; they took on duties with regard to a range of finance, personnel and ancillary services. This was extended to all primary schools in October 1990 and Circular 7/91 *Local Management of Schools: further guidance* extended local management to special schools, to take effect from April 1994.

A parallel development to the devolution of responsibility to the governors for the management of their schools was the increasing extension of parental rights. The 1980 Education Act allowed parents to express a preference for schools and gave them access to local appeal committees, to determine the merit of their cases. The 1986 Education (No.2) Act extended similar rights to be heard to parents of children excluded from school. However, with the 1981 Education Act, parents of children with special educational needs were not given the freedom to express a preference for a school. They were to be involved in the process of their child's assessment for special needs and could have their cases heard by an appeals panel — but not one which had the same powers as that for school admissions. The rights of parents of children with special educational needs are addressed in the Education Bill (1992) in particular with regard to the creation of the (national) Special Educational Needs Tribunal, with local tribunals working under it.

From the 1988 Education Reform Act it would appear that parents' rights were to be strengthened with the clauses dealing with open enrolment. The details of the legislation and the tensions between parental choice and the autonomy of the school meant, however, that this did not always happen consistently across the country. The same Act also gave parents the right to complain about the National Curriculum, religious education and against charging for school activities — a first step in treating parents as consumers.

The autonomous school was a major creation of the 1980s. Many welcomed the development of local management of schools because it transferred responsibility and decision making to the point of service delivery and the freedom to deploy resources to provide a quality education to meet individual needs. It brought about a revolution in the management of schools and caused education authorities to review their activities and carry out major restructuring of their departments.

Grant-maintained schools

While many authorities were adapting to the changes caused by the development of local management of schools, for example, 23 LEAs had introduced local financial management before the Education Reform Act appeared as a Bill, very few were prepared for the impact of another section of the Education Reform Act: the creation of grant-maintained schools.

To meet the needs of this new category of school, over 50 sections were written into the Act to deal mainly with the mechanisms of governance and incorporation of grant-maintained schools. In enhancing the importance of governors and parents by emphasising the role of the ballot, together with the arrangements for funding the grant-maintained school, the Education Reform Act was to set the agenda for the Government's White Paper *Choice and Diversity* four years later. Whether the Secretary of State for Education and Science at the time was aware of this can only be open to conjecture.

Initially, secondary schools and primary schools with over 300 pupils were to be allowed to become grant-maintained. On 10 October 1990 John MacGregor, then Secretary of State for Education and Science, announced that all primary schools could make application to become grant-maintained. The White Paper and subsequent Education Bill proposed that special schools should be eligible to become grant-maintained after 1994.

In the Education Bill the powers of the governing body of a grant-maintained school are spelt out. These include all previous responsibilities as governors, plus powers to acquire and dispose of land and property, enter into contracts and invest money and receive gifts. It does not, however, confer a general power to borrow money. In addition, responsibilities consistent in many cases with LEA schools, for example, religious education and collective acts of worship, are identified.

Five years after the Royal Assent to the Education Reform Act, some 350 schools have been incorporated as grant-maintained schools; the majority of them are in the secondary sector. During 1992 Hillingdon had the highest proportion of grant-maintained schools in any one sector and has therefore been used as an example of their impact on the service. Reasons for schools becoming grant-maintained have been given as school autonomy and the financial security offered by the Department for Education. Research by the University of Leicester, *Managing Autonomous Schools: The Grant Maintained Experience* by T. Bush, M. Coleman and D. Glover, published early in 1993, suggests that schools give greater priority to autonomy. However, one of the schools in Hillingdon selected for the case study became grant-maintained in September 1991, shortly after the introduction of local management of schools in the Borough, and therefore had little opportunity to experience the freedom provided by LMS.

The slow evolution of the grant-maintained school has led in many cases to local education authorities clarifying their approach to this category of school and the activity they need to undertake to address the debate. Authorities have tended to adopt different stances, depending in many cases on the political leadership of the local administration. A number of authorities have chosen to adopt a neutral stance, i.e. to ensure parents make an informed choice. In most authorities there has been a public debate of the issue which has drawn in the services of the Grant-maintained Schools Foundation and the Local Schools Information Service. This may result in some areas in the local authority officer identifying the functions and role of the LEA. To assist officers in this activity, the Society of Education Officers set up a group to exchange information and advice. At its meeting in October 1992 it prepared a position statement on the work of the Local Education Authority in the context of the White Paper, and advice to local authorities on managing the debate on GM: *Choice and Diversity – Changing Relationships.*

The autonomy of the grant-maintained school has been a key element of the Government's policy. It is interesting to note an aspect of legislation with regard to the category of school: under s. 15(3) of the Further and Higher Education Act 1992 the Funding Council will have responsibility for a GM school when the institution falls within this subsection 'if on 17 January 1991 not less than 60 per cent of the pupils at the institution were receiving full time education suitable to the requirements of persons over compulsory school age who have not attained the age of nineteen years'. This wording applies to any sixth-form college (technically a school) which attained GM status before April 1993.

To secure the autonomous school the Government recognised the need to establish a basis for funding. In Circular 10/88 the funding arrangements were set in the context of local management of schools:

> . . . the acquisition by a school of grant-maintained status should not change the financial position either of the school or of . . . community charge payers in the LEA which previously maintained the school. The maintenance grant from the Department payable under s. 79 of the Education Reform Act will be calculated so as to reflect as far as possible the level at which the school would have been funded had it continued to be maintained by the LEA, including provision for services provided centrally, and an approved scheme for the local management of schools in place in the authority. The amount of maintenance grant will be determined by reference to the formula determining the funding of comparable maintained schools in the authority.

It soon became clear that the 'level at which the school would have been funded had it continued to be maintained by the LEA' as determined by officials at the Department of Education and Science was not intended to create the now famous 'level playing field'. Indeed, in his announcement of 10 October 1990, John MacGregor:

- doubled the maximum amount of transitional grant payable to grant-maintained schools to £60,000 to help them prepare for their new responsibilities;
- increased the annual amount of specific grant paid to grant-maintained schools by the average of £10,000, a 50 per cent increase on existing plans;
- increased by 50 per cent, to an average of £25,000, the formula capital allocation made to each grant-maintained school for equipment and small scale capital projects.

To provide grant-maintained schools with financial support to reflect the services they would have received from the LEA the Department for Education adopted a simple device. It was this introduction of a percentage of the Aggregated Schools Budget in April 1991 which caused consternation among local education authority officers: it was arbitrary; it did not reflect the local expenditure on central administration; it impacted directly on economies of scale. In a consultation document in October 1991 (*Annual maintenance grant for grant-maintained schools 1992–1993*) the Secretary of State proposed lowering the existing 16 per cent of the ASB to 15 per cent and, under certain circumstances, allow LEAs to operate at a lower percentage.

However, within the Department for Education paper on the calculation of AMG for grant-maintained schools for 1992/93, paragraph 26 states that '. . . in the case of schools which were in operation as GM prior to April 1992, the amount of central AMG in 1992/93 cannot be lower than the cash amount calculated by the Department as the school's full year central AMG for 1991/92' remained in place thus penalising authorities which had grant-maintained schools prior to April 1992.

In the case of the first of Hillingdon's schools the central AMG as a percentage of the ASB to reflect actual central costs would have been in the region of £277,103; the amount they received because of paragraph 26 was £342,000. The total effect of this mismatch on the budget of the LEA was an additional cost of £179,600 over all the secondary grant-maintained schools which fell within this category.

For students of financial management who wish to examine in detail the funding arrangements for grant-maintained schools recommended reading is 'Statutory Instrument 1992/555: The Education (Grant Maintained Schools) (Finance) Regulations 1992'. This covers the basis for calculations of the annual maintenance grant, school meals, contingencies and the provision of nursery education and capital and specific purpose grants.

An element appears in the Education Bill (Clause 72 (b)) which restated the Education Reform Act (s.79(3)(a)(ii)) with regard to grant funding to schools in respect of 'any special needs of the area'. It remains a matter of important local controversy how 'the special needs of an area' will be identified.

The issue of funding has been a matter of concern for the local authorities and grant-maintained schools alike. In the case of the former the concern has been its apparent unfairness and impact on the local authority budget; in the case of the latter there does appear to be an irony in using as a basis for funding the LMS formula of an authority from which the school has opted out.

In an attempt to address these issues, the White Paper suggested the introduction of 'a common funding formula (CFF) for GM schools when there are sufficient primary and secondary schools to justify it. The formula will distribute between GM schools in an LEA area a total based on the relevant share of the Government's Standard Spending Assessment (SSA) for the LEA concerned' (Para.13.8).

While LEAs will welcome the assurance that 'the Secretary of State will apply the CFF to an area only after consultation with the GM schools in that area and the LEA', only time will tell if this matter will be effectively resolved. The debate over the Summer of 1992 on SSAs and GM funding, and responses to the White Paper, caused John Patten, Education Secretary, to write to all headteachers of all maintained schools in England in October 1992, to state that 'there is no basis for the suggestion that schools opting for GM status will be worse off under the CFF than they are now. The CFF will . . . provide for GM schools to receive funding to reflect their additional responsibilities compared with LEA schools'. The Education Bill 1992, refers only to 'the total amount . . . determined . . . in accordance with regulations made by the Secretary of State'. Regulations based on the consultation document issued at the end of 1992 will have to address this very carefully since most LEAs currently fund schools at a level above SSA, so a move to fund them on a CFF based on SSA could leave schools worse off even taking into account their share of the LEA's central costs.

A new feature in the Education Bill is the discontinuance of grant-maintained schools in the case of extremely low school roll or failure to meet the requirements imposed by legislation. The governing body or Funding Agency for Schools will publish proposals and consult on the discontinuance of a school. The decision will be made by the Secretary of State. The matter of public consultation has only partially been recognised in the Bill where reference to 'ten or more objectors' is reproduced. However, how the transfer of pupils to other schools will be managed is not addressed.

The relationship with grant-maintained schools

The funding of grant-maintained schools, because it was not seen by LEAs as either equitable or fair, caused a tension between authorities and the schools. Given that a significant proportion of schools chose to opt out because of threat of closure by the LEA or dissatisfaction with the authority, often over finance, it was not surprising that relations with the grant-maintained sector were not always as harmonious as they could have been.

The increasing autonomy of these schools and locally managed ones caused most authorities to review their working relationships with schools. Hillingdon has always adopted a neutral stance to grant-maintained schools. It has also wished to work in co-operation with these schools since they educate children in the area and offer a range of services to the local community. This has shown itself in a variety of ways:

- grant-maintained schools' representation on the Education and Community Services Committee;
- attendance by grant-maintained headteachers at meetings and conferences;
- membership by grant-maintained schools' staff and governors of working groups;
- involvement of grant-maintained schools in discussions with the Director of Education on issues of mutual interest;
- buying LEA support services.

The authority worked in partnership with grant-maintained schools to guarantee community facilities such as dual use of sports halls when the contracts were put out to tender.

Authorities have responded differently to having grant-maintained schools within their areas; one of the interesting examples has been the different approaches to selling services. Some authorities have taken the view that they will have nothing to do with these new customers while others, like Hillingdon, have gone out to sell to this new market. Because of the funding arrangements for grant-maintained schools, Hillingdon in 1992–93 stood to lose £2.2million from its education budget to grant-maintained schools. To ensure that elements of this money were not lost and to secure services for local authority schools, the authority started on an ambitious programme of consultation on services and the preparation of a portfolio of services entitled *Hillingdon Services to Schools*, the second edition of which was launched in April 1992. Grant-maintained schools have indicated a willingness to purchase local authority services if they are of quality and at the right price. Up to date there has been considerable interest in purchasing a wide range of services from personnel support to a computer programme for identifying a child's home address in relation to the local school. The long term value of this exercise is open to question in the context of the White Paper with the Government's apparent intention to change the funding arrangements for grant-maintained schools and its unwillingness to amend the Local Authorities (Goods and Services) Act 1970 to allow local authorities to trade other than at the margin. The Education Bill proposes a minor change for two years: that an authority may be allowed by the Secretary of State to provide services either in 'the area of the authority and the area of any other local education authority which shares any boundary with the authority'.

John Patten, in his letter to headteachers and Chairmen of Governors of all maintained schools in England, has stated that authorities, in addition to those services required by the legislation 'will also be able to supply other services, such as peripatetic music provision and payroll services, for a specified period of time, if schools wish to purchase them. After that, we would expect individuals or organisations in the private sector to supply them'.

If they do not, what will be the impact on the quality of education? It would appear that the Government's view is that local education authorities exist only to provide statutory services. Traditionally, the authorities have provided services, whether or not they are statutory, to meet local need. It is hoped that this local delivery continues; in the absence of local authority provision and alternative providers coming forward, schools and children could be the losers.

The creation of grant-maintained schools provided the Government with an opportunity to reassess the work of schools and the responsibilities of local education authorities. Within Circular 10/88 the role of the local authority in relation to individual needs is identified. The responsibilities, as amended by the 1988 Act, include:

(a) the duty to secure that there are sufficient schools available for the area (taking into account the contribution made by any grant-maintained schools in the area), and that the facilities for their area include adequate facilities for recreation and social and physical training;

(b) the duty to ensure that parents comply with the law on school attendance;

(c) the duty to make such arrangements for the provision of free transport as the LEA considers necessary or as the Secretary of State may direct (in accordance with the guidance in the Department's letter of 15 December 1981, SS(1) 17/96/03, School Transport and Choice of School);

(d) the duty to reimburse the governing body of a grant-maintained school for board and lodging charges incurred in respect of a pupil where the LEA would have remitted them had the school continued as an LEA-maintained school;

(e) the duties given to LEAs under the Education Act 1981 and, in particular, the duty to secure that appropriate provision is made for pupils who have special educational needs, with or without statements.

The LEA is under a statutory obligation to perform each of these duties in such a way that they treat the pupils at a grant-maintained school no less favourably than those at schools which they maintain (s.100 of the 1988 Education Reform Act). This wording is reiterated in the Education Bill, which deals with the provision of benefits and services by the LEA and now includes reference to persons other than pupils. Such persons could include adults attending classes at the school.

In addition to these duties, LEAs retain certain statutory powers in respect of grant-maintained schools, including the following:

(a) they may provide board and lodging for pupils in order that they may benefit from the education provided by a particular school;

(b) they may defray such expenses as may be necessary to enable pupils to take part in any school activities;

(c) they may provide clothing for pupils.

It is the duty of the LEA to exercise these powers in such a way that they treat the pupils at a grant-maintained school no less favourably than those at schools which they maintain.

No charge can be made for these activities and it is interesting to note that the Government recognises that grant-maintained schools and local authorities will need to work together:

The governing body of a grant-maintained school will be required to give the LEA any information it may need in order to exercise its functions in relation to the school, or a pupil at the school. (Circular 10/88, para. 66)

A key role for the local authority has been and will continue to be that of advocate — defending the rights of the individual and securing those services to ensure that the child or young person benefits from her or his education.

In its advocacy role the local authority has also worked with parents to safeguard their rights and to ensure the balance between these and the autonomy of the schools. There have been occasions when grant-maintained schools have had to be reminded of their responsibilities, for example, for school admissions or exclusions. The local authority will safeguard its responsibility towards parents and ensure procedures are adhered to and individuals are treated with equity and fairness.

The White Paper and grant-maintained schools

The 1988 Education Reform Act created the grant-maintained school: the White Paper and subsequent legislation will provide the framework for its funding and management.

The development of grant-maintained schools was a key feature in the Conservative manifesto for the General Election in 1992. To increase the numbers the Conservatives promised to 'make it easier for small schools to enjoy the benefit of GM status by grouping together' (*The Best Future for Britain*, p. 17). In addition, they were to be the key to the creation of a diverse system of education.

> GM schools will be able to change their character if that is what parents clearly want and the change fits in with the wider needs of the local area . . . Existing schools which opt for GM status will be able to emulate city technology colleges and attract private technology sponsorship. (p. 18)

When the White Paper *Choice and Diversity* was published on 27 July 1992 it contained very few surprises since much had been pointed up in earlier regulations and circulars, and in the manifesto. Discussions with Department for Education officials prior to the publication of the White Paper had indicated that the approach to the relative growth of GM schools and decline of local authorities would be evolutionary and would be dependent on the parental ballot.

To make the move towards grant-maintained status easier, the White Paper proposed that the two resolutions of governing bodies be replaced by one. The general reaction to this, including that of some headteachers of grant-maintained schools, was that the two resolutions at this level were necessary, to allow full debate to take place and the LEA to be consulted. Equally it was felt, if it was important it was essential to give time to it. The White Paper proposed to carry out the Conservative manifesto promise of making it easier for small schools to opt out, by going out in clusters of two or more primary schools. Responses to this element would suggest that the practicalities need to be resolved, as too does the issue of having one headteacher-governor on annual rotation for a group of autonomous schools, as provided in the Education Bill.

While these changes are important, far more important are changes to the character of schools which are so much at the heart of the Government's proposals. Initially, schools going grant-maintained were not expected to change their character for five years. This was amended in 1991 by Kenneth Clarke as Secretary of State for Education; the White Paper proposed legislation for schools to change character at the time they are becoming grant-maintained. Given the importance of seeking this step, and the need to prepare the statutory proposals and the statements which have to be annexed to, and to accompany, them, it could be seen as asking a great deal of governors to consider a change of character at this time. There could also be the danger of the consultation exercise with parents being sidetracked away from the main issue of becoming grant-maintained.

There appears to be an assumption in the White Paper that secondary schools are not already diverse, this is far from true; each school offers the National Curriculum but draws upon the expertise of its staff and local community to create its own ethos and identity. If the agenda is to turn back the developments since Circular 10/65 *The Organisation of Secondary Schools* the assent of headteachers, governing bodies and the community will need to be secured.

In Chapter 10, *Specialisation and diversity in schools*, the White Paper builds on good practice in terms of education–business links by suggesting two new roles for industry — sponsors and sponsor-governors. This new category of governor — the sponsor-governor — will bring about representation on the governing body of private sector persons and organisations drawn from a local education–business partnership. The Education Bill proposes that aided secondary schools could have sponsor-governors. What is not clear is why the sponsor-governor should be on the governing body of grant-maintained and voluntary schools but not on county schools.

The powers of the Secretary of State are clarified in relation to the governing bodies of grant-maintained schools in the Education Bill which restates s. 53(6)(a) of the Education Reform Act:

> the instrument of government ... of a grant-maintained school shall enable the Secretary of State to approve not more than two additional governors if it appears to him that the governing body are not adequately carrying out their responsibilities in respect of the conduct or management of the school.

The new power to enable LEAs to contribute to governors' capital costs at technology colleges and voluntary-aided schools would enhance the relationship with these bodies only if there were sufficient capital funds to meet the authority's needs and those of the voluntary sector.

While the steps proposed in the White Paper are designed to secure the funding base to ensure diversity in schools and enhance the quality of children's learning, it is not so easy to detect the impact of one of the more important sections which deals with the creation of the FAS, for England. The Bill subsequently proposed a differently named body but with similar functions, to be set up in Wales, 'The Schools Funding Council for Wales'.

The rationale for such a body is clear if the Government's projection of the number of grant-maintained schools is to be achieved, on the basis of 300 grant-maintained schools at the time of the publication of the White Paper, the Government estimates that there will be 1,500 by April 1994 and that, by 1996 most of the 3,900 maintained secondary schools and a significant proportion of the 19,000 primary schools could be grant-maintained (para. 3.2. White Paper). Since the responsibility for grant-maintained schools falls within the remit of the Department for Education, 'as the number of GM schools grow, it will become increasingly inefficient and inappropriate for these essentially executive tasks to be performed by a Department of State' (para. 3.5).

The Funding Agency for Schools will have ten to fifteen members appointed by the Secretary of State 'who appear to him to have experience of, and to have shown capacity in, industrial, commercial or financial matters or the practice of any profession' (Education Bill). The budget and staffing complement will be approved annually by the Secretary of State 'with a view to ensuring that it operates with maximum efficiency' (para. 3.8 White Paper).

The Funding Agency will acquire functions as the number of grant-maintained schools increases. Its main function will be the allocation of grant and financial monitoring of such schools. The Funding Agency will have responsibility for ensuring no financial impropriety takes place; will it carry out its own investigations?

It will play a significant role in provision of school places, in school rationalisation plans which will require information from the local authority to discharge this responsibility. Under the Education Bill the FAS 'may establish grant-maintained schools for the purpose of providing relevant education, including grant-maintained special schools'. It may also purchase land compulsorily for this purpose. This has significant implications for the strategic planning in a local area and the nature of the relationship with the LEA.

The section (3.12) in the White Paper which proposes common instruments and articles of government for grant-maintained schools is to be welcomed as this step should greatly assist parents to raise issues with schools. It is hoped that these will be available in public libraries for ease of access. The Secretary of State recognises that there may be a need to have a variation within this common format to meet the school's circumstances and he will have the power to give his consent; it is hoped that this will be given only in exceptional circumstances if the impact of this development is not to be diluted. This point is not touched on in the Bill.

Responsibility for quality assurance will be with the governing body and the assessment of school's performance will be carried out by the Office for Standards in Education (OFSTED). For the schools (i.e. sixth form colleges) which fall within s. 15(3) of the Further and Higher Education Act (1992) the school will normally be inspected by the inspectors from FEFC. The FAS, unlike the Further Education Funding Council, will not retain its own inspectorate. It will, however, be consulted by the Secretary of State in the case of a parental complaint against a grant-maintained school. On what basis will it be able to give advice to the Secretary of State if it is not involved in the quality assurance work of schools? The complaints mechanism for parents is not spelt out and it is unclear what practical help parents will be offered and by whom.

The issue of a grant-maintained school at risk of failing is addressed in paragraph 3.15 of the White Paper and in the Education Bill. In such an event, and the conditions will be spelt out, the Secretary of State may be given powers to replace some or all of the first governors. Will parents be consulted in this process and when will normal arrangements be resumed? This brief reference to failing grant-maintained schools is in sharp contrast to Chapter 11, *Tackling failing schools,* and the chapter of the Education Bill 1992 which deals in detail with local authority schools and proposes the creation of education associations to turn schools around. Then, without benefit of the parental ballot, the 'normal expectation is that the school will then become grant-maintained' (para. 11.13, White Paper). The Bill also allows for the Secretary of State to determine the closure of such schools after the intervention of an education association has failed to achieve turnaround.

The most contentious aspects of the proposals with regard to the FAS are for those which deal with securing sufficient places and with the relationship with LEAs. 'The Funding Agency will share with the LEA the duty to secure sufficient secondary and primary places in the areas, from the point where 10 per cent of those pupils in the LEA are in GM schools. The Funding Agency will discharge the duty by itself when 75 per cent of secondary (and primary) pupils in the LEA are in GM schools, though the LEA may apply to be relieved of this responsibility well before that point is reached' (introduction to Chapter 3, White Paper).

The Association of Metropolitan Authorities and the Association of County Councils in particular raised concerns about having exit and entry points and the confusion that could be caused by having two such points. However, the Education Bill makes reference to those stages, albeit in more formal language. There is no information on the proposed working relationship between the Funding Agency and the LEA even though both are likely to have shared responsibility for some considerable time. It is unclear whether they will be equal partners or whether one will take the lead in the case of consultation on school closures.

How the local authority will discharge its responsibilities after the 75 per cent point and the Funding Agency involvement in the detail of parental choice will need to be addressed. The new power proposed for LEAs (in paragraph 5.11 of the White Paper) to direct any maintained school to admit a child who would otherwise be without a place may be welcomed, in the interests of children and parents, but there would not seem to be any advantage to parents in transferring this power to the Funding Agency at the 75 per cent point. This would involve the Agency in the detail of individual cases with parents in assessing the relative scope for various schools in a locality to admit an extra pupil. This is a time-consuming task and requires detailed local knowledge (e.g. of school accommodation and public transport routes).

Apart from relying on the LEA for the supply of information, how much use will the Funding Agency wish to make of the locally based skills and expertise which the LEA is able to offer? Will the Funding Agency wish to sub-contract work to the LEA, both before and after the 75 per cent point? Local authorities have significant experience of public consultation and if the FAS is to embark on this sensitive area of work it could do worse that learn from the experience of local authority staff.

It is unclear from the White Paper and the Education Bill how the new partnership with the Funding Agency will work when surplus places need to be removed and the public consulted. Who will chair the understandably volatile public meetings when the proposal is to close the local school? Who will be the accountable body when the decision is taken to close it and manage the complex, myriad and sensitive tasks associated with the closure of schools? Chapter 4 of the White Paper on the supply of school places seems to indicate that the Funding Agency for Schools and local authorities will be acting in parallel and produce annual reports on their respective sectors. Therefore, partnership would seem to be the solution. How this will work in reality and improve the dialogue with parents and the local community will need to be clarified in legislation and in practice. Building on current good practice would be useful.

The Education Bill, following on from the White Paper, proposes a public inquiry system when the Secretary of State has put forward counter-proposals. While the concept of a public inquiry system may be welcomed as securing objectivity and giving a voice to the local community, its timescale must be such as to ensure that schools under threat of closure do not wither while the inquiry deliberates on issues critical to children's futures.

The proposal for voluntary bodies to establish new grant-maintained schools will need to have clear criteria created if they are to offer the National Curriculum, meet community needs and not add to the stock of surplus places in the local area. How the framework will achieve the Government's goals will be a matter of time and there is still much in the White Paper and the Education Bill which needs to be clarified in subsequent regulations. The operation of the Funding Agency for Schools is critical if the framework is to succeed. In his letter of 15 October 1992 John Patten attempts to spell out the role of the Funding Agency: 'The agency will proceed on the basis of minimal interference in the day to day affairs of grant-maintained schools, its principal task is simply to distribute grant to schools on the basis of an agreed formula'. This would appear to echo the comments in Chapter 13 where the costs of the Funding Agency are expected to be 'modest' and will be 'offsetting savings in local authority administration and DFE staff costs'. How this will happen will need to be identified in the legislation, not least because of the confusion in the working relationship of the FAS and LEAs and the debate on levels of expenditure in LEAs and the potential for making savings. The Explanatory Memorandum to the Education Bill claimed:

> The expansion of the grant-maintained sector for which the Bill provides should lead to a reduction in public service manpower: the funding authorities for schools will employ substantially fewer administrative staff than LEAs, and grant-maintained schools will increasingly look to the private sector to provide the range of support services for which they previously relied on their LEAs.

Further confusion is caused by the reference in paragraph 3.10 of the White Paper to the possible setting up of regional offices 'as the number of GM schools grow, to carry out its closely prescribed duties'. However, this is not clear in the Education Bill. Is it the case that local authorities are being scaled down and a shadow organisation being created? Only time will tell.

In preparing for the general election, the Conservative Party manifesto indicated an intention to smooth the path for schools to become grant-maintained. The White Paper and Education Bill propose the extension of grant-maintained status to special schools. The White Paper proposes restrictions to the activities of local authorities; these include documentation to be circulated at the time of the ballot.

The constraints will be financial: the Bill refers to LEA spending within 'the prescribed amounts'. The Secretary of State will be able to pay governing bodies 'reasonable' expenses incurred in promoting grant-maintained status. The Bill refers to 'payments . . . on such terms as the Secretary of State may determine'. These proposals appear to imply that local authorities need to be restrained while governors and headteachers of prospective grant-maintained schools do not. Yet the education legislation assumes that all bodies will normally act reasonably.

The White Paper proposed that grant-maintained schools would be given the power to provide part-time as well as full-time nursery education. What was particularly worrying was the reference in paragraph 7.11: 'A GM school will be free to use its annual maintenance grant for this purpose, but its grant would not be increased to take account of part-time nursery pupils'. This raised the prospect of underfunded nursery education, to which Hillingdon Council amongst others strongly objected. The proposal was not, however, pursued in the first print of the Bill and a case initiated by Lewisham at the end of 1992 indicated unexpectedly that GM schools have always had the power to continue part-time nursery education. There remains uncertainty about new nursery provision at GM schools and how that might be funded.

The role of the local education authority

As local management of schools and grant-maintained schools have developed, with increasing delegation of budgets and functions to autonomous schools, it has become clearer that the role of the local authority has changed.

From being a service provider, it has given greater focus to the role of advocate — defending the rights of the individual and securing those services to ensure that the child benefits from her or his education. It is interesting to note in the White Paper that this key role is identified and the tasks of the LEA are spelt out:

- to ensure that all children secure a place at school;
- to assess and meet special educational need;
- to meet the duty to secure education otherwise than at school;
- to intervene in schools 'at risk of failing';
- to provide youth and adult education and careers advice;
- for the time being, to provide other pupil specific and support services such as board and lodging and clothing, education psychology, welfare services and home to school transport — the last service to be exposed to competition. (paragraph 6.2–6.5 White Paper).

The duty to provide careers advice was soon to be removed from LEAs to the Secretary of State under the proposals contained in the Trade Union Reform and Employment Rights Bill (1992).

How these duties are to be carried out in a local context, where such budgetting is delegated to schools and the authority is working with the Funding Agency, is unclear. Even at the 75 per cent 'exit point' it is clear that these duties remain with the local authority.

Parents and governors and the staff of schools have increasingly shown that they can work together and with officers of local authorities. The introduction of the Funding Agency for Schools will broaden this base and create a new infrastructure for the service. Its accountability to parents, the community and schools need clear definition if it is to establish its credibility for the strategic planning of services in a local community and not add a further level of bureaucracy. Equally, what safeguards will be put in place to ensure local decisions are made locally and not by a national body?

Clearly, the Education White Paper, the Education Bill and the Schools and Further and Higher Education Acts foretell significant changes in the future work of local authorities — not just local education authorities, given the scale of the budget involved and range of functions potentially lost to the service. In a number of councils discussions are taking place to identify the future configuration of local government. In the light of the proposals in this White Paper about the Goods and Services legislation, authorities are addressing the issue of the medium term service delivery.

There will be a requirement to examine the principles behind local government and to focus on the four cornerstones of: advocacy, arbitration, access and accountability, with the child and other clients at the centre. At the same time, any structure must include devolution to the institution or service, local information gathering and opportunity for identification of local need, and integration and co-ordination of services. This will require a change in style of service delivery which will be about enabling and empowering people and partnership with the individual and the community.

The conclusion to be drawn from this exercise — which builds on an analysis of the authority's functions and client focused activities — is that services may be delivered elsewhere in five years' time and the monitoring done externally. This means, in effect, that advocacy/arbitration is the residual role of the authority.

There is much discussion at the moment which would suggest that the authorities pursuing the advocacy path should simply merge education and social services departments and create a Welfare State 'safety net'. However, this must address the issues of quality of the child's education and the perspective the educationalist brings to the child's educational experience. In an age in which increasingly the non-professional is determining policy, e.g. the governing body, it is essential that professional advice and support are available.

Life without local education authorities

The Government's White Paper *Choice and Diversity* is subtitled *A Framework for Schools*. With the document's emphasis on evolution and the creation of an infrastructure for grant-maintained schools, the title might equally apply to local authorities since the approach reinforces the diversity of local authorities especially those with a significant proportion of grant-maintained schools.

There is reference in the White Paper to the Local Government Review. However, it would appear that the Government also expects local education authorities to undertake their own review:

> In general, as the number of GM schools increases, local authorities will need to consider carefully the most effective way of delivering their continuing responsibilities for education in the light of their particular circumstances. At present there are statutory obstacles which deny local authorities the organisational flexibility which they need to respond properly to the evolution of their educational functions. The Government proposes to remove such obstacles, in particular the requirement to establish an Education Committee. (para. 6.5)

Any authority contemplating such a step will need to assess the impact on the services within the area, local accountability and how it would be perceived by these schools who have chosen to remain within the local education authority.

A key step in the debate must be to examine the nature of service provision in the area should the Education Committee cease to exist. Past and recent legislation has seen the creation of a number of bodies with responsibility for the quality of education:

OFSTED
FEFC
TECs
Governing bodies
University and examination boards
the autonomous school
private companies.

To this list the Education Bill proposes to add the newly merged National Curriculum Council and School Examinations and Assessment Council (to be called the School Curriculum and Assessment Authority), the FAS and the education associations.

These bodies, in many cases, are quangos, non-elected, government appointed and a mixture of regional or national organisations. Only governing bodies reflect local accountability to their client groups. They do not have a responsibility to the whole of the local community and the White Paper is unfortunately deficient in addressing community needs.

The autonomous school has a very busy agenda delivering the National Curriculum, meeting diverse needs and managing itself and may have difficulty in giving sufficient priority to networking and accountability or have the time and expertise to tap into these bodies, all of which have different terms of reference and priorities. At the LMS National Conference on 3 October 1992, a DFE assistant secretary, paraphrasing the Secretary of State claimed 'The grant-maintained schools are accountable to the local community and serviced by the Funding Agency for Schools'. Unfortunately he did not identify how they would discharge this accountability.

Before anyone takes any precipitate steps to end local accountability the tensions in the White Paper, reinforced in the Education Bill, need to be addressed.

1   The first of these is that of the autonomy of schools and meeting children's needs. This is best demonstrated in the area of school admissions. Hillingdon was pleased to note that the Department listened to some of its concerns and addressed them in Chapter 5 of the White Paper and Clause 8 of the Education Bill 1992. It, along with other authorities, was disappointed that there was no mention of the Greenwich Judgement (*R v. Greenwich LBC ex parte Governors of the John Ball Primary School* (1989), which Geoffrey Williams discusses in Chapter 7). In addition, authorities remained concerned that the fundamental tension between school

autonomy and parental choice had not been addressed. In January 1993 there were some 450 parents in Hillingdon who will not have had an offer of a school place for their child and this situation continue for some months.

Hopefully, the clause in the Education Bill which refers to 'co-ordinated arrangement for admissions' may resolve this issue if grant-maintained schools and local authorities can be persuaded of the value of drawing up a scheme of co-ordination. With a slightly different example, in the context of clusters of schools opting out, how will autonomy of schools and parental choice be safeguarded?

2 Another tension is that of autonomy and the balance between co-operation and competition. As autonomous schools have developed, despite the competition for pupils and resources, they have demonstrated a willingness to co-operate on a range of areas, for example, curriculum activities such as the Technical and Vocational Education Initiative and consortium arrangements.

3 Increasingly, schools and local authorities have had to demonstrate their accountability to parents by keeping them informed. The regulations on publication of schools' attainments, The Education (School Performance Information) (England) Regulations 1992 have identified the information and requirements which schools will meet to discharge these responsibilities. In the debate on the value of league tables it is essential that effective communication is achieved with parents and that they do not feel they are inundated with data.

4 The emphasis in the White Paper on what I have described as the advocacy role of education authorities and the requirement for them to meet certain needs of all children in the area highlights a long standing traditional tension: between advocacy and service delivery.

This is perhaps best exemplified in the position of educational psychologists who have traditionally identified a child's needs and then determined how they should be met within a cash-limited budget. If the local authority is to become the 'purchaser' this may address the tension, but this solution presupposes that 'providers' exist to meet the special educational needs.

5 The major tension in the White Paper is between the increasing centralisation of education and devolution to the schools. How these two can work in tandem without the creation of layers of bureaucracy will need to be evaluated as the legislation is drafted and implemented.

Perhaps one method to examine the best way in which this can be achieved is to assess what is and should be the proper role of the LEA in the context of the White Paper. What is clear is that such an examination may be to focus on the next five years because the long term future of local education authorities is by no means guaranteed or clear. The 1944 Education Act laid many of the foundations of the local education authority system and paramount among its provision was the requirement on it to secure adequate provision (ss.7 and 8 1944 Education Act).

This responsibility is reiterated in the White Paper and Education Bill, somewhat obliquely, with its requirement to deal with surplus places and to keep the Funding Agency for Schools informed about demographic trends so that it can discharge its responsibilities for planning in the area.

A key role of the authority must be to secure the quality of children's learning. In the education service there are many groups of people — professional and non-professional — who can be called upon to promote the quality of schools. In the recent past, local education authority inspection teams have been called in by schools and by LEAs to assess the quality of the work of schools and to provide advice and support on improving it. Equally, inspections have been invaluable in promoting good practice at a formal and informal level. In some authorities, grant-maintained schools have valued this expertise and brought in local services, while LEA headteachers have worked in partnership with inspection teams. Will the Schools Act mirror the track record of these local teams? Will it provide a programme for the future enhancement of children's learning in a range of curriculum areas and promote good practice at a local level?

Even with the work of OFSTED and the four yearly inspection of schools, there will remain certain responsibilities to be discharged by local authorities. The duty to provide education other than at school and to identify and support schools requiring special measures will demand not only an assessment of the quality of activities in these areas, but also skills in intervention and quality assurance. The duties with regard to the National Curriculum still remain with the local authorities and they will need to be satisfied that the schools which remain within their area discharge their responsibilities and are supported in their activities. The work of local authorities in inservice training, preparation of advice, support for the standard assessment tasks and dissemination of information are all well known and valued by the teaching profession. If local authorities cease to deliver in this area, what will be the impact on the quality of children's learning?

A changing role for the local authority, highlighted in the Children Act, is the need to befriend and work closely with the individual child. At a time when schools are changing and taking on new responsibilities it is important that there is a body which recognises it has a role to support the individual who might otherwise be rejected by the school. The reason for the child experiencing difficulty could be because of non-conforming behaviour and it might also be because the child is 'vulnerable' and has a variety of needs, the response to which will have to be co-ordinated and require expertise not readily available in the school situation.

While the autonomous or self managing school is a desirable goal, there is a danger that schools may be isolated and staff and children may not benefit from an exchange of ideas. Professional expertise is enhanced by networking and sharing good practice. It is interesting to note that in Hillingdon, for example, where at the time of the publication of the White Paper, some 53 per cent of secondary school children were in grant-maintained schools, partnerships have developed and relationships between locally managed and grant-maintained schools are good. It is significant that all the secondary headteachers in Hillingdon still meet with the Director of Education and her officers since everyone in the area is committed to the education of the young people in the community.

One issue which is not mentioned in the White Paper or the Education Bill is that of crisis management. It is not clear what will happen when a school's buildings are in danger of collapsing and everyone needs to work together urgently to resolve the situation to keep the school open. This will often require co-ordination of a range of services and co-operation with others to secure emergency accommodation for the school. Local education authorities have a proven track record in this area of work and it is doubtful if there is any body which could match it.

Equally, there is a substantial body of expertise and experience which is on a daily basis made available in the form of advice and support to governing bodies and headteachers and staff generally. How will this be provided in the future? The Government in the White Paper sees a diminishing role for local education authorities and, in particular, with regard to direct service delivery 'The Government expects that increasingly the private sector will step in to provide such services' (para. 6.8, White Paper). This presupposes that the sector is in a position to deliver these services. If schools are not to suffer because that is not the case, action will be needed to secure these services. The whole area of supplying services under the Local Authorities (Goods and Services) Act 1970 is fraught with difficulty. The Compulsory Competitive Tendering regulations ensure that services are competitive and these regulations could be held as a model enabling LEAs to sell services across their boundaries.

Local authority experience is that the LEA offers services to grant-maintained schools and the schools buy them because they are of quality, meet their needs and cannot be provided by commercial firms which do not have the capacity to offer services which reflect the complex statutory requirements governing the locally managed, autonomous school. It is important that this matter is resolved and that authorities be allowed to operate in the market place if schools are to access these services.

The proposals in the Education Bill only offer a short term solution and only time will tell if this meets the needs of schools, and more importantly, children.

7   Admissions to schools
Geoffrey Williams

Admissions Policies

The admissions policy of a school (including in particular the admissions criteria) and the way in which the policy is implemented determine more than any other policy the character of the school. The Department for Education's December 1992 draft circular on admissions, designed to replace 11/88 and 6/91, implicity recognises this.

It is self-evident that the criteria for admission to a school will, if the school is oversubscribed and some selection of entrants must take place, determine who is actually admitted to the school and who is not. The way in which the selection is carried out may mean that it is easier for some pupils (or their parents) to fulfil the admissions criteria than for others.

The rhetoric behind some of the primary legislation and regulations about admissions is that choice should be enhanced (that is, there should be more of it and that it should be easier for parents to obtain their choice of school). The reality is somewhat different. The language of 'choice' tends to be used in ministerial statements and in press releases, or, hedged with safeguards, in charter documents. Statues and regulation generally refer to the word 'preference'. The provision of different kinds of school is distributed very unevenly across the country — a parent in a town 30 miles from a CTC is not likely to be impressed with any rhetoric which tells him or her that CTCs are available and accessible as part of a pattern of choice.

Responsibilities of those involved in the process

The broad responsibilites of those involved in admissions are these. The admissions authority is responsible for deciding both the criteria and the arrangements for admissions including provision for appeals against decisions.

The admissions authority also has to carry out certain consultations: annually upon its admissions arrangements, and when it is proposing certain changes, including any formal variation of the standard number (that is, the number to be admitted into the intake year, or any subsequent year if there are formal arrangements to admit pupils, say, at a later year — certain schools may have formal admissions to admit at years 7 and 9, for example, and an admission number must in those cases be published for each of the years in question).

For county schools the local education authority is the admissions authority; for voluntary controlled schools the governing body is the authority, unless governors decide otherwise; for voluntary aided schools, grant-maintained schools and city technology colleges the governing body is the admissions authority.

Admissions numbers ('standard numbers')

An admissions authority must decide how many children it intends to admit. The authority must establish the 'standard number', which is the number of children that they must admit. For secondary schools, the number is fixed by whichever of the following three methods gives the larges number:

1 the number admitted for 1979/80 (the school year that preceded the implementation of the 1980 Education Act);
2 the number admitted for 1989/90 (the school year that followed the implementation of the 1988 Education Act);
3 the number of pupils that a statutory reorganisation noticed, subsequently approved, indicated that it was proposed to admit to the school in question.

For primary schools, the number is fixed by one of the following calculations:

1 the total number of pupils on roll at the school at May 1991 (not including pupils receiving nursery education) divided by the number of age groups in the school (not including pupils receiving nursery education), rounded down to the nearest whole number. There are special provisions for calculating the number for schools where there are two relevant age groups for entry. Separate figures are calculated for these. The figures for the first relevant age group should be the numbers of pupils in the age groups up to but not including the second relevant age group divided by the number of age groups, again up to but not including the second relevant age group. The figure for the second relevant age group should be the number of pupils in the

second relevant age group and higher age groups divided by the number of these age groups minus the figure for the first relevant age group;

2 the number produced by applying the formula at Annex A of DES Circular 6/91 which provides a device for calculating the physical capacity of the school and deriving from this an admission number;

3 the number published by the admissions authority as the number of pupils in the age group intended to be admitted into the school in the 1990/91 school year;

4 the number of pupils that a statutory reorganisation notice, subsequently approved, stated as the number it was proposed to admit to the school in question.

For grant-maintained schools the number is fixed by the Secretary of State, who considers the admission number proposed by the governors of the school seeking grant-maintained status and modifies it if he sees fit.

If the Secretary of State subsequently approves proposals for a significant change in the character of, or a significant enlargement to, a grant-maintained school, the approved admission number will be governed by those proposals. The Secretary of State will also have powers to approve variations in the admission numbers in relation to any relevant age group at a grant-maintained school proposed by the school.

The admissions authority must admit up to the standard number of children before the formal appeal stage, at which point an appeal committee considers whether or not appeals should be allowed and more children admitted. The admissions authority cannot allocate a number of places less than the standard number at the pre-formal appeal stage and then allow the appeal committee to allocate places up to the number.

The admissions authority can admit in excess of the standard number if it wishes, and the formal appeal process then takes its course in the same way once allocations in accordance with the published criteria for admission have been completed.

The admissions authority can also make changes in the standard number, but reductions can be carried out only with the approval of the Secretary of State. An admissions authority can increase the number in one of the following ways:

1 a local education authority can consult the governing body, and subject to this consultation, publish a larger number (a governing body which is not an admissions authority can request the admissions authority to increase the number);

2 a governing body of a voluntary-aided school or grant-maintained school can publish a larger number (the governing body of a voluntary school must consult the local education authority).

To reduce the standard number, an admissions authority must publish a notice of their intention so to do, notify the Secretary of State of this and allow a period for objections to their proposal (in effect, a process similar to that required for the reorganisation of schools).

The Secretary of State will then determine the proposal. He can (and experience shows that he does) modify the number that the governors or the local education authority (if they are the admissions authority) propose. Generally he goes about this by indicating that he is 'minded to' approve the proposal subject to a particular modification. In effect, he is substituting at that point his judgement for the judgement of these making the proposal.

The Secretary of State also uses this approach when he is fixing the admissions arrangements (including the admissions criteria and the admissions number) for grant-maintained schools when they are being established. For grant-maintained schools, the Secretary of State uses the term 'approved admissions number' rather than 'standard number'.

The Secretary of State is altering criteria for admission which governors propose in their published arrangements (even where these criteria exactly or nearly reflect the ones that were previously in use by the governing body or the maintaining local education authority). The law allows him to take a different role from that taken by local authorities in the process of agreeing admissions arrangements for voluntary aided schools with the governing body concerned, where the process of agreement was precisely that, and without dictation. The stop press section at the end of the chapter refers to this.

He will normally expect to fix an admissions number for these schools which is related to the capacity of the school and the intake number derived from calculations using the 'workplace' formula for the assessment of accommodation at secondary schools which was promulgated in DES Circular 11/88, and the formula for assessing the capacity of primary schools which was promulgated in DES Circular 6/91.

These methods of calculations may often produce higher standard numbers than other methods of assessing school capacity, since the Secretary of State takes a less generous view of accommodation needs than the view normally taken by governing bodies and local education authorities.

For admissions into years other than the admission year, the admissions authority must use their published criteria to decide applications if there are more applications than there are places available. An unsuccessful applicant may appeal to a statutory appeal committee. The appeal is likely to succeed if the appeal committee are considering a case where the number of children in the year for which application is being made has not reached the standard number, even though that number applies strictly to the intake year (or years, if there are formal arrangements to admit pupils at more than one point into the school).

The annual consultations required for county and controlled schools, and for aided schools (but not for grant-maintained schools) include consultation about the actual criteria used for admission to schools in the case of oversubscription, and any changes proposed in these. Following consultations the admissions authority must publish details of their admissions arrangements (including the criteria) no later than 6 weeks before the date by which parents are required to make application for places at the school or schools concerned, in the case of secondary schools. For primary schools, the legislation does not require the publication to take place 6 weeks before the date, but the draft DFE circular of December 1992 on admissions advises that a similar period represents good practice.

Selection and specialisation, and recent DFE draft advice about criteria

The draft admissions circular introduces the concept of specialisation being secured, without a formal change of character of the school (which would require public consultation in the case of a maintained school, and the publication of notices, with the opportunity for objections to be made). The draft discusses the practice of interviewing applicants (pupils and parents) which has been a noticeable feature of the admissions arrangements for a number of non-selective non-denominational voluntary-aided schools and has been adopted with enthusiasm by certain non-selective grant-maintained schools once they have been incorporated.

The draft suggests that 'schools which do not select on the basis of ability or aptitude need to consider carefully whether the use of reports or interviews can properly form a part of their formal admission arrangements. In general this should be avoided except in the case of church schools, where reports or interviews may help to judge the family's religious background and the child's suitability for the religious ethos of the school'. It goes on to advise: 'discussions with the headteacher are of course extremely valuable for parents wishing to know in detail about a school and allow the headteacher in turn to explain the attitudes, values and expectations of the school. Such interviews are to be encouraged; the admissions policy and prospectus should however make it clear that the interview will not affect the child's chances of gaining a place at the school, except in the limited circumstances of church schools set out above'.

The question of specialisation by a school in relation to admissions is discussed in the draft circular. The Secretary of State's expectation is that 'he would not, other than in exceptional cases, expect schools which decide to specialise in some curricular area to apply to select pupils on the basis of ability or aptitude . . . in general it should be sufficient for any school which wishes to state in its prospectus that it seeks to attract applications from children with a particular interest in a specific subject. It should not be necessary to use aptitude or ability in that subject as an oversubscription criterion, which will amount to selection'.

In passing it is worth noting that the Secretary of State appears to allow this process to develop unplanned by the local education authority and the funding authority (and indeed his own department) since clearly much unproductive duplication is likely to result from a situation where a variety of different agencies both propose and act upon individual initiatives with no mechanism for collaboration.

The draft circular sets out the arrangements for the introduction of a 'strictly limited amount of selection, involving the selection of a total of not more than 10 per cent of pupils on the basis of ability or aptitude in one or more of music, art, drama and physical education'. To propose the allocation of more than 10 per cent would trigger the requirement for a maintained school to consult and publish proposals for a significant change of character, and for the Secretary of State, in the case of a grant-maintained school, to decide whether or not publication of proposals is necessary.

Where it is decided to introduce an element of selection, whether for 10 per cent or less, or for more than that figure, the statutory proposals (if required) and the admissions policy each year should state:

1 the number of places affected;
2 how ability or aptitude in the subject or subjects concerned will be assessed;
3 how the admissions authority intend to choose between applicants for 'specialist' places;
4 whether pupils selected in this way will be given special treatment once admitted to the school — for example given access to specialised courses not open to other pupils.

With regard to criteria, the draft admissions circular also gives advice on criteria used in determining applications when schools are oversubscribed.

The draft classifies certain criteria as 'objective', where if given a statement of the rule to be applied two people operating independently would rank applicants in exactly the same order. Examples of these are sibling links, family links or staff links (provided that the exact nature of the family link is set out for the avoidance of doubt); distance from the school; catchment areas; named feeder primary, first, nursery or middle schools; ability (for selective schools). There is then a group of possible criteria which involve a measure of judgement. Examples of these are medical, social or compassionate grounds; educational reasons, contribution to the life of the school, pastoral benefit; wish for single sex education; religious affiliation. The draft then gives guidance on those criteria which seem to the Secretary of State to be unacceptable. Examples of these are the admissions authority reserving the right to make the final decision on all admissions, taking into account but not being bound by their published criteria; exclusion of the potentially disruptive; exclusion of those with special needs; fees in connection with admission (in relation to this the draft helpfully explains that parents should not be invited to commit themselves to any degree of voluntary financial support for the school, however conditional, before admissions decisions are taken: this could be misinterpreted as a disguised fee); drawing lots.

The consideration of applications for places

In considering applications for places at schools the admissions authority must have regard to the reasons which are expressed by parents and judge these in accordance with the criteria which they have published. The criteria must be expressed in order of priority. It follows that, if regard has to be paid to the reasons which are expressed by parents, parents must be asked to state the reasons which they wish to have taken into account. No arrangements may be made in such a way as to constitute unlawful discrimination under the Race Relations Act.

In considering applications, the admissions authority cannot have regard to local authority boundaries and either exclude from consideration applicants from a neighbouring area altogether or accord them a lower priority if their application otherwise meets the established criteria for admission. This is the practical effect of the so-called 'Greenwich judgement'. Prior to this judgement, admissions authorities often as a matter of routine gave priority to applicants from their own local authority area. The judgement applies to admissions into all years, not only intake years.

Admissions authorities must consider applications for entry into years other than intake years in accordance with published criteria and arrangements.

A child must be admitted into a school for which his or her parents have expressed a preference unless the admission of the child would prejudice the provision of efficient education or the efficient use of resources.

In addition, a child need not be admitted if the school is, or was, an aided or special agreement school which had an agreement with the local education authority designed to preserve its (generally religious) character or (in the case of such a school which has become grant-maintained) has been allowed by the Secretary of State to include such an arrangement in its approved admission arrangements.

Such arrangements may for example allow a child of a different faith from the trustees of the school to be refused admission once a fixed proportion of places have been offered to pupils of different faiths.

Finally, if a school admits pupils with reference to their ability or aptitude, and the admission of a pupil would not be compatible with these arrangements (in other words, although places are available, the child has not passed an entry examination), the pupil need not be admitted.

Appeals mechanisms

There is a statutory appeals process which admissions authorities must organise and make known to parents. Apart from this appeals process the Secretary of State considers that is is good practice that there should be a process that operates on an informal basis to try and reconcile difficulties before the statutory appeals process is put in train.

Admissions authorities must be careful not to confuse these two distinct steps. The informal process must not be seen either as a substitute for the formal appeal or as a mechanism to bully or persuade parents not to lodge a formal appeal. As noted above, the formal appeal process begins to operate at the level when all places have been allocated up to the standard number (or in excess of it if the admissions authority for any reason decide that they will allocate over and above the standard number). The admissions authority must take steps to ensure that at every stage applicants are aware of the next appeal stage and how they can obtain access to it (this statutory requirement is to be extended by the Secretary of State, after consultation, to grant-maintained school governing bodies). The composition of appeals committees is regulated. A committee must consist of 3, 5 or 7 persons. For a county school, the members who are members of the authority or of any education committee of the authority must not outnumber the other members by more than one, and the chairman of the committee must not be a member of any education committee of the authority. A member of any education subcommittee should also not be appointed chairman.

For a voluntary-aided school an appeal committee must consist of 3, 5 or 7 persons of whom half the members, excluding the chairman, must be nominated from among those in the list drawn up by the local education authority. Panels may include one or more of the governors, but shall not include employees of the local education authority and should not include employees of the governors other than teachers. None of the governors must be the chairman of an appeal committee. A teacher at the school must not be a member of an appeal committee dealing with admissions (the provision for teachers to serve on appeal committees referred to above relates to those appeal committees which deal with issues other than admissions).

For a grant-maintained school the composition of the appeal committee reflects that of the composition of an appeal committee for an aided school save that there is no requirement to include any member from the local education authority. The model provisions lay down that a committee shall consist of an odd number of members appointed by the governing body. The persons comprise:

(a) members of the governing body other than such members who are also members of the relevant committee (save that no member of the staff of the school may be a member of an appeal committee); and

(b) persons chosen from the governing body from an independent panel.

Members of the committee who are members of the governing body may not outnumber the other members by more than one; the definition of 'relevant committee' means in the case of admission appeals the governors' Admissions Committee. A governor may not chair the appeal committee.

The admissions authority must take steps to ensure that there is a degree of independence in the process. The local education authority may not service the committee by using an officer who is concerned with admissions to schools. The committee may not contain any authority member or governor who has had any involvement in admissions to the school or schools concerned.

Admissions authorities should have particular regard to the way that procedures are handled to avoid any conflict of interest or possible bias in the membership of committees; for example, a person who is married to or closely related to a person excluded from membership of an appeal committee should not normally be a member; husbands and wives should not serve on the same committee, nor should members who are related in any way to children who are the subject of an appeal.

The best reference work on this area of operations is the Code of Practice document (1992) produced on appeals for admissions, exclusions, reinstatements and special needs by the local authority associations. It is obtainable from either of the associations concerned (Association of County Councils or Association of Metropolitan Authorities). The Department for Education has also (November 1992) issued a Code of Practice for governors of grant-maintained schools. Documents of this nature are likely to be referred to by the Ombudsman in his consideration of any allegations of maladministration. Those involved in any part of the work of an appeal committee, whether setting one up, acting as clerk or chairman, or dealing with giving evidence to a committee or presenting the appeal statement are strongly recommended to read these documents.

The appeal committee must undertake its work in two distinct steps. Apart from the qualification which relates to selective schools, the duty that an admissions authority is under is to admit unless to do so were to 'prejudice the provision of efficient education or cause the uneconomic use of resources'. The first decision that an appeal committee must come to therefore is whether or not the admissions authority has, in the judgement of the committee, proved prejudice. If the admissions authority has not been able to prove prejudice, then the appeal must be allowed; if, however, the admissions authority has proved prejudice, the question then that the appeal committee must consider is whether, balancing the degree of prejudice and the strength of the case, the appeal or appeals before it must be allowed. The decision and the reason for it must be communicated in writing to the appellant.

Further appellate provisions

Parents who are not satisfied about the decisions reached about admissions may ask the Secretary of State to investigate the actions of the admissions authority, or may ask the local government ombudsman to consider whether or not to investigate an individual case where a local authority is the admissions authority to see whether or not there has been maladministration.

The Secretary of State may investigate the actions of an admissions authority, but his investigation is limited under existing legislation to determining whether or not the authority has properly followed its own published procedures. He may not substitute his judgement for the judgement about an individual application — that is, that applicant A should have been admitted rather than applicant B. He may comment upon the procedures.

The Ombudsman, in deciding whether or not formally to investigate a case, is concerned to establish whether or not there is a *prima facie* case that maladministration has occurred. Maladministration can occur when a local authority does something in the wrong way, or does something they should not have done or fails to do something they should have done.

Examples of this could be unreasonable delay, bias against an applicant, failure to follow the correct procedures. The Ombudsman cannot question what an authority has done simply because the applicant does not agree with the decision in question. The Ombudsman may award compensation, and in a recent case (November 1992, involving Bolton Metropolitan Council) has recommended in the report of a formal investigation into admissions decisions that the local authority should make restitution by admitting the appellants to the school to which they sought admission. This latter appears to be a significant development, prior to this recommendation, a judicial review granted to the London Borough of Croydon had established that there were limits on the powers of the Ombudsman and that in particular his recommendation that an admission appeal should be reheard some considerable time after the original appeal was of doubtful legal status.

A parent or parents (or an applicant — an application may be lodged in the name of the pupil) may apply for leave for a judicial review of the admissions authority's decision. There is limited experience at the time of writing of this particular route for review. It is likely that it is the process (and compliance with the admissions authority's published procedures in particular) which would be the subject of scrutiny by the court.

Other general matters related to admissions

There is an expectation in the 1992 White Paper (supported by a reserve power for the Secretary of State in the 1992 Bill) that agreements can be and will be struck between admissions authorities about the coordination of admissions arrangements where there is a multiplicity of admissions authorities in particular involving grant-maintained schools. The Secretary of State's target for these agreements simply appears to be that of co-ordinating announcements about decisions, a target rather too low for the high ambitions normally claimed by Government. This issue is dealt with in more detail in Chapter 6 on grant-maintained schools.

Admissions to nursery classes and schools should also be described in published arrangements. Since there is not universal coverage of nursery places, admissions arrangements need to spell out criteria for admission with care. In particular, the arrangements for admitting any children with any priority assigned to them by degrees of social need, and any arrangements whereby a nursery class at a primary school performs an area role and does not guarantee admission to the primary school to which the class is attached must be set out in the published arrangements.

Exclusions

The powers of the various bodies involved, including the powers of the head of the school, will be set out in the articles of government. There are three kinds of exclusion: temporary, indefinite and permanent.

The 1992 Bill introduces measures designed to assist with the admission to schools of pupils with a history of having been excluded.

The local education authority will be able to give a direction, specifying a school which is a reasonable distance from the child's home and from which he has not been permanently excluded. Before deciding to give a direction, the LEA must consult the parent, the governing body of the school (whether county, voluntary or grant-maintained) and the 'home' local authority. In this area the powers given to a local education authority are also given to the Funding Agency for Schools.

The local education authority will be able to specify any maintained school (county, voluntary or grant-maintained) in a school attendance order. Before naming a school, the local education authority must consult the governing body (and, if the school is in the area of another local education authority, the other LEA). A governing body or LEA upon whom notice is served may apply to the Secretary of State for a direction (if they do this they must inform the local education authority who served the notice upon them).

Notwithstanding these generally welcome provisions, there is however little doubt that the process of seeking to ensure admission to schools of pupils who have been excluded will be, as now, a long and fraught process of negotiation.

Appellate provision in relation to exclusions

Appeals arrangements are required to enable parents to appeal against exclusion decisions. The Local Authority Associations Code of Practice (already cited) deals fully with the procedures that need to be followed and is invaluable for those involved in establishing and operating these appeal committees.

Admission to schools of pupils who are the subject of a statement of special educational needs

This chapter is not designed to deal with appellate provision in relation to statutory assessment and the process of preparing a statement of special educational needs, but only with admissions to schools.

The 1992 Education Bill proposes significant changes to the existing arrangements for admissions to schools of pupils who are the subject of a statement of special educational needs and for the appeal provisions in relation to these pupils.

A local education authority will be required to make arrangements for enabling a parent of a child who it is proposed should have a statement of special educational needs to express a preference about the maintained or grant-maintained school which he wishes the child to attend (and give reasons for this). The governing body of any school it is proposed should be thus named in a statement must be consulted before the school is named (and if the school is in the area of another local education authority they must also be consulted).

The authority is not under a duty to comply with the parent's preference where:

(a) the school is unsuitable to the child's age, ability or aptitude or to his special educational needs, or
(b) the attendance of the child at the school would be incompatible with the provision of efficient education for the children with whom he would be educated or the efficient use of resources.

If the preference expressed by the parent is not then complied with, the parent will have the right of appeal to a regional Special Education Needs Tribunal.

The Tribunal will have the power to order the local education authority to comply with the preference, rather than, as under the existing appellate provisions, require reconsideration only of the original decision.

Stop Press

There have been very recent developments about the approval of admissions criteria by the Secretary of State, where these have been put forward by governors as part of a proposal for grant maintained status being acquired. The Secretary of State would appear to have moved governors to a position where they have in effect been caused to accept a mixture of criteria, regarded by the Secretary of State as objective, but including selection by ability (performance in entrance examinations and/or tests).

In two cases up to 50% of entrants are being admitted by reference to ability by schools which are non-selective. The Secretary of State has taken the view that this does not constitute a change of character and thus requires no consultation, nor public notices, notwithstanding the previous character of the schools concerned, as proposed in notices his predecessors approved.

At the time of writing these interpretations have not been tested by the courts. It is difficult to reconcile them either with the principal legislation, or with the logic of the draft circular on admissions — it is clearly not in accord with the wording of the draft in relation to selection on grounds of ability. A number of references in this chapter refer to the controls being exercised by the Secretary of State over admissions arrangements proposed by governors making grant-maintained school proposals — it is early yet to judge what controls he may wish to exercise over existing grant-maintained schools, since the system is still relatively young.

8 Personnel Matters
Michael P. Brunt

General

Introduction

Employment law is among the most complex areas of law generally and of educational law in particular. It is affected by common law principles but has been diversified by successive enactments since the 1960s in three particular areas:

1 general employment law;
2 educational law; and
3 the European dimension.

This chapter seeks to cover some of the most important areas: important because of the frequency of their occurrence in practice, or important because of the potential financial or other consequences of ignorance.

The most important enactments and regulations to be covered include:

- The Education Act 1944 (the 1944 Act) (notably ss.22 to 30 concerning voluntary schools and religion);
- The Education (No.2) Act 1986 (the 1986 Act);
- The Education Reform Act 1988 (the 1988 Act) (in particular ss.33 to 51 on local management of schools (LMS), ss.52 to 104 on grant-maintained status (GMS) and s.222 on the Secretary of State's powers to modify employment legislation for schools subject to a delegation scheme);
- The Education Act 1993 (the 1993 Act);
- The Equal Pay Act 1970;
- The Sex Discrimination Act 1975 (SDA);
- The Race Relations Act 1976 (RRA);
- The Employment Protection (Consolidation) Act 1978 (EP(C)A);

- The Education (Modification of Enactments Relating to Employment) Order 1989 (SI 1989 No 901) made under s.222 of the 1988 Act;
- The Education (School Government) Regulations 1989, in particular the right of headteachers and teacher-governors to attend governors' meetings;
- The Employment Act 1990; and
- The School Teachers' Pay and Conditions Act 1991 (STPCA).

Employment relationships in education

The various employment powers and responsibilities in respect of different types of schools, when subject, or not subject, to a scheme of local management (LMS) are set out in Tables 8.1 to 8.7 as follows:

- Table 8.1　The employer
- Table 8.2　The staffing complement
- Table 8.3　Conditions of service
- Table 8.4　Headteacher (and deputy headteacher) appointment procedure
- Table 8.5　Other staff appointment procedures
- Table 8.6　Suspension
- Table 8.7　Dismissal

Abbreviations used in the tables and elsewhere in this chapter are explained at the end of the chapter.

As regards Table 8.4, s.36(1)(c) of the 1986 Act provides for the governing body and the local education authority (LEA) to have the power to replace at any time any member of the (headteacher and/or deputy headteacher) selection panel whom they have appointed. It should be noted that in *Regina v. Birmingham City Council ex parte McKenna* it was ruled that the panel could not operate without its full complement. It is therefore incumbent on both governing body and LEA to make suitable arrangements for substitutes.

Although the 1993 Act entails incorporation for LEA-maintained governing bodies, this does not extend to the employment of staff.

Teachers and religion

Under s.30 of the 1944 Act, teachers in maintained schools may not be paid less, nor be placed at a disadvantage for:

- giving religious education; or
- holding religious opinions; or
- attending religious worship.

Table 8.1 Who is the employer?

	Non-LMS	LMS
Nursery	LEA (1944 Act; the 1986 Act does not apply to nursery schools)	LEA (There is no provision in the 1988 Act for nursery schools to become subject to a delegation scheme)
County	LEA (1944 Act as amended by the 1986 Act s.35)	LEA, but many of the employment rights and duties accrue to the governing body (1988 Act ss.33–51)
Maintained Special	LEA (1944 Act as amended by the 1986 Act s.35)	LEA, but the 1988 Act permits the extension of delegation schemes to maintained special schools, in which case many of the employment rights will accrue to the governing body. (1988 Act s.43)
Voluntary Controlled	LEA (1944 Act as amended by the 1986 Act s.35)	LEA, but many of the employment rights and duties accrue to the governing body (1988 Act ss.33–51)
Voluntary Special Agreement	LEA (1944 Act as amended by the 1986 Act s.35)	LEA, but many of the employment rights and duties accrue to the governing body (1988 Act ss.33–51)
Voluntary Aided	Governing body subject to Articles of Government, except for DLO or DSO staff, if any (compulsory competitive tendering does not apply to voluntary-aided schools) (1944 Act)	Governing body subject to Articles of Government, except for DLO or DSO staff, if any (compulsory competitive tendering does not apply to voluntary-aided schools) (1944 Act)
Grant-maintained	Governing body, but some of the staff may be employed by contractor companies or an LEA's DLO or DSO (1988 Act s.57(3)(c))	

Table 8.2 Who determines the staffing complement? (Full time teachers, part-time teachers employed solely at school and all non-teaching staff, but excludes school meals and midday supervisors)

	Non-LMS	LMS
Nursery	LEA (1944 Act)	LEA (There is no provision in the 1988 Act for nursery schools to become subject to a delegation scheme)
County	LEA (1986 Act s.34)	Governing body (1988 Act s.44(2))
Maintained special	LEA (1986 Act s.34)	On introduction of local managment of special education, governing body. (1988 Act s.43)
Voluntary controlled	LEA (1986 Act s.34) Reserved teachers: subject to maximum of 20% of teaching force, by foundation governors (1944 Act s.27(4))	Governing body (1988 Act s.44(2))
Voluntary special agreement	LEA (1986 Act s.34) Reserved teachers: subject to maximum of 20% of teaching force, by foundation governors (1944 Act s.28(3))	Governing body (1988 Act s.44(2))
Voluntary aided	LEA (1944 Act s.24(2)(a)) Caretaking staff: governors, subject to directions from the LEA (1944 Act s.22(4))	Governing body (1988 Act s.44(2)) Caretaking staff: governing body (1988 Act s.45(2)(a))
Grant-maintained	Governing body, but on the establishment of a GM school, all staff employed by the former governing body (aided school) or by the LEA to work at the school (all other schools) transfer to the GM school (1988 Act s.75)	

Table 8.3 Who determines the conditions of service? (See also 'Teachers and religion')

	Non-LMS	LMS
Nursery	LEA (1944 Act)	LEA (There is no provision in the 1988 Act for nursery schools to become subject to a delegation scheme)
County	LEA (1986 Act s.42)	Governing body on grades currently applicable in relation to employment with the LEA (1988 Act s.44(2))
Maintained special	LEA (1986 Act s.42)	On introduction of local management of special education, governing body (1988 Act s.43)
Voluntary controlled	LEA (1986 Act s.42)	Governing body on grades currently applicable in relation to employment with the LEA (1988 Act s.44(2))
Voluntary special agreement	LEA (1986 Act s.42)	Governing body on grades currently applicable in relation to employment with the LEA (1988 Act s.44(2))
Voluntary aided	Subject to articles of government. Caretaking staff: Governing body, subject to directions from LEA. (1944 Act s.22(4))	Governing body on grades currently applicable in relation to employment with the LEA (1988 Act s.45(2))
Grant-maintained	Governing body, but on the establishment of a new GM school, all the former employer's 'rights, duties, powers and liabilities' transfer to the GM school governing body. (1988 Act s.75(6)&(7).	

Table 8.4 What is the appointment procedure for head teachers? (Also for deputy headteachers in some circumstances)

	Non-LMS	LMS
Nursery	Set out in articles of government (1944 Act; the 1986 Act does not apply to nursery schools)	Set out in articles of government (There is no provision in the 1988 Act for nursery schools to become subject to a delegation scheme)
County	Panel of equal numbers of governors and LEA representatives. (1986 Act s.35–37) Articles of government may also provide for this procedure to apply to deputy head-teachers (1986 Act s.41)	Panel of at least three governors, appointment subject to approval by full governing body (1988 Act s.44 and Schedule 3 para. 1)
Maintained special	Panel of equal numbers of governors and LEA representatives. (1986 Act s.35–37) Articles of government may also provide for this procedure to apply to deputy head-teachers (1986 Act s.41)	Panel of at least three governors, appointment subject to approval by full governing body (1988 Act s.44 and Schedule 3 para. 1)
Voluntary controlled	Panel of equal numbers of governors and LEA representatives. (1986 Act s.35–37) Articles of government may also provide for this procedure to apply to deputy head-teachers (1986 Act s.41)	Panel of at least three governors, appointment subject to approval by full governing body (1988 Act s.44 and Schedule 3 para. 1)
Voluntary special agreement	Panel of equal numbers of governors and LEA representatives. (1986 Act s.35–37) Articles of government may also provide for this procedure to apply to deputy head-teachers (1986 Act s.41)	Panel of at least three governors, appointment subject to approval by full governing body (1988 Act s.44 and Schedule 3 Para. 1)
Voluntary-aided	Determined in articles of government, subject to prohibition by LEA in case of teachers employed to give secular instruction (1944 Act s.24(2)(b))	Panel of at least three governors, appointment subject to approval by full governing body (1988 Act s.44 and Schedule 3 para. 1)
Grant-maintained	Determined in articles of government (1988 Act s.58)	

Table 8.5 What is the appointment procedure for other staff? (Including deputy headteachers in some circumstances)

	Non-LMS	LMS
Nursery	Set out in articles of government (1944 Act; the 1986 Act does not apply to nursery schools)	Set out in articles of government (There is no provision in the 1988 Act for nursery schools to become subject to a delegation scheme)
County	LEA may redeploy existing employee. Subject to LEA veto, by governing body which may delegate functions to one or more governors, or to the headteacher, or both (1986 Act s.37)	Governing body may delegate functions to one or more governors, or to the headteacher, or both acting together (1988 Act s.44 and Schedule 3) School Meals: LEA (1988 Act Schedule 3)
Maintained Special	LEA may redeploy existing employee. Subject to LEA veto, by governing body which may delegate functions to one or more governors, or to the headteacher, or both (1986 Act s.37)	Governing body may delegate functions to one or more governors, or to the headteacher, or both acting together (1988 Act s.44 and Schedule 3) School Meals: LEA (1988 Act Schedule 3)
Voluntary controlled	LEA may redeploy existing employee. Subject to LEA veto, by governing body which may delegate functions to one or more governors, or to the headteacher, or both (1986 Act s.37)	Governing body may delegate functions to one or more governors, or to the headteacher, or both acting together (1988 Act s.44 and Schedule 3) School Meals: LEA (1988 Act Schedule 3)
Voluntary special agreement	LEA may redeploy existing employee. Subject to LEA veto, by governing body which may delegate functions to one or more governors, or to the headteacher, or both (1986 Act s.37)	Governing body may delegate functions to one or more governors, or to the headteacher, or both acting together (1988 Act s.44 and Schedule 3) School Meals: LEA (1988 Act Schedule 3)
Voluntary aided	Determined in articles of government, subject to veto by LEA in case of teachers employed to give secular instruction (1944 Act s.24(2)(b))	Governing body may delegate functions to one or more governors, or to the headteacher, or both acting together (1988 Act s.44 and Schedule 3) School Meals: LEA (1988 Act Schedule 3)
Grant-maintained	Determined in articles of government (1988 Act s.58)	

Table 8.6   Who may suspend staff?

	Non-LMS	LMS
Nursery	LEA (1944 Act; the 1986 Act does not apply to nursery schools)	LEA (There is no provision in the 1988 Act for nursery schools to become subject to a delegation scheme)
County	Both governing body and headteacher have power to suspend staff, subject to informing the LEA, the head and the governing body, and subject to re-instatement by LEA (1986 Act s.41)	Both governing body and headteacher have power of suspension of staff (1988 Act Schedule 3 para. 7)
Maintained special	Both governing body and headteacher have power to suspend staff, subject to informing the LEA, the head and the governing body, and subject to re-instatement by LEA (1986 Act s.41)	Both governing body and headteacher have power of suspension of staff (1988 Act Schedule 3 para. 7)
Voluntary controlled	Both governing body and headteacher have power to suspend staff, subject to informing the LEA, the head and the governing body, and subject to re-instatement by LEA (1986 Act s.41)	Both governing body and headteacher have power of suspension of staff (1988 Act Schedule 3 para. 7)
Voluntary special agreement	Both governing body and headteacher have power to suspend staff, subject to informing the LEA, the head and the governing body, and subject to re-instatement by LEA (1986 Act s.41)	Both governing body and headteacher have power of suspension of staff (1988 Act Schedule 3 para. 7)
Voluntary aided	Determined by articles of government (1944 Act)	The governing body has the power of suspension of staff. Further provisions may be in articles of government. (1988 Act s.45 (3))
Grant-maintained	Determined by articles of government (1988 Act s.58)	

Table 8.7 Who may dismiss? (Includes requiring LEA to dismiss or requiring person to cease to work at the school or permitting person to retire with compensation)

	Non-LMS	LMS
Nursery	LEA (1944 Act; the 1986 Act does not apply to nursery schools)	LEA (There is no provision in the 1988 Act for nursery schools to become subject to a delegation scheme)
County	LEA subject to consultation with headteacher and governing body (1986 Act s.41)	Governing body and it may determine the amount of any severance payment (1988 Act s.44(2)(b) and s.46(2))
Maintained special	LEA subject to consultation with headteacher and governing body (1986 Act s.41)	Governing body and it may determine the amount of any severance payment (1988 Act s.44(2)(b) and s.46(2))
Voluntary controlled	LEA subject to consultation with headteacher and governing body (1986 Act s.41) Reserved teachers: foundation governors, if for failing to give RE efficiently and suitably (1944 Act s.27(5))	Governing body and it may determine the amount of any severance payment (1988 Act s.44(2)(b) and s.46(2))
Voluntary special agreement	LEA subject to consultation with headteacher and governing body (1986 Act s.41) Reserved teachers: foundation governors, if for failing to give RE efficiently and suitably (1944 Act s.28(4))	Governing body and it may determine the amount of any severance payment (1988 Act s.44(2)(b) and s.46(2))
Voluntary aided	Secular teachers: governing body, subject to veto by LEA (1944 Act, s.24(2)(a)) RE teachers: governing body, not subject to approval of LEA if on ground of failing to give RE suitably and efficiently (1944 Act s.28(2))	Governing body and it may determine the amount of any severance payment (1988 Act s.44(2)(b) and s.46(2))
Grant-maintained	Governing body, determined by articles of government (1988 Act s.58)	

However, teachers in voluntary-aided and 'reserved' teachers in voluntary controlled or voluntary special agreement schools may be paid less or disqualified for promotion or other advantage for:

- not giving religious education; or
- not holding religious opinions; or
- not attending religious worship.

The 1993 Act applies similar conscience clauses to teachers in grant-maintained schools.

Qualifications

Under the Education (Teachers) Regulations 1989 (Statutory Instrument (SI) 1989 No.1319), no person shall be employed as a teacher at a maintained school unless he or she is a qualified teacher. Qualified teacher status may be achieved by:

- obtaining a Bachelor of Education, Certificate in Education, Postgraduate Certificate in Education or equivalent;
- the licensed teacher route;
- completing a course of initial teacher training or being recognised as a teacher in Scotland or Northern Ireland; or
- the possession of a Higher Education diploma from a European Community country. (Croner 1992, p. 2–1).

Licensed teachers

Under the Education (Teachers) (Amendment) Regulations 1991 (SI 1991 No.1840) applications for a teacher to have licensed teacher status may be submitted by:

- the LEA for non-LMS schools;
- the governing body with the consent of the LEA for a LMS school; and
- the governing body for a grant-maintained (GM) school or non-maintained special school.

Through this route, qualified teacher status may be achieved after two years or more. (Croner 1992, p. 2–2).

Articled teachers

Under this scheme, instead of joining a Postgraduate Certificate in Education course, a person may undergo two years' training as a teacher in a school rather than as a student on a course (Croner 1992, p. 2–2).

School teacher probation

The school teacher probation requirements set out in Regulation 14 and Schedule 6 of the Education (Teachers) Regulations 1989 were revoked with effect from 1 September 1992, on the ground, among other considerations, that the arrangements made under s.49 of the 1986 Act for the introduction of school teacher appraisal (Education (School Teacher Appraisal) Regulations 1991) were sufficient to replace the probationary period. This, notwithstanding the fact that the appraisal regulations allowed for the phased introduction of appraisal which need not apply until September 1995 in any of the schools to which teachers new to teaching were being appointed.

As a result of the abolition of the statutory probation period, teachers new to teaching will in future have to be treated in the same way as any longer serving teachers when it comes to dismissal on grounds such as competence or redundancy. They will be entitled to the normal rights of appeal against dismissal and there will be a statutory requirement to consult with recognised trades unions under s.99 of EPA (see below). They will also come within the scope of the relevant disciplinary and grievance procedures.

Appointment

The employment relationship

The legal basis for an employment relationship is the contract between employer and employee. This legally enforceable bargain involves a promise to work in return for a promise to pay. Like all contracts (except those for real estate) in England and Wales, the contract does not have to be in writing to be enforceable in law. It may be oral or it may be established by conduct. If one of the parties fails to abide by the agreement, the other may sue for damages and, in serious cases, treat the contract as having ended. The value of this protection to the employee is not substantial as it is normally limited to the length of notice required to terminate the contract. These generalisations of common law are modified in the case of employment contracts by the existence of collective bargaining and the proliferation since the 1960s of employment legislation.

Statements of particulars

s.1 of the Employment Protection (Consolidation) Act 1978, requires that, within 13 weeks of the start of employment, each employee, whether permanent or temporary, be issued with a statement of particulars. The minimum requirements of the statement are:

- the identity of the parties;
- when the employment began;
- the date recognised as the beginning of continuous service with the employer or within local government whichever is the earlier;
- the date recognised as the beginning of service recognisable for the purpose of a redundancy payment;
- the scale or rate of pay;
- the frequency of the payment;
- the hours of work;
- the holiday entitlement;
- the effect of sickness or injury including sick pay arrangements;
- details of pensions and pension schemes;
- the notice required to terminate the contract;
- whether the employment is subject to a contracting-out certificate;
- the job title;
- references to disciplinary and grievance procedures; and
- if the contract is for a fixed term, the date of expiry. (Scowcroft, unpublished)

The EP(C)A provides (ss.2(3) and 5) that no statement of particulars need be given if the employee is either referred to another document which is reasonably accessible to him or her or is given a copy of a written contract of employment.

Under the European Directive on the Proof of Employment Relationship with effect from 30 June 1993 every employee working over 8 hours per week is entitled to a statement of particulars within 8 (rather than 13) weeks of starting work.

Implied contract terms

Some rights and obligations are so fundamental to the relationship that they are implied automatically into the contract, even if they have not been specified in the contract or statement of particulars, for example:

Employees must:

- act reasonably;
- display a duty of care to all others affected by their work;
- provide personal service;
- obey instructions which are lawful and reasonable;
- act in good faith; and
- preserve the confidentiality of the employer's information.

Employers must:

- pay wages;
- ensure safety under the common law and under the Health and Safety at Work etc Act 1974 (HSWA) (Scowcroft, unpublished); and
- refrain from unreasonable behaviour.

Conditions of service

The conditions of service for school teachers in maintained schools in England and Wales are determined by Parliament by means of an Order (SI 1992 No.989) made under s.2 of the School Teachers' Pay and Conditions Act 1991 (STPCA), except for teachers in GM schools which have opted out of the provisions of the STPCA by means of an Order made under s.3(4) of that Act. The current provisions are contained in the School Teachers' Pay and Conditions Document 1992, which sets out overriding requirements, general functions and professional duties for headteachers and has sections on the exercise of general professional duties, the exercise of particular duties, professional duties and working time for school teachers.

Under the Education (School Teachers' Pay and Conditions of Employment) Order 1987 (SI 1987 No.650), there is a requirement to provide cover for any teacher not available to teach his or her class for a period of more than three days:

- if the absence is known 48 hours or more in advance — for the whole of the absence;
- if the absence is not known 48 hours or more in advance — from the fourth day.
  (Croner 1992, p. 2–4).

STPCA has not set aside the conditions of service set out in 'the Conditions of Service for Schoolteachers in England and Wales' (the 'Burgundy Book') which continue in operation to the extent that they are not incompatible with the STPCA and Orders made under that Act.

The conditions of service for administrative, professional, technical and clerical (APT&C) staff in most maintained schools are contained in the National Joint Council for Local Authorities' Professional, Technical and Clerical Services Scheme of Conditions of Service ('the Purple Book').

The conditions of service of manual staff in most maintained schools are contained in the National Joint Council for Local Authorities' Services (Manual Workers) Handbook ('the Green Book').

Time off for public duties

Apart from time off work for trade union officials (see below) an employer has a duty to allow employees holding public positions (e.g. Justice of the Peace, maintained school governor, local authority councillor) to have reasonable paid time off to perform their duties. The full list of public offices is set out in s.29(1) and (2) of EP(C)A. 'Time off' does not mean switching the employee's work to another time (*Ratcliffe v. Dorset County Council* (1978) (Scowcroft, unpublished). Conversely, it does not mean that the employee is entitled to time off to compensate for public duties undertaken outside normal working hours (*Hairsine v. Kingston-upon-Hull City Council*). In the case of local authority employees (which includes teachers and other employees in maintained schools except VA and GM schools), the annual paid time off is limited to 208 hours per year (Local Government and Housing Act 1989).

Fixed term and other temporary contracts

Fixed term contracts

An employment contract is regarded as 'fixed term' if the agreement which led to its establishment determined that it would end on a specified date. If the employer or the employee wish to allow for the contract to be terminated before the specified date, provision must be made for this eventuality in the contract. Failing this, the employee may claim damages amounting to the sum of the unpaid remuneration for the unexpired remainder of the contract.

EP(C)A ss.55(2) and 83(2) prevents employers from using a series of fixed term contracts as a device to deny employees remedy against unfair dismissal. An employee on a fixed term contract has the same rights to claim unfair dismissal compensation as other dismissed employees. The same conditions apply in respect of continuous service (qualifying period of 2 years for 16 hours per week or more; 5

years for 8 hours per week or more), and the dismissal may or may not be adjudged to be fair by an industrial tribunal (IT).

Waiver clauses

All this is subject to an important exception. Under s.142 of the EP(C)A, an employee being offered a contract for a single term of one year or more may be asked in writing to waive his or her right to bring, at the end of (but not during) the contract term, a claim for unfair dismissal. If the contract is for a period of two years or more, the employee may, in the same way, be asked to waive in writing his or her right to claim for a redundancy payment.

If the fixed term contract is renewed, the waiver can also be renewed, provided that the contract offered for renewal is for two years or more (redundancy payment waiver) or for one year or more (unfair dismissal waiver). If the contract is for a shorter period, the waiver may not be renewed, with the result that the right to claim for recompense for unfair dismissal or redundancy will then apply to the whole of the period of continuous service, not just to the period of the last renewal.

On seeking to renew a fixed term contract to which no waivers previously applied, an employer may seek to introduce the waiver clauses. The employee may refuse to accept the waiver clause, in which case the earlier contract will end, a dismissal occurs, and it will fall to the employer to establish a substantial reason for the dismissal. A fixed term contract as alternative employment for a long serving employee will seldom be reasonable if it is made conditional on the employee agreeing to sign away his or her unfair dismissal and/or redundancy rights. However, if the employee accepts such a condition, it may be sustainable in law as a suitable alternative.

Because waiver clauses are not available for contracts of less than twelve months' duration, employers need to exercise care when renewing temporary contracts, as claims for unfair dismissal or redundancy pay could arise.

Non-renewal of fixed-term contracts

The non-renewal of an expiring fixed term contract is still a dismissal in law. Whether the dismissal is fair or not depends on the circumstances of the individual case, and may fall to be determined in an IT.

In practice, fixed term contracts are frequently used for work of limited duration, for which reason the ground for dismissal will normally be redundancy and (if handled properly) intrinsically fair, but in such cases employers will need to follow the normal consultation procedures (see *AUT v. Newcastle-Upon-Tyne* (Employment Appeal Tribunal (EAT) (1987, Industrial Cases Reports (ICR) 317)) (see 'Redundancy: consultation with trade unions' below). The costs of such redundancy payments may nonetheless be considerable as, in the absence of a waiver clause, they may relate to many years of continuous service with various public sector employers (see the Redundancy Payments (Local Government Modification) Order 1983 (as amended)).

Where the fixed term contract is not renewed for reasons other than redundancy, the reasonableness of the dismissal may fall to be tested in an IT, unless the employee has waived this right.

Rarer contract forms

Very rare in the education sector are contracts for the performance of a specific task. On completion, they are 'discharged by performance', there is no dismissal and therefore no potential claim for unfair dismissal or redundancy; but, if the contract is terminated earlier, there may be grounds for such a claim, unless the contract includes a provision to give notice.

Contracts terminable on the occurrence or non-occurrence of a specified event may be of use in the education sector, as the continuation of projects increasingly depends on the availability of external funding. In the case of *Brown et al. v. Knowsley Borough Council* (EAT (1986 Industrial Relations Law Reports (IRLR) 102)) dismissal was found to be fair and no redundancy was payable, but care should be exercised in the use of such contracts as this is an area largely untested by the courts.

Contracts of the types referred to above (fixed term appointments, those for a specific task or those terminable on the occurrence or non-occurrence of a future event) should only be used when the job genuinely requires their use, otherwise they may be subject to challenge in the courts. If used incorrectly (e.g. *Wiltshire County Council v. NATFHE and Guy* (Court of Appeal (CA) (1980, IRLR 198)), they can be overturned and unfair dismissal and/or redundancy compensation may result (Scowcroft, unpublished).

Temporary appointments

Standard temporary contracts of indefinite duration must be distinguished from fixed term contracts. Temporary contracts should clearly state the nature of the contract and the circumstances which will bring the contract to an end (e.g. the return of a staff member absent on sick leave). Unlike contracts terminable on the future happening or non-happening of a specified event, temporary contracts do not automatically terminate without dismissal, and a period of notice may therefore be necessary. Temporary appointments made to cover maternity leave absences and suspensions on medical grounds are specifically covered by s.61 of EP(C)A; dismissals are regarded as being for a substantial reason, and therefore as fair, provided the employer has otherwise acted reasonably by giving appropriate notice and seeking suitable alternative work for the employee.

When appointing to a temporary post, it is important to establish at the outset that the potential employee understands:

- that the employment is temporary;
- why it is temporary;
- how long it is likely to last;
- what event will bring it to an end; and
- any special conditions of service and or pension provisions.

In the case of an appointment to a fixed term contract, to these understandings must be added:

- the date on which the contract will expire; and
- the effect of waiver clauses, if used.

Teachers on temporary contracts for a term or less ('supply teachers') covering the absence of a permanent teacher are covered by all the conditions of the 'Burgundy Book' except:

- the notice provisions;
- dismissal procedures other than incompetence or capability; and
- maternity leave.

Short-term hourly rate teachers are not covered by:

- the grievance procedure;
- compensation for assaults and losses;
- travelling expenses;
- medical suspension and termination;
- leave for public duties;
- holidays and the working day; and
- disciplinary procedure.

Termination of contract

Rights and duties on termination

The employment contract normally ends in one of two ways: resignation or dismissal. Occasionally it will end by expiration of time or under an express term in the contract or by 'frustration' (e.g. permanent illness) but employers will need to exercise care before relying on this doctrine. The most important issues are those to do with dismissal and it is on dismissal in its various forms that this section concentrates.

Notice of termination

An employee is entitled to a minimum period of notice of termination depending on the length of his or her continuous employment with the same employer, as follows:

- 4 weeks' to 2 years' employment: 1 week's notice;
- 2 to 12 years' employment: 1 week for each year of employment;
- over 12 years' employment: 12 weeks.

In the education service, many contracts have longer notice periods, notably for most teachers whose notice period is of two months at the end of the Autumn or Spring terms or three months ending on 31 August.

The dismissed employee

With the exception of the remedies available to the employee through the IT (see below), which do not ensure that the employee gets his or her job back, there are means available to dismissed employees to challenge dismissals made improperly. These may include obtaining an injunction against the employer from dismissing; a second involves seeking to have the dismissal declared null and void as being contrary to the rules of natural justice or *ultra vires*. Such cases are extremely rare (Morris 1990). In certain circumstances, the contract may be terminated by either party on the ground that the other has repudiated it.

Redundancy

Redundancy occurs when an employer ceases or intends to cease carrying out the business temporarily or permanently, or the requirements of the business cease or diminish. A redundant employee is entitled to a payment if he or she has been in continuous employment with the employer for at least 2 years at 16 hours per week but excluding any period before the employee's 18th birthday. The continuity is not broken by sickness, pregnancy or strikes. Entitlement is lost after the employee's 65th birthday; and during the employee's 65th year the payment diminishes by one-twelfth each month.

An employee who refuses a reasonable alternative offer of employment in a situation of potential redundancy may lose entitlement to a redundancy payment. The length of the contract and whether it is for regular employment are material factors in determining whether the employee's refusal is reasonable. In *Morganite Crucible Ltd v. Street* (National Industrial Relations Court (NIRC) 1972 Industrial Tribunal Reports (ITR) 182) the refusal of a job offer lasting 12 to 18 months was considered unreasonable, but the refusal of one lasting 2 months was recognised as justified. In *Pritchard-Rhodes Ltd v. Boon & Milton* (1979 IRLR 19) a 7 month period of work was recognised as suitable alternative employment.

A dismissal on the grounds of redundancy may or may not be fair. If it is unfair (for example because of unfair selection for redundancy), there is provision for an award or re-instatement. If it is fair, there is an entitlement to redundancy pay, if the employee has the requisite number of years' service and the requisite number of hours worked per week (2 years at 16 hours per week, 5 years at 8 hours per week). An employee under notice of dismissal for redundancy is entitled to reasonable time off to look for new employment or re-training, if he or she has achieved the 2 year qualifying limit.

Summary dismissal

Summary dismissal, that is dismissal without notice, may only be imposed if the employee has committed an act of gross misconduct, examples of which are usually and advisably set out in disciplinary rules and will often include:

- wilful disobedience to lawful and reasonable instructions at a level of seriousness so great that it strikes at the heart of the contract; or
- misconduct incompatible with the continuation of the employment or prejudicial to the employer's business; or
- dishonesty; or
- immorality or drunkenness prejudicial to the performance of the employee's duties (Scowcroft, unpublished).

Summary dismissal does not obviate the need for a thorough investigation and a fair hearing in accordance with agreed procedures.

Protection againt unfair dismissal

After a period of 2 years of continuous employment, an employee working 16 or more hours per week gains protection against, and the right of remedy for, unfair dismissal. Similar safeguards apply to employees working 8 or more hours per week, but only after a period of 5 years of continuous employment. Contracts for separate employments in various jobs in the same school or in the same employing authority may not be aggregated to achieve the 8 or 16 hour qualifying limits, providing the contracts are genuinely independent and self-standing. This will be a matter on which the IT may need to make a judgement depending on the facts of the individual case (*Surrey County Council v. Lewis* (1987 IRLR 509)) (Scowcroft, unpublished) Teachers' 'preparation time', even if the preparation was carried out off the school premises, may be reckoned as part of the 8 or 16 hours, but this must be decided in the context of the whole contract (*Lake v. Essex County Council* (1977)). Break periods and a weekly discussion period with a head of department could be added to the contracted hours of a part-time teacher with pastoral duties to take her (or him) above the 16 hours' requirement (*Girls' Public Day School Trust v. Khanna* (1987)) (Scowcroft, unpublished).

If an employee:

- has worked for the requisite period; and
- is under the normal retirement age for the job or under 65 (whichever is the lower);

he or she has a right not to be unfairly dismissed.

The establishment of employment protection rights depends on a sufficient number of hours being worked each week and a sufficient length of continuous service. The qualifying period is 2 years in the case of an employee working 16 hours per week, and 5 years in the case of an employee working 8 hours per week. The Equal Opportunities Commission has challenged these differential qualifying periods as being indirectly discriminatory (for definition, see below), but at the time of writing the issue has not been fully resolved through the courts and may even become the subject of an

European Court of Justice (ECJ) ruling (LGMB No. 264, *Independent* 1992).

Continuity is not broken when one employment contract follows another with the same employer or even in some instances when there is a break between contracts. A break arising from a temporary cessation of work or arising in circumstances such that, by arrangement or custom, the employee is regarded as continuing in the employment of his or her employer for all or any purpose, will not affect the continuity of employment (EP(C)A Schedule 13, para. 9(1)(b) and (c)).

This provision was of particular importance in the case of *Ford v. Warwickshire County Council* (1983 IRLR 126) (Croner 1992, p. 2–33), where it was held, on appeal to the House of Lords, that the gap between two September to July contracts was short in relation to the combined duration of the two contracts, that it therefore counted as 'a temporary cessation of work' and continuity of employment was not broken. If, however, irregular or uneven breaks occur over a period of years, the courts may adopt the broad approach established in *Fitzgerald v. Hall, Russell and Company Ltd* (1970 Appeal Cases (AC) 984), entailing consideration of all the relevant evidence, including: the nature of the employment, the length of the prior and subsequent service, the duration of the break, what was said when the break occurred, what happened during the break, what happened on re-engagement and the expectations of both employer and employee when the gap or gaps began.

Temporary cessations do not break the continuity of the employment; neither do they contribute to the duration of the employment, for which reason an employee on, say, successive September to July contracts would require more than two calendar years to achieve the necessary milestone. The above-mentioned case and the accompanying considerations may be particularly important for supply teachers employed on a term-by-term basis, as they may establish continuity of employment if the appointment is renewed beyond two years' employment.

There are special (but exceptional) circumstances in which continuity of service is preserved despite a break in service. These include the following sets of circumstances:

- for manual workers a break of up to 6 weeks does not affect annual leave or sick pay entitlements;
- APT&C staff returning to local government service after a break for maternity leave of up to eight years may preserve continuity of entitlement to certain benefits, if no permanent full-time paid employment has intervened.

Unfair dismissal

To complain of unfair dismissal, the former employee must prove that there has been a dismissal, which is defined in s.55 of EP(C)A as:

- where a fixed term contract expires and is not renewed;
- where the contract is ended by the employer, and
- where the contract is ended by the employee in circumstances which justify that resignation 'constructive dismissal' (see below).

Once the employee proves that he or she has been dismissed, it falls to the employer to show the reason for the dismissal and that it is one specified by EP(C)A. The IT then decides whether in all the circumstances it was reasonable for the employer to use that reason as a basis for dismissal.

Permissible reasons for dismissal are:

- the capability or conduct of the employee;
- redundancy;
- a statutory restriction against the continued employment of the employee; and
- some other substantial reason.

The tribunal then considers the procedural aspects of the employer's actions, in particular whether the employer acted as a 'reasonable employer' would. This implies a range of possible behaviours and it is not for the IT to substitute its own view for that of the employer.

The primary remedy was meant to be re-instatement. In practice, this may not always be possible and the employer may refuse to comply with a re-instatement order, but in so doing will incur the additional expense of an award of compensation in addition to the basic award which is calculated on the basis of age and length of service but with a maximum irrespective of the actual salary level.

Constructive dismissal

Constructive dismissal may arise if an employee resigns, with or without giving notice, in response to a fundamental breach of an important term of his or her contract of employment. It may also occur if the employee believes that the employer intends to breach the contract. Putting pressure on an employee to resign will normally constitute constructive dismissal, but constructive dismissal may also arise from a failure to provide support to allow an employee to do his or her job, or a failure to deal adequately with a health and safety or a harassment issue. Constructive dismissal is often very difficult for the employee to establish at an IT, unless it is blatant.

Resignations in the heat of the moment

In *Kwik-Fit (GB) v. Linehame* (1992 IRLR 156) the court advised employers that a reasonable period should be allowed to elapse before a resignation given in the heat of the moment is accepted (LACSAB Advisory Bulletin No. 276)

Disciplinary action

The legal position relating to disciplinary action is complex and changing as new cases chart fresh terrain on a daily basis. Two principles of common law are fundamental to the fair hearing of any disciplinary case. They are *nemo in causa sua iudex* (no-one may be judge in his or her own cause) and *audi alteram partem* (hear the other side). These principles have been elaborated in statutory codes of practice drawn up by ACAS.

Disciplinary procedure

Each employer must adopt an appropriate disciplinary process after consultation with relevant trades unions. In the case of locally managed schools (LMS), GM and voluntary-aided (VA) schools, the responsible body for establishing disciplinary, suspension and dismissal procedures is the school governing body. Important principles to be maintained in the drafting of such disciplinary procedures or codes include:

- the right of the employee subject to the disciplinary case ('the employee') to attend, and be heard at, a hearing of the case;
- the employee's right to be accompanied, advised and represented by a 'friend' of his or her choosing at any hearing or interview connected with the case;
- the right to know, at reasonable advance notice, the nature of the complaints to which he or she has to answer;
- the right to confront and cross-examine his or her accusers (though this principle is modified by *British Home Stores Ltd v. Burchell* (1978 LRLR 379) see below) (LACSAB Advisory Bulletin No. 219);
- the principle that the 'accuser' or 'prosecutor' on the one hand and the 'judge' on the other shall be different people;
- the right to an appeal to be heard by a different person or body

of persons from those who reached the decision of first instance;
- a restriction of the range of penalties which a disciplinary body may impose, normally including:
— the issue of an oral warning which normally remains extant for six months;
— the issue of a written warning which usually remains 'live' for twelve months;
— the issue of a final written warning whose life depends on the agreement contained in the relevant disciplinary code;
— dismissal with notice (cumulative misconduct); and
— summary dismissal (gross misconduct).

It should be noted that disciplinary codes in the education sector do not normally allow for the imposition of anything which might be conceived as a 'fine'. The procedures must comply with the Advisory, Conciliation and Arbitration Service (ACAS) Code of Practice No. 1 Disciplinary Practice and Procedures in Employment. The dismissed employee has a right to be provided, on request with a written statement of the reasons for dismissal in accordance with EP(C)A. If there is more than one reason, the over-riding reason must be identified.

Clark v. Civil Aviation Authority (1991) resulted in some useful guidance for those conducting disciplinary hearings:

- explain the purpose of the meeting;
- identify those present;
- arrange representation if appropriate;
- inform the employee of the allegation or allegations being made;
- make the primary documents available to both sides before the meeting;
- indicate the evidence whether in statement form or by the calling of witnesses;
- allow the employee or representative to ask questions;
- ask if the employee wishes any witnesses to be called;
- allow the employee to explain or argue the case;
- listen to argument from both sides upon the allegations and any possible consequence including any mitigation;
- ask the employee whether there is any further evidence or enquiry which could help his or her case;
- offer both sides the facility to sum up; and
- after deliberation, reduce the decision to writing whether or not an earlier oral indication has been given.

If there are defects in the manner in which the original decision was reached, it is possible for these to be made good, but only by the appeal body completely re-hearing the case.

The importance of disciplinary procedures cannot be underestimated in any disciplinary case. An early case in the education sector had seen a teacher forced to write his resignation ('constructive dismissal', see below, because of an improper relationship with a pupil. The dismissal was upheld because it would not have made any difference — the employee would have been dismissed anyway, even if the full disciplinary procedure had been invoked. However, in 1987, the House of Lords in *Polkey v. AE Dayton Services Ltd* (1987 IRLR 503) re-established the principle that an employer could not justify a failure to follow disciplinary procedures on the grounds that the employee would have been dismissed anyway (LGMB No. 259, No. 274).

Governing body procedures

The interaction of the principles of *Clark v. Civil Aviation Authority* (1991) with the delegation requirements of the 1988 Act cause substantial difficulties for governing bodies seeking to establish appropriate mechanisms to ensure that there is an appeal body separate from the disciplinary body which first heard the case. Some attempt is made in the Education (School Government) Regulations 1989 to clarify the various roles, by providing (Regulations 25(3) and 26(5)(a)) that the initial decision as to the dismissal of a member of staff may be delegated to a committee of not fewer than three members of the governing body but not to an individual, and that the appeal may be delegated to a committee with no fewer members than the first committee. Although Department of Education and Science (DES) Circular 7/88 states that 'an external element in appeals is not excluded by the legislation', it is not clear that the governing body may enter into a binding agreement with the LEA for the latter to handle appeals against dismissal or removal (for 'removal' see 'Removal of DLO etc. staff' below). This is because of the principle of *delegatus non potest delegare*, namely that it is not lawful to delegate a power which is conferred by statute.

The Education (School Government) Regulations 1989 establish an unsatisfactory arrangement for the involvement of the headteacher (and potentially also the clerk to the governors) in the initial disciplinary and appeal hearings. Given that, in the great majority of disciplinary issues, the case will have been instigated by the headteacher, or at the very least, with his or her approval, the presence of the headteacher at the disciplinary and appeal hearings is at variance with the principle of *nemo in causa sua iudex*. It is unthinkable that any case against a member of staff will have been brought to the governing body without the headteacher's involvement as a witness or as an advocate or as one who has given permission for the case to be brought. For this reason, it is inappropriate that the headteacher should be permitted to remain in with the governing body when it has heard the evidence and is meeting in private to determine the outcome of the case. The situation is only in part improved by para. 5 of the Schedule to the 1989 Regulations which confirms the right of the headteacher to attend throughout such meetings but restricts his or her role to the giving of advice and withdraws the right to vote on the issue. These regulations do not yet appear to have been tested in an IT, but offer the potential of some interesting (and, for the lawyers, rewarding) litigation, if a headteacher, remaining in the meeting, transgresses the rules about the level of his or her involvement in the governing body's decision. Similar considerations apply to the clerk to the governing body if he or she has been involved in the disciplinary case, but this set of circumstances is, in practice, less likely to arise.

Validity of warnings

Some issues relating to the validity and life expectancy of disciplinary warnings are important to note.

The first is that care needs to be exercised if the governing body is to use disciplinary warnings about totally unrelated disciplinary issues as a ground for dismissal. Although a teacher issued with a final written warning for, say, striking a pupil, may later automatically be subject to dismissal for, say, a subsequent case or cases of lateness, it is safer to impose an appropriate staged series of warnings. This was made clear in the case of *Auguste Noel Ltd v. Curtis* (EAT 1990 IRLR, 326). An employee was dismissed for mishandling company property. In reaching the decision to dismiss, the employer had regard to the fact that the employee was already subject to two final warnings, one for his relations with fellow employees, the other for unsatisfactory documentation and absenteeism. The IT found that the earlier warnings should have been disregarded. The EAT over-ruled it, stating: 'it is essentially a matter of balance, of doing that which is fair and just in the circumstances and an employee is entitled to consider the existence of the warnings'. That this case was only resolved at a second appeal is an indication of the degree of caution required in this area. The important principle which must not be breached is that spent warnings must not be allowed to count again for the totting up of cumulative penalties.

The second issue is that the records of disciplinary cases should not be destroyed when the warning expires. If the employee is later the subject of a further disciplinary action about a related issue, it is important that those deciding whether or not to proceed with a case should have a reliable, objective, contemporaneous written record on which to base their decision whether or not to proceed with a case, rather than the imperfect memories of participants. The absence of such records does not necessarily favour the employee and can make a miscarriage of justice more, rather than less, likely.

A third consideration is that spent warnings may be used as one of the criteria for the selection of candidates for redundancy, a contentious practice which was upheld in the Court of Appeal in *Spel Manpower Services Ltd v. Waters*.

The fourth consideration relating to the retention of records is that, although a warning may no longer be extant and useable in the context of disciplinary proceedings, it may still be appropriate for use in other domains, notably decisions relating to career promotion and the contents of confidential references. This issue achieved significance in the case of the appointment of the former Director of Social Services of a Metropolitan Borough Council, whose spent disciplinary record had not been made available to the appointing body, a fact which was criticised when similar allegations made at a later date led to his resignation (LACSAB Advisory Bulletin No. 231). There is also a danger that, in the giving of a reference, the employer, having divested himself or herself of the records, may be liable for negligent mis-statement in the provision of any subsequent reference (see *Spring v. Guardian Assurance plc* and others (1992) IRLR 173). (LACSAB Advisory Bulletin No. 276).

In many disciplinary cases, dismissal arises from a protracted series of warnings, oral, written and final, each subject to a process of appeal. Notwithstanding the difficulties of such protracted procedures, consideration should be given to allowing each warning and appeal to take its course, before an escalation of the disciplinary warnings is imposed. Thus, in the case of *Tower Hamlets Health Authority v. Anthony* (1988 IRLR 321) it was ruled that a dismissal while appeal proceedings against a final warning were pending could be unfair. In this case, the disciplinary procedure provided for a final warning before dismissal other than dismissal for gross misconduct. Two of the warnings which had been imposed on Ms Anthony were, at the time of her dismissal, still the subject of appeal and a hearing had been scheduled for a few days later. The facts that the appeals were outstanding and were to be heard shortly were factors which a reasonable employer ought to have taken into account. Since their validity was a necessary precondition of her fair dismissal, the Court of Appeal remitted the case to the IT. This should not be construed as meaning that the employer has to wait months for the appeal to be heard, but rather that a reasonable employer must make a judgement on the issue.

As regards the fairness of proceeding without allowing the employee to cross-examine the witness, the EAT in *British Home Stores Ltd v. Burchell* (1978 IRLR 379) provides a procedure for maintaining a proper balance between the desirability to protect informants who are genuinely in fear and providing a fair hearing of issues for employees who are accused of misconduct. This includes:

- taking full statements with a view to later circulation after the omission of those parts which would lead to the identification of the informant;
- further investigation to confirm or undermine the information;
- information about the character of the informant;
- if during the disciplinary hearings the employee raises any particularly relevant issue which should be raised with the informant, the chair should adjourn the meeting to make further enquiries of the informant;
- the importance of written statements (LACSAB Advisory Bulletin No. 219).

The points summarised above were by way of an '*obiter dictum*' at the EAT and are not therefore a binding authority. It should also be stressed that the EAT in *Louies v. Coventry Hood and Seating Co Ltd* (EAT 1990 IRLR 324) envisaged very few circumstances in which an employer would be acting fairly in withholding statements.

It is also important to note that some of the principles of criminal law do not apply to employment law. Most important among these is the issue of balance of proof. As is widely known, in criminal law, the case has to be proven 'beyond all reasonable doubt', whereas in employment law, the burden of proof is 'the balance of probabilities' and the disciplinary body must show a reasonable belief, based on reasonable grounds that the employee was incompetent or had committed an act of misconduct.

Part performance of contract

Sometimes, in pursuit of a trade dispute the employee will engage in 'working to rule' or 'withdrawal of good will', with the result that some tasks normally achieved are not completed. From the employer's perspective, this may be considered to be a 'part peformance of contract' resulting in one of two legal remedies. The first is for the employer to sue the employee in the hope of recovering damages. The assessment of such damages in the education sector is difficult. The alternative is for the employer to pay a partial salary for the part peformance of the contract, a course of action upheld in *Royle v. Trafford Borough Council* (1984 IRLR 184). In *Sim v. Rotherham Metropolitan Borough Council* (1986 IRLR 391) this course of action was confirmed in relation to an implied contract term, namely covering for absent colleagues.

Equal Opportunities

General

'An employer may refuse to employ [a worker] for the most mistaken, capricious, malicious or morally reprehensible motives that can be conceived, but the workman has no right of action against him ... A man has no right to be employed by any particular employer, and has no right to any particular employment if it depends on the will of another.' (Lord Davey 1898)

That is clearly no longer an accurate statement of the law.

The responsibilities of employers in respect of equal treatment as regards race run in parallel with those set out below in respect of sex.

It should be noted that neither RRA nor SDA addresses motive in the determination of whether an act of discrimination (whether direct or indirect) is unlawful. This has been made clear in *Ace Mini Cars v. Albertie* (1991 IRLR 425) as regards race and *Bain v Bowles* and others (1991 IRLR 356) as regards sex (LGMB No 261).

Anyone who believes that he or she has suffered discrimination in an employment case can file a complaint in an IT. Complainants may apply to the Commission for Racial Equality or the Equal Opportunities Commission for assistance which can take the forms of advice, procuring a settlement or legal representation.

By virtue of being the employer in the case of VA schools and GM schools and as a result of LMS delegation regulations in the case of locally managed schools, the governing body has the effective power of recruitment. In consequence, it also has the duty to ensure compliance with sex and race discrimination legislation in respect of employment. RRA and SDA have been modified in such a way as to make the governing body the respondent in cases where:

- discrimination against applicants, employees or contract workers is alleged, or
- challenge is made to the governing body's decision to impose a requirement for candidates of a particular sex or race under the

'genuine occupational qualification' provision of the two Acts, or

- the employer may incur 'vicarious liability' for the discriminatory acts alleged to have been committed by an employee.

Race Relations Act 1976

This Act applies to England, Scotland and Wales but not to Northern Ireland. s.1(1)(a) of RRA defines 'direct discrimination' as 'treating a person less favourably than others on racial grounds'.

Under s.1(1)(b) of RRA, indirect discrimination occurs when a condition or requirement is applied to all people, irrespective of race, but that condition or requirement is of such a type that a smaller proportion of a particular racial group can comply with it than others and it constitutes a detriment to those who cannot comply and it cannot be justified.

The definition of racial grounds given in s.3 of RRA, namely that racial grounds are grounds of race, colour, nationality (including citizenship) or ethnic or national origins, has been refined by the House of Lords. In consequence, essential characteristics are defined as a long shared history and a cultural tradition of its own, but other relevant characteristics are a common geographical origin or descent from a small number of common ancestors, a common language, a common literature, a common religion and being either a majority or a minority in a larger community (Mandla and Mandla v. Lee and Park Grove Private School Ltd (1983) IRLR 17) (Commission for Racial Equality 1991, p.11).

In consequence, gypsies, Sikhs and Jews have been defined as racial groups whereas Rastafarians and Muslims have not.

The responsibility to ensure fairness extends throughout the recruitment process. In April 1987, Ms Ranjit Arora applied for the post of Head of Teaching Studies at the Bradford and Ilkley College where she had been Head of Multicultural Education since 1983. After a 'biographical' interview, only one candidate was selected for the second interview and was appointed. On complaint to the IT alleging discrimination under both the RRA and the SDA, it was found that:

- undue emphasis had been placed on Ms Arora's cultural and ethnic background;
- no account had been taken of her extensive research experience; and
- too little attention had been paid to her managerial experience.

The discrimination in this case did not consist in the fact that Ms Arora was not appointed, but rather in that the way she had been questioned in the first interview had prevented her from moving on to the next stage of the selection interview (*Arora v. Bradford Metropolitan Council* ICR 226) (Commission for Racial Equality 1991, p. 34).

In 1987, the London Borough of Newham LEA wrote to secondary headteachers advising them not to consider teachers appointed under s.11 of the Local Government Act 1966 for any internal promotions, as they were not ordinary members of staff, but only attached to particular schools. In consequence a case was successfully brought before the IT (*Singh v. London Borough of Newham* (Director of Education) on the grounds of indirect discrimination, the exclusion of s.11 teachers being a requirement with which a smaller proportion of ethnic minority teachers could comply than others and the requirement could not be justified. The tribunal rejected the LEA's justifications that the s.11 posts were 'above ratio' posts, that the promotion of such teachers would lead to difficulties over Home Office funding and that financial considerations and budgetary restrictions forced the LEA to consider internal applicants only. This is an example of the way in which indirect racial discrimination can operate in the education service (Commission for Racial Equality 1991, p.32).

Vicarious liability and incitement to discriminate

Under s.32 of RRA, an employer is liable for any discriminatory acts committed by an employee ('vicarious liability'), unless the employer has taken reasonable steps to prevent such discrimination.

Under ss.30 and 31 of the RRA, it is unlawful to instruct or put pressure on others to discriminate. In *Commission for Racial Equality v. Fearn and British Electrical Repairs* (BER) it was found that a teacher had been put under a degree of pressure from a potential work experience placement not to place two 'West Indian' boys with the firm. Had the teacher complied with the request, he would have been in breach of s.17 of the Act (by not affording equal access to educational facilities) and the employing authority would have been vicariously liable (Commission for Racial Equality 1991, p.28).

The RRA is intended to eradicate discrimination. Although it allows for favourable provision to be made for members of racial groups, s.5 (which permits discrimination where being of a particular racial group is a genuine occupational qualification for the job) only permits positive discrimination in exceptional cases. It is not intended as a means of promoting social engineering.

The Sex Discrimination Act 1975

The SDA renders unlawful discrimination on the grounds of sex or marital status. Discrimination can be direct or indirect. Direct discrimination is where a person of one sex is treated less favourably, because of his or her sex, than a person of the opposite sex in similar circumstances is or would be treated. Indirect discrimination occurs when a condition or requirement is applied to both sexes but disproportionately few people of one sex can comply with the condition or requirement and that condition cannot be shown to be justifiable irrespective of sex, while the inability to comply is a disadvantage to the individual concerned (s.1(1)(b)).

The principle applies equally to men being treated unfavourably because a considerably smaller proportion of men can comply with the condition than the proportion of women.

It is unlawful to discriminate either directly or indirectly on the grounds of sex or marriage:

- in the arrangements for recruitment;
- in the terms on which employment is offered;
- by refusing or deliberately omitting to offer employment;
- in the manner of offering, or by refusing or deliberately omitting to offer, access to promotion, transfer or training or any other benefits, facilities or services; or
- by dismissing an employee or by subjecting him or her to any other detriment.

Employers must exercise care when prefering candidates for selection on the grounds that they will better 'fit in' with the existing environment. In *Baker v. Cornwall County Council* (1990 ICR 452 CA) when Mrs Baker complained of being three times passed over for promotion, the Council indicated that a man was thought better suited to fitting in with the all-male section of the Council's workforce. The court held that there were 'circumstances consistent with the treatment being based on grounds of sex . . .' This evidence, in the absence of counter-evidence, entitled the IT to conclude that direct discrimination had occurred and then the onus of proof shifted to the employer to give an innocent explanation supported by evidence. Appointing authorities will need to exercise care when requiring a commitment to extra-curricular activities. In *Briggs v. North-Eastern Education and Library Board* (1990 IRLR 181) it was held that a requirement to coach sports after school amounted to indirect discrimination against women. However, this being a case of indirect discrimination, the employer was entitled to argue (successfully in this case) that this requirement was justified.

Appointment panels must be careful in avoiding sexist questions at interview. To ask the same questions of all candidates is not enough, for even apparently innocuous questions may enable unlawful direct sex discrimination to be inferred. Ms Ambrose, the only woman on a shortlist of five for appointment as a technical and design adviser (a traditionally male dominated area) was asked 'given your opinions on equal opportunities and as a woman design and technology adviser, how would you deal with reactionary male teachers in the CDT departments?' and subsequently brought and won a sex discrimination case against the London Borough of Hackney.

Likewise in *Gates v. Wirral Metropolitan Borough Council* the complainant won her case on the grounds of objectionable questions having been put to her in breach of s.6(1)(a) of the SDA, which provides that it is unlawful for employers, unless the job is covered by an exception, to discriminate directly or indirectly on the grounds of sex or marriage in the arrangements they make for deciding who should be offered a job (Equal Opportunities Commission (a), undated).

There is an unresolved dilemma for governing bodies of VA church (particularly Roman Catholic) schools when failing to appoint otherwise suitable divorced applicants. The issue does not yet appear to have been resolved in the courts, but it remains unlawful, under ss.3 and 6 of the SDA, for governors to treat a person 'on the grounds of his or her marital status' less favourably than they would treat an unmarried person of the same sex, and no express exceptions have been written into any enactment since 1975. The arguments are finely balanced and revolve around:

- the legality in Great Britain (but not in Northern Ireland) of discriminating on religious grounds;
- the special status of denominational schools by virtue of s.114 of the 1944 Act, and the importance of the Trust Deed;
- in the case of teachers already in post, the effect of the usual contractual term 'to have regard to the Roman Catholic character of the school and not to do anything in any way detrimental or prejudicial to the school'; and
- the assertion that to discriminate on the grounds of marital status between a single and a married person may be unlawful, but to discriminate between a married person and a (divorced and re-) married person is not.

(Bradley 1991)

Unlawful indirect discrimination may also arise in selection for redundancy. In *Dick v the University of Dundee* it was established that by reviewing part-time and temporary jobs (rather than all jobs) without sound justification amounted to unlawful indirect sex discrimination because more women than men would be detrimentally affected by the decision (Equal Opportunities Commission (b), undated).

In *Bullock v. Alice Otley School* (1991, IRLR 324), the EAT found that the school was not permitted to maintain different ages of retirement for different groups of employees; their teaching and domestic staff being required to retire at age 60, gardeners and maintenance staff at age 65. It was ruled that to allow such categorisation would undermine the purposes of the SDA and that the school had directly discriminated on the ground of sex, contrary to s.1(1)(a) of the Act (*Education and the Law*, 1st edn, p. 209). In the Court of Appeal, however, it was held that different retirement ages for different categories of staff did not amount to unlawful sex discrimination if the categories and the different retirement ages were not gender based and the different retirement ages were objectively justified (in this case because of the difficulties of recruiting staff with certain specialist skills) (*Independent* 11 November 1992).

Age restrictions

Unnecessary age restrictions have been found to be indirect discrimination on the grounds of sex. Many LEAs impose conditions that candidates in receipt of occupational pensions may not be re-employed. As a result of *Greater Manchester Police Authority v. Lea*. LEAs or governing bodies continuing to pursue such restrictions (for whatever worthy social objectives) risk a complaint of indirect sex discrimination before an IT. The restriction is such that a smaller proportion of men can comply with it than the proportion of women and the condition is not justifiable irrespective of sex and the application of the condition to the case of a man would be to his detriment because he could not comply with it (LACSAB Advisory Bulletin No. 237).

Genuine occupational qualification

There are exceptions for certain jobs for which a person's sex is a genuine occupational qualification. There are very few instances in which a job in education will qualify for a genuine occupational qualification on the ground of sex. Exceptions may occur where considerations of privacy or decency are involved.

A case from an area outside education may yet have implications for schools. In *Etam plc v. Rowan* (1989 IRLR 150) the EAT upheld an IT finding that being a woman was not a genuine occupational qualification for the job of a sales assistant in a women's clothes shop. Whether this case has parallels in the case of women sports teachers remains to be seen. The genuine occupational qualification will not be valid if members of the appropriate sex are already employed in sufficient numbers to meet the employer's likely requirements without undue inconvenience. Genuine occupational qualifications may apply to recruitment, promotion, transfer or training, but cannot be used to justify a dismissal.

General issues

It is unlawful to instruct or put pressure on others to discriminate on the grounds of sex or marriage unless the job is subject to an exception (ss.39 and 40). A person who knowingly aids another person to do an act made unlawful by the SDA is treated as himself or herself committing a similar unlawful act (s.42(1)).

It is unlawful to victimise an individual for a complaint made in good faith about sex or marriage discrimination or for giving evidence about such a complaint.

It is lawful, where there have been comparatively small numbers of persons of one sex in particular work for the previous 12 months, to give special encouragement to, and provide specific training for, the minority sex.

Pregnancy

Employers must ensure that women are not treated unfavourably because of their pregnancy, as this can give rise to both unfair dismissal and sex discrimination claims. Under s.60(1) of the EP(C)A dismissals for reasons connected with a woman's pregnancy are automatically unfair. In the case of *Brown v. Stockton-on-Tees Borough Council* (1988 IRLR 263). Mrs Brown successfully claimed unfair dismissal on the grounds that she was not selected for one of three one-year contracts because of her pregnancy and consequent need of maternity leave early in her employment (Morris 1990, p. 60).

The area of sex discrimination is rendered the more complicated by the interaction with European case law. As a result of *Dekker v. Stichting Vormingscentrum Voor Jong Volwassenen (VJV-Centrum) Plus*, (ECJ, 1991 IRLR 27), it has been established that unfavourable treatment on the grounds of a woman's pregnancy is unfavourable treatment on the grounds of sex and therefore direct discrimination, since pregnancy is unique to the female sex. (LACSAB Advisory Bulletin No. 249).

The British Courts have tended to apply the principle that any unfavourable treatment on the ground of a woman's pregnancy will contravene the SDA, if it can be shown that a male comparator in similar circumstances would have been treated more favourably. The male comparator used by the courts is usually a sick man requiring a similar amount of time off work as a pregnant woman would require.

Equally, restrictions on the employment prospects of women returning to work after child-rearing are direct discrimination and therefore unlawful. A headteacher of an independent school sought to impose on a woman teacher returning to work after the birth of her baby a restriction that she could only work part-time and was found to have discriminated unlawfully on the grounds of sex.

An apparent paradox, however, is the case of *Berrisford v. Woodward Schools (Midland Division) Ltd* (1991). The dismissal of an unmarried pregnant matron of a church school was upheld as fair at both the IT and the EAT. The majority of the EAT found that the employer's real objection to the employee's continued employment was the outward and visible sign of her conduct. For there to be a comparable male situation there would have to be a visible sign; that, it was said, was the answer to the argument that because a man could not become pregnant, there necessarily was discrimination on the ground of sex (*Education and the Law*, 1st Edn, p. 209). The decision appears to be at variance with the over-riding European Court of Justice precept that dismissals on the ground of pregnancy (being a condition unknown in the male) are *ipso facto* unfair.

All this is to be clarified in the Trade Union Reform and Employment Rights Bill, which will, subject to the will of Parliament, make it automatically unfair to dismiss a woman:

- because she is pregnant or for reason connected with pregnancy;
- during or at the end of her maternity leave because she has given birth or for reasons connected with the birth;
- after her maternity leave, because she has taken, or seeks to avail herself of the benefits of, maternity leave;
- because of a requirement or recommendation that she is suspended from work on maternity ground;
- where the maternity leave is ended by dismissal on the grounds of redundancy and the special statutory provisions relating to this situation have not been complied with.

There are neither qualifying service provisions nor qualifying hours for enjoying these rights.

Equal Pay Act 1970

Under the Equal Pay Act 1970, employees of one sex are entitled to bring a claim for equal pay for 'like work' (i.e. work of a broadly similar nature) or for 'work of equal value' (i.e. work rated as equal after a job evaluation study) using as comparators members of the opposite sex employed by the same employer. If successful in the claim, the complainant's contract is deemed to include an equality clause. An example was the case of Mrs Gill who won her case against Doncaster Metropolitan Borough Council (*Gill v. Doncaster MBC* 1989). Notwithstanding the substantial powers delegated to governing bodies under the local management of schools provisions of the ERA 1988, the effective employer and respondent before the IT for the purpose of the Equal Pay Act 1970 remains, in the cases of county, voluntary controlled, voluntary special agreement and maintained special schools, the LEA, rather than the governing body of the individual school. The 1988 Act essentially removes the LEA's powers to ensure that employees carrying out like work or work of equal value receive equal pay — even in the case of posts subject to a job evaluation scheme, the evaluation is not binding on the governing body.

The Secretary of State has powers under s. 222 of the 1988 Act to make regulations modifying employment legislation in such a way as to make the two bodies of legislation consistent. He has exercised his powers under this section of the 1988 Act by issuing regulations modifying employment legislation in such a way as to make the governing body the effective employer in the following areas:

- dismissal;
- trade disputes; and
- 'small employer' provisions of employment law;

but he has not modified the Equal Pay Act 1970, with the result that employees of either sex may seek comparators of the other sex in any institution in the same LEA and bring a claim for equal pay. Mrs Gill's case above was one of these cases, albeit pre-LMS. Although it remains important to ensure that men and women are treated equally in matters of remuneration, particularly in small schools where there may be no available comparator, it is singularly inappropriate that LEAs are being brought to task for matters over which they have no control.

When defending an equal pay for like work or equal pay for work of equal value claim, the employers may enter a defence that a 'genuine material factor' (as defined by s. 1(3) of the Equal Pay Act 1970) caused the difference between the pay rates. In *Clark and Enderby v. Bexley and Frenchay Health Authorities* (LACSAB Advisory Bulletin No. 216) the IT held that the existence of different pay bargaining bodies, each of which reached decisions in a non-discriminatory manner, justified a difference in pay. This case has now been referred by the House of Lords to the ECJ. When eventually resolved it could find use in the domain of education if, for example, a nursery nurse sought to claim like work or work of equal value with a school teacher.

Disabled people

The Disabled Persons (Employment) Act 1944 requires an employer not to fill a vacant job with anyone other than a registered disabled person, unless at least 3 per cent of the existing workforce is registered disabled. A permit, obtainable from the Secretary of State for Employment, enables an employer to recruit to vacancies even when the 3 per cent quota has not been reached. Although the governing body has the responsibility under LMS for staff selection, it is to the LEA (being of course, the Council as a whole rather than just the education department and schools) that this 3 per cent quota requirement falls. This provision appears, however, to be falling into disuse. The original (1944) maximum fine of £100 has never been increased and no employer has been prosecuted since 1975.

Repeated, but unsuccessful, attempts have been made in Parliament to amend and reinforce the law, but it remains lawful to discriminate against a job applicant on the grounds of any disability he or she may have.

Local management of schools

Official guidance

Local management of schools (LMS), established under ss. 33 to 51 of the 1988 Act, has substantially altered the management of the personnel function in the education service. Official guidance on its implications is set out in Department of Education and Science (DES) Circular 7/88, and DES Circular 13/89 gives guidance on governing bodies' responsibilities under employment law. The Local Authorities Conditions of Service Advisory Board (LACSAB) has set out very useful guidance on the implications of LMS in its booklet *Personnel Management Implications* (LACSAB 1990).

Delegated and non-delegated functions

The delegation of powers and duties to all governing bodies will take place by stages and in due course it is intended that special as well as mainstream schools will have been included. As each school becomes subject to LMS, it will be the governing body, rather than the LEA, which will exercise all of the key functions of the employer. It is the governing body of a school subject to a scheme of delegation which:

- decides on the number of employees of each type at the school;
- decides on the job description for each;
- determines, at the time of the appointment, the remuneration (which term is not defined in the Act, but is clearly wider than just the grade of the post and includes the choice of start point);
- chooses the grade structure to be used for each post by selecting from among those used by the LEA;
- makes appointments to all vacancies;
- is responsible for fair recruitment decisions;
- must consult as required with the headteacher and chief education officer (who is entitled to be involved personally or through representatives in all stages of the recruitment procedure); and
- must take into account (but need not necessarily comply with) any advice given.
(LACSAB 1990).

In practice, the discretions relate only to new employees and to existing employees promoted or transferred.

The LEA, meanwhile, though remaining in law the employing authority, can only advise as to the numbers of each type of worker to employ, can, and sometimes must, in the person of its chief education officer (CEO), offer advice to the governing body, and must appoint the governing body's chosen candidate unless certain staff qualification requirements fail to be met. These requirements relate to (academic) qualifications, health and physical capacity or conduct and are specified in regulations made under ss.218 and 235 of the 1988 Act, notably the Education (Teachers) Regulations 1989 (SI 1989 No. 1319). These regulations are in this case relevant not only to teachers but also to other staff whose work brings them regularly into contact with children and young adults under nineteen years of age. They provide for the maintenance of health standards on appointment and during employment (Regulations 8 and 9), barring by the Secretary of State on medical, misconduct or educational grounds (Regulations 10 and 11) and teacher qualifications (Regulations 12 to 18 and Schedules 1, 3, 4 and 5).

Conditions of service remain the province of the LEA, thus permitting the LEA to determine, for example, that a school clerk's post should be paid on an APT&C rather than a manual grade and to prevent the granting of additional leave to members of staff. Whether a contract is for a fixed term and whether unfair dismissal and redundancy waiver clauses should be inserted (see above) are conditions of service issues and therefore matters for the LEA.

The role of the governing body is not entirely unbridled. The governing body is required to honour the contracts of employment of existing staff. Although it may set the hours of work of part-time staff, the hours of work of full-time staff are largely determined by the various conditions of service documents referred to above. There is provision for the LEA to nominate to a teaching post any employee whom it considers qualified to fill the post in question, but the governing body is not constrained to accept the nomination. Strangely, there is no parallel provision in respect of non-teaching staff. Combined, these provisions effectively set aside redeployment procedures adopted by LEAs during the 1970s and 1980s to respond to the effects of falling rolls, and also make more problematic the arrangements for school closures and reorganisations.

Although the LEA has lost many of its employment rights, many of its responsibilities remain. The LEA continues to be responsible for contracts of employment on terms and conditions which they set and also for issuing written particulars of the terms of employment in compliance with s.1 of EP(C)A. To carry out the latter responsibility, the LEA will need full information from the governing body including, for example, the grievance procedure adopted by the governors. This requirement would have been administratively unmanageable, had not the great majority of governing bodies accepted LEA recommendations as to appropriate procedures in each case. Although the LEA would be the respondent at the IT in respect of a complaint that written terms of employment (including disciplinary and grievance procedures) had not been given to the employee, paradoxically the 1988 Act provides for the governing body rather than the LEA to notify all employees at the school of those procedures.

Grievance procedures are within the ambit of the governing body, although there may be matters of dispute which the governing body is powerless to resolve (e.g. conditions of service issues). It is permissible for the governing body and the LEA to establish procedures which will encompass a right of appeal to the LEA, thus enabling a resolution to be achieved in areas legally within the remit of the LEA and enabling an appeal mechanism to be established beyond the governing body in matters within the latter's remit.

Introducing new terms and conditions

New terms and conditions of employment cannot be imposed unilaterally on existing staff, but can be negotiated with the concurrence of the LEA. If new conditions of service are introduced only for newly appointed and/or promoted staff, there is a potential for complaint under the Equal Pay Act 1970, using comparators both within and outside the school (see *Gill v. Doncaster MBC* above).

Power of dismissal

The power to dismiss employees at locally managed schools is effectively delegated to the governing body. The CEO has the right to advise the governing body and, if a dismissal were to proceed in spite of the CEO's contrary advice, the LEA has a right to deduct (under s.46 of the 1988 Act) the costs arising from the dismissal from the school's delegated budget share. Although this provision amounts to a substantial disincentive, it does not amount to a veto. The only further courses of action available to the LEA in the case of a disagreement over a dismissal are:

(a) to complain to the Secretary of State under s.68 of the 1944 Act, that the governing body has acted or is proposing to act unreasonably; or

(b) to suspend the governing body's right to a delegated budget in accordance with s.37 of the 1988 Act.

In the latter case, the school has the right of appeal to the Secretary of State.

The right to declare redundancies rests with the governing body but the local authority has the power to deduct the costs of redundancies from the school's budget share if they are excessive in relation to the LEA's own practice, but the LEA may not make deductions solely on the grounds that it has a 'no redundancy' policy (1988 Act, s.46(6)) (LACSAB 1990).

Criminal records

Although the LEA should carry out a check on the existence and content of any criminal record of a prospective employee for a post having substantial access to children and young adults under the age of 19, it remains the decision of the LMS school governing body as to whether or not the employee is appointed, and the LEA cannot normally refuse to appoint unless the candidate's name appears on DES List 99 (the list of teachers and others banned by the Secretary of

State from working in schools and other employment involving significant access to children and young adults under the age of 19) or unless the teacher fails the qualification requirements set out in the Education (Teachers) Regulations 1989.

Medical records

A further responsibility of the LEA arises from the Access to Medical Records Act 1988, which applies to medical reports obtained with a view to assessing a candidate's suitability for employment. This involves obtaining the candidate's consent if a report is to be obtained from the applicant's General Practitioner, allowing the candidate sight of the report, the right to annotate the report, and in the final analysis, the right to withdraw consent for it to be supplied. (Croner 1992, p. 2–11; LGMB No. 264).

Ill-health dismissals

For staff already in post, the LEA can take action to dismiss on grounds of ill health teachers and others employed to work with children and young adults under the age of 19 without the intervention or consent of the governing body. The dismissal will need to be handled fairly and comply with the provisions of the Access to Medical Reports Act 1988 (see above).

Removal of DLO etc. staff

Although the governing body does not retain effective disciplinary and dismissal rights in respect of staff employed in direct service organisations (DSOs), direct labour organisations (DLOs) or peripatetic services (e.g. remedial or music), it can determine that any employee engaged to work at the school should cease to work there. Before it may invoke this provision, the governing body must inform the LEA, giving its reasons, and afford the employee the opportunity to make representations (including oral representations) to it, before reaching a final decision. If the employee is employed to work solely at the school, this will entail the dismissal of the employee.

Although the local authority remains the employer of DLO and DSO staff, the appointment, rate of remuneration and dismissal of DLO or DSO staff employed to work at one school rest with the governing body even though they are managed by the LEA's DLO or DSO and terms and conditions are mainly determined by the LEA. The DES Circulars state that any decision about the replacement of DLO or DSO staff must be cost-neutral. This last-mentioned provision does not extend to peripatetic staff employed to work in various schools on an irregular part-time basis. For such staff, the appointment power continues to rest with the LEA.

The 1988 Act has had relatively little impact on the employment duties and rights of VA school governing bodies, since they were already the employers of their staff under the 1944 Act. Because the governing body, rather than the LEA, is the employer, the compulsory competitive provisions of the Local Government Act 1988 do not apply to manual staff in VA schools. The only staff who are potentially affected by the LMS provisions of the 1988 Act are those employed by the LEA to work at a school (e.g. peripatetic music staff) and these would be affected in the same way as staff at locally managed county and voluntary controlled schools (see above).

Voluntary-aided schools

The advisory rights in respect of the appointment of teaching staff accorded to the CEO apply in the case of VA schools only if the governing body so determines, and it may withdraw its agreement by giving the LEA written notification. The Act is silent on advisory rights for non-teaching staff in VA schools, but there is nothing to prevent parallel arrangements being made.

Trade Unions

Trade union rights

The governing body of the locally managed school is the responsible authority in respect of most issues to do with the recognition of trade union rights. It:

- must recognise trade unions recognised by the LEA;
- may recognise additional trades unions;
- must comply with disclosure of information provisions in relation to recognised trade unions (EPA ss.17 to 21);
- must provide reasonable facilities for recognised trades unions to carry out workplace ballots; and
- is to be regarded as the effective employer in respect of any 'trade dispute' in relation to matters for which it has delegated LMS powers (Trade Union and Labour Relations Act 1974, as amended by the Education (Modification of Enactments relating to Employment) Order, 1989, SI 1989 No. 901). (LACSAB 1990, p.21).

The governing body normally carries out these duties through the headteacher, a function recognised by the allocation to the headteacher of a professional duty 'liaison with staff unions and associations' (School Teachers' Pay and Conditions Document, paragraph 30(4) 'maintaining relationships with organisations representing teachers and other persons on the staff of the school'.

It is for the LEA to set provisions for time-off for trades union duties or activities in accordance with ss.27 and 28 of EP(C)A.

The duties for which time off may be required by officials have been amended by the Employment Act 1989 (LACSAB No.236). The duties must concern 'negotiations with the employer that are related to, or connected with, any matters which fall within s.29(1) of the Trade Union and Labour Relations Act 1974 (definition of trade dispute) and in relation to which the trade union is recognised by the employer.

Reasonable time off may therefore be requested for negotiations about:

- terms and conditions of employment (which includes pay, hours, conditions of service or physical working conditions);
- the recruitment, dismissal or suspension of one or more employees;
- the allocation and organisation of work or the grading of jobs;
- disciplinary matters including representing members at disciplinary interviews, hearings etc;
- trade union membership or non-membership;
- trade union facilities; and
- negotiation or consultative machinery or procedures.

Officials may also request paid time off to prepare for negotiations on the above, but a trade union official is not necessarily entitled to time off to attend a meeting simply because it is in connection with collective bargaining; the employer, when considering whether the employee's request for time off is reasonable, can take account of other factors such as the overall history, timing and agenda of the meeting (*London Ambulance Service v. Charlton* and others (EAT 1992) (*Independent* 28 October 1992).

Trade union duties must be distinguished from trade union activities, which might include branch, area or regional meetings, national executive committees or annual conferences. For trade union activities the requirement is for reasonable time off, but not necessarily with pay. There is no entitlement to time off to participate in industrial action!

Protection against unfair dismissal: trade union activities

The Employment Act 1990 makes it unlawful to refuse a person employment because he or she is, or is not, a trade union member or because he or she will not agree to become or cease to be a member. If a complaint to an IT is upheld, compensation may be awarded and the respondent may be recommended to take remedial action. If it is alleged that the trade union or another person put pressure on the employer to refuse an applicant by threatening industrial action, that union or person may be joined to the proceedings and may be ordered to pay part or all of any compensation awarded (LACSAB No.246).

In *Fitzpatrick v. British Railways Board* (LGMB No.259) the Court of Appeal overturned decisions of the lower tribunals and established that a dismissal based on an employee's trade union activities in a former employment were unfair, there being 'no reason for a rational and reasonable employer to object to the previous activities of an employee except insofar as they will impinge on the employee's current employment'.

A claim of unfair dismissal on the grounds of union membership or union activities has no qualifying period of continuous service, only a requirement that the claimant is an employee.

Redundancy: consultation with trades unions

Under ss.99 and 100 of EPA (as amended by the Employment Protection (Handling of Redundancies) Variation Order 1979), notification and consultation is required with recognised trades unions where there is a proposal for dismissal on the grounds of redundancy. The notice and consultation period required depends on the number of redundancies envisaged:

- there is no notice period where fewer than 10 redundancies are proposed;
- the notice period is of 30 days when more than 9 but fewer than 99 redundancies are proposed; and
- where 100 or more redundancies are envisaged, 90 days' notice and consultation is required.

Cases in education such as *NUT v. Avon County Council* (1978 IRLR 55), *AUT v. Newcastle-upon-Tyne* (1987 ICR 317) and *NUT (Solihull Branch) v. Solihull MBC* (1984 IT 26231/84) highlight the need to initiate consultations at the earliest opportunity and irrespective of the part-time or temporary or fixed-term nature of the contract).

DES Circular 13/89 explains that the responsibility for carrying out the s.99 consultations falls to the governing body in respect of staff who are contracted to work solely at the school and to the LEA in the case of staff who are contracted to work anywhere in the LEA. In either case, the employee identified as vulnerable to redundancy is entitled under the EP(C)A to paid time off to seek alternative employment.

Two ITs ((a) *NATFHE v. (1) the Governing Body of Rycotewood College* and (2) *Oxfordshire County Council:* and (b) *BCS Cooke and others* v (1) the *Governors of Horsell High School* and (2) *Surrey County Council*) have upheld this distinction based on s.235(3) of the 1988 Act and the Education (Modification of Enactments Relating to Employment) Order 1989.

The trades unions are entitled to the following information:

- the reasons for the proposals;
- the total numbers of employees of each description employed by the employer at the establishment in question;
- the proposed method of selection;
- the proposed method of carrying out the dismissals with due regard to any agreed procedure, including the period over which the dismissals are to take effect.

During the course of consultation, the employer must consider any representations made by the trade union representatives and reply to those representations, and, if he or she rejects any of those representations, give reasons.

These notice and consultation periods do not over-ride the notice requirements under the employees' contracts of employment and it may be necessary to issue notices of redundancy during, but not before, the consultation period.

The requirement for notification and consultation persists irrespective of the number of hours worked by each employee each week (see *NATFHE v. Manchester City Council* (EAT 1978 ICR 1190)) and irrespective of the amount of continuous service acquired. It also applies to temporary employment, but not to employees on fixed term contracts of three months or less or those engaged to perform a specific task not expected to last for more than three months. It should be noted that this consultation requirement relates only to dismissals on the grounds of redundancy. No prior consultation is required in law for dismissals of temporary staff on other grounds (e.g. staff who are employed to fill a maternity leave vacancy and who are dismissed on the return of the permanent member of staff).

Health and safety

HSWA places obligations on employers, employees, governing bodies and the LEA in respect of health and safety of workers and visitors (which includes pupils). The responsibilities for health and safety continued to be shared between those four groups after the introduction of LMS, but those of the governing body increase because of its greater control over spending and management. The LEA, meanwhile, continues to have responsibility for a safety policy under s.2(3) of HSWA, continues to be the employer as far as the establishment of safety committees (under s.2(7)) is concerned and continues to set time off (with pay) provisions for safety representatives to enable them to perform their functions or undergo training in accordance with the Safety Representatives and Safety Committees Regulations 1977 (SI 1977 No. 5000).

With effect from 31 December 1992 the Health and Safety at Work Directive for Temporary Workers requires temporary workers to be given the same health and safety information, training and protective equipment as permanent employees on the same work.

European community law

The impact of European legislation is growing and employers will need to be increasingly sensitive to the potential implications of their personnel policies and practices in an increasingly complex domain. Whether or not small institutions with an increasing range of devolved responsibilities and powers can equip themselves adequately to meet those challenges remains to be seen.

Abbreviations

AC	Appeal Cases
ACAS	the Advisory, Conciliation and Arbitration Service
APT&C	Administrative, Professional, Technical and Clerical
CA	the Court of Appeal
CEO	chief education officer
DES	Department of Education and Science (since 1992 DfE)
DfE	Department for Education (replaced DES in 1992)
DLO	Direct Labour Organisation

DSO	Direct Services Organisation
EAT	the Employment Appeal Tribunal
ECJ	European Court of Justice
EPA	the Employment Protection Act 1975
EP(C)A	the Employment Protection (Consolidation) Act 1978
ERA	Education Reform Act 1988
GM	grant-maintained
GMS	grant-maintained status
HSWA	the Health and Safety at Work etc. Act 1974
ICR	Industrial Cases Reports
IRLR	Industrial Relations Law Reports
IT	Industrial Tribunal
ITR	Industrial Tribunal Reports
LMS	local management scheme or local management of schools (as the context requires)
LEA	local education authority
NIRC	national industrial relations court
RRA	The Race Relations Act 1976
SDA	The Sex Discrimination Act 1975
s.	section (of an Act of Parliament)
SI	Statutory Instrument
ss.	sections (of an Act of Parliament)
STPCA	the School Teachers' Pay and Conditions Act 1991
The 1944 Act	the Education Act 1944
The 1986 Act	the Education (No. 2) Act 1986
The 1988 Act	the Education Reform Act 1988
VA	voluntary-aided (school)
VC	voluntary controlled (school)
VSA	voluntary special agreement (school).

References

Bradley, A. (1991) 'Through the legal maze' *The Times, Educational Supplement* 1 November.

Commission for Racial Equality (1991) *Lessons of the Law: A Casebook of Racial Discrimination in Education.*

Berrisford (1991) 'Case survey' *Education and the Law* 3 (4) p. 209.

Croner (1992) *The Head's Legal Guide* Croner Publications. Equal Opportunities Commission (undated a) The Case of *Gates v. Wirral Borough Council,* Sex Discrimination Decisions No. 1 Employment Interviews.

Equal Opportunities Commission (undated b) The Case of *Dick v. University of Dundee*, Sex Discrimination Decisions No. 2 Selection for Redundancy.

Equal Opportunititres Commission (1991) *Equal Opportunities in Schools: A Guide for School Governors in the Elimination of Sex Discrimination and the Promotion of Equal Opportunities.*

LACSAB (1990) *Local Managment of Schools and Colleges: Personnel Management Implications.*

LACSAB Advisory Bulletins:
  193   3 June 1988
  216   May 1989
  219   July 1989
  231   2 March 1990
  236   22 May 1990
  237   May 1990
  241   25 May 1990
  245   October 1990
  246   26 November 1990
  249   December 1990
  253   February/March 1991

Local Government Employment (1990) Ill Health Dismissals December.

LGMB Advisory Bulletins:
  259   August 1991
  261   September 1991
  264   November 1991
  270   February 1992
  274   March 1992
  276   April 1992

Morris, A (1990) 'Employment law: surveying the terrain' *Education and the Law* 2(2) pp. 55–65.

Scowcroft, P. L. (undated) *Employment Legislation* Unpublished.

Walton, F. (1990) 'How sexist was his question?' *Local Government Employment.*

9 Further education

Chris Brooks

The setting

At 5.30 pm on Thursday 21 March 1991, the Secretary of State for Education and Science, Mr Kenneth Clarke, rose in the House of Commons to make a statement about the future funding and organisation of further education. It took the education service completely by surprise. There had been no formal Government consultation with the colleges or the local education authorities, no outline proposals, and no manifesto commitment to pave the way for Mr Clarke's statement. The only authoritative indication of Government intentions had been a well-informed article published by *The Independent* earlier that day.

Mr Clarke announced that the Government proposed to introduce legislation to create a new further education sector in April 1993 by taking further education and sixth form colleges out of the local authority sector. These colleges would be funded directly by Government through a national council appointed by and responsible to the Secretary of State. The colleges would be the responsibility of free-standing corporate bodies vested with the land, buildings and plant currently in use and existing staff would be given a right of transfer of employment to the new colleges. He added that it would be important that the colleges should work in close co-operation with the training and enterprise councils (TECs).

The justification for these changes provided by Mr Clarke was thin. While the Education Reform Act 1988 had given colleges greater managerial autonomy, he said, they were 'still subject to bureaucratic controls from local authorities. They lack the full freedom which we gave the polytechnics and higher education colleges in 1989 to respond to the demands of students and of the labour market'. He added that the polytechnics had demonstrated that higher student enrolments and increased efficiency could be achieved without loss of academic standards following freedom from the local authority sector.

Throughout the following twelve months, this rather odd

justification emerged periodically from spokesmen and supporters. Little heed was paid to the fact that the local authority controls in question had, in the main, been the subject of formal specification and approval by Mr Clarke's predecessor, nor that an important part of the polytechnic expansion had been achieved during the period of local authority responsibility for non-university higher education.

Mr Clarke's statement also reiterated a number of themes which had characterised ministerial and departmental utterances for several years. These included the concern that insufficient numbers of school-leavers participated in further education and training, the belief that further education had a vital role in providing knowledge and skills for the workplace, and the need for links between the colleges and employment interests to be strengthened. Ironically, these themes had also been reflected in the then Government's education White Paper of 1943 (President of the Board of Education 1943) which heralded the momentous changes in the structure and development of the education service provided by the Education Act 1944. The conclusion drawn by the legislators of 1944, however, was that local education authorities should be given greater rather than fewer responsibilities for the development of further education.

The Government's White Paper (Secretaries of State 1991) which followed in May 1991 elaborated substantially upon the detail of the Secretary of State's announcement, if not upon the justification. It indicated, for example, that the Government would use its 'reserve powers' under s.24 of the Education Reform Act to control the qualifications and syllabuses to be put on offer in the new further education sector. Colleges in the new sector would be obliged to publish their examination results. Schools would be enabled to admit part-time and full-time students, including adults. The training and enterprise councils would 'secure coherence in vocational education and training provision' through their continued involvement in the planning of work-related provision made by colleges and by representation on the proposed national further education funding councils and on new governing bodies of colleges. A national system of training credits for young people in employment would be promoted, providing greater motivation and choice. The colleges' funding regime would provide a powerful incentive to recruit additional students and reduce unit costs. Colleges would be responsible for setting their own tuition fee levels. The Secretary of State would specify conditions on which funding would be made available to the funding councils. The councils would also be accountable for the quality of provision funded by them.

These are by no means all of the main provisions included in the White Paper, but they serve to illustrate the characteristics of the new further education sector which the Government envisaged. There would be a considerable potential for increased determination by Government of what should be provided by the colleges. The colleges would operate in a local context of increased competition, increased influence by the TECs, and heightened public accountability for the quality of their provision. And the mechanisms for the central funding of the colleges would provide incentives to enrol greater numbers of students, coupled with pressures to make efficiency gains.

The message which the White Paper clearly conveyed was the Government's belief that a further education sector of this kind would be achieved more rapidly and sustained more successfully without the continued involvement of the local education authorities. The values characterised by local government — equity in resource allocation, co-ordination and planning across wide areas, equality of opportunity, and control of inter-institutional competition — would not deliver this kind of further education sector. It was not freedom from local authority bureaucracy or the analogy with the polytechnics which motivated Government policy, but a desire to promote a sector in which market-related disciplines, incentives, accountabilities and pressures would create greater effectiveness, efficiency and economy.

The law of further education

Between 1944 and 1988, the law relating to further education was ambitious, unimplemented and, subsequently, benevolently ignored. The optimism of the Education Act 1944, which envisaged the creation of a new national system of county colleges, to be attended compulsorily by all young people in work, and planned and provided by local authorities under statutorily approved schemes of further education, soon gave way to the economic realities of the post-war period. By 1981, a review by officers of the Department of Education and Science, the Welsh Office and Local Authorities (Thompson 1981) concluded that 'Because authorities have neither the duty nor the power to make FE provision except through schemes endorsed by the Secretary of State [which had lapsed], much of the existing FE is almost certainly *ultra vires*. It would be inadvisable to allow such a situation to continue.'

However, continue it did, until the Education Reform Act 1988 clarified the statutory duties and powers of local education authorities, provided greater powers of delegated decision-making to college governing bodies, and introduced new funding arrangements for colleges by means of a formula common to all colleges within the responsibility of an individual local education authority. The Act also placed an obligation on authorities to prepare and implement schemes for the planning of further education, the delegation of powers to governing bodies and the adoption of a formula for the annual funding of individual colleges. In many respects, these provisions prepared colleges for the greater autonomy provided subseqently by the Further and Higher Education Act 1992.

The Further and Higher Education Bill

The Further and Higher Education Bill was introduced in the House of Lords in November 1991 and completed its Lords stages three months later. In many ways, these debates exemplified the seriousness, cogency and rigour which the House of Lords was able to bring to educational matters during that period. Debates were well-informed and contributors on all sides often displayed a close and up-to-date knowledge of the issues under consideration.

At the same time, the Lords stages also highlighted the difficulties encountered by ministers in the Lords who are required to speak on matters for which they hold no current departmental responsibility. Neither of the Government's spokesmen in the Lords was a minister at the Department of Education and Science. Their Lordships were able to secure amendments to the Bill relating to the provision of an act of collective worship and the teaching of religious education in sixth form colleges, and another which gave the further education funding councils responsibility for the funding of some provision for students with special educational needs. However, they were less than successful in eliciting from Government spokesmen any indication of Government intentions which went substantially further than what was already known. For example, the case put forward from the Government benches for the inclusion of sixth form colleges in the new sector was weak. Government spokesmen were not able to put forward a convincing argument to support the Government's refusal to include provisions in the Bill which would oblige colleges not to charge tuition fees for full-time students aged 16–19. Nor did they cast any general light on the nature of the funding methodology to be adopted by the funding councils, nor the likely guidance the councils would receive from the Secretary of State.

By the time the Bill reached the House of Commons, a pre-general election atmosphere had developed and much of the debate, particularly in committee, was characterised by arguments already well-rehearsed in the Lords, polemic and good-humoured banter. Some clarification of the Bill's effects on community and adult colleges was obtained, but once the Bill was guillotined by the Government, the proceedings flagged. Education ministers gave little by way of concession and came out of the Bill's proceedings having encountered very limited pressure.

Thus it was that during the passage of the Bill through Parliament, those parliamentarians with persistently cogent arguments and questions were responded to by ministers having no educational responsibilities, albeit with great courtesy and charm, but with little if any room for manoeuvre, while those parliamentarians with most to gain from direct exchanges with Education Department Ministers in the Commons put up a fair showing but allowed their attention to be distracted by the prospect of a spring election.

The Further and Higher Education Act 1992

The Bill completed its Parliamentary stages and received Royal Assent on 6 March 1992. As the Further and Higher Education Act 1992, it now provides the statutory framework within which the new further education sector will develop.

The further education funding councils

The Act established a further education funding council (FEFC) for England and, separately, for Wales. It provided that FEFC Chairmen and members would be appointed by the Secretary of State. Schedule 1 of the Act outlines details of the tenure of members, supplementary FEFC powers and stipulations relating to the appointment of staff, the Councils' proceedings and committee structure, and the keeping of accounts. In particular, Schedule 1 specifies that the FEFC for England will have regional advisory committees, the location and members of which are for determination by the Secretary of State. Schedule 1 also provides for the appointment of the first chief officer by the Secretary of State and for the appointment of each subsequent chief officer by the Council but with the approval of the Secretary of State. This provides a remarkably high degree of central Government control over the determination of who shall be both members and principal advisers to the FEFCs.

The Act also provides for the establishment by both FEFCs of a quality assessment committee, the membership of which is not for determination by the Secretary of State but by the funding council. Funding councils have a statutory duty to secure arrangements for assessing the quality of education provided in the new sector and the quality assessment committees (QACs) will advise on the discharge of this responsibility. Interestingly, the FEFC for England has decided that this advice should be given by a group acting independently of the council and that no member of the council should also be in membership of the QAC (FEFC 1992a). This may well provide a most interesting example of value tension management within a large and powerful public body, particularly as quality assessment staff are likely to need to relate both to the council and its independent advisory committee on quality. It remains to be seen whether the advice of the QAC is made public and whether it will press for quality assessments of colleges to be reflected in their future budgetary allocations.

Statutory duties and powers

Far less straightforward are the provisions made in the Act relating to the statutory duties and powers of the FEFCs and LEAs. These provisions bear the hallmarks of transitional provisions. They will be difficult to realise in practice and the settling of ambiguities will be a time consuming task for both the councils and the LEAs.

The FEFCs have a duty to secure sufficient facilities for full-time education suitable for those aged 16 (over compulsory school age) and under 19 years of age who may want it (s.2). In so doing, they must have regard to provision of this kind which is made in schools and other providers of 16–18 education. Consequently, while the vast majority of full-time 16–18 year olds in education are currently found in the LEA schools sector and not the FEFC further education sector, it is the FEFC and not the LEA which has the statutory duty to secure these facilities.

The FEFCs are also given statutory duties to secure adequate provision of part-time education suitable for persons of any age over 16 years and full-time education for those over 19. But the duty is limited to the types of courses set out in Schedule 2 of the Act. These form the vast bulk of current mainstream provision made by further education colleges and are as follows:

(a) a course which prepares students to obtain a vocational qualification which is, or falls within a class, for the time being approved for the purposes of this sub-paragraph by the Secretary of State,
(b) a course which prepares students to qualify for:
   (i) the General Certificate of Secondary Education, or
   (ii) the General Certificate of Education at Advanced Level or Advanced Supplementary Level (including Special Papers),
(c) a course for the time being approved for the purposes of this

sub-paragraph by the Secretary of State which prepares students for entry to a course of higher education,

(d) a course which prepares students for entry to another course falling within paragraphs (a) to (c) above,

(e) a course for basic literacy in English,

(f) a course to improve the knowledge of English of those for whom English is not the language spoken at home,

(g) a course to teach the basic principles of mathematics,

(h) in relation to Wales, a course for proficiency or literacy in Welsh,

(j) a course to teach independent living and communication skills to persons having learning difficulties which prepares them for entry to another course falling within paragraphs (d) to (h) above.

Courses in categories (a) and (c) have received formal approval by the Secretary of State (conveyed in a letter dated 10 August 1992 from Mr E.R. Morgan, Department for Education). In addition, the funding council advice to colleges has been sensibly circumspect in respect of courses referred to at (d) and (j). Given the development of course progression routes in further education over the past ten years, almost any type of provision made by colleges could be regarded as falling into either of these categories. FEFC have made it clear (FEFC 1992b) that the student progressions implied in (d) and (j) must constitute a demonstrable course objective, that the course should include assessment of student preparedness to progress to other courses, and that evidence of progress should be provided to the council.

Section 60 provides that no statutory duty of an FEFC shall extend to any person detained, other than at a school, in pursuance of an order made by a court or an order of recall made by the Secretary of State. Education in prison establishments does not therefore come within the duties of FEFC but remains the responsibility of the Home Office.

The FEFC's statutory duties therefore extend to all full-time provision made for 16–19 year olds and Schedule 2 provision for all part-time over-16s and full-time over-19s. Running concurrently with these FEFC duties, s.11 provides local education authorities with a statutory duty to secure adequate facilities for further education in their areas, subject to two provisos. First, this duty does not extend to full-time education for 16–19 year olds; s.10(2) provides LEAs with a power rather than a duty to make such provision, thus enabling local education authorities to continue to provide sixth form education in schools. Second, the duty does not extend to the provision of Schedule 2 courses for part-time students over 16 years of age and full-time students of 19 years and over. However, s.11 empowers LEAs to continue to secure provision which falls within Schedule 2, if they choose to do so.

Section 11 also defines further education as 'full-time and part-time education suitable to the requirements of persons over compulsory school age (including vocational, social, physical and recreational training)' and 'organised leisure-time occupation provided in connection with the provision of such education'.

LEAs therefore have power to secure provision for which the FEFCs have a duty to secure, together with a duty to secure further education defined in s.11 which falls outside the duties of the FEFC. Consequently, LEAs retain a duty to secure adequate adult non-vocational provision not covered by Schedule 2, and the functions of authorities in respect of the Youth Service (under s.11 of the FHE Act and s.53 of the 1944 Act) remain unchanged.

Special educational needs

In exercising their powers and duties, FEFCs and LEAs must have regard to the requirements of persons having learning difficulties.

LEAs will therefore need to retain arrangements for the assessment of special educational needs in respect of young people up to the age of 16 and for those above that age for whom the FEFC does not have responsibility. These will include young people over 16 who remain in the schools sector and adults whose provision is not covered by Schedule 2. At the same time, the FEFC will need to establish assessment and placement services for those with special educational needs falling within their remit, and, for example, will be responsible for funding the placement of such full-time students aged 16–18 at institutions which are currently located outside the students' home authorities.

How the LEAs' and the FEFC's assessment and placement services will work in practice remains to be seen and is currently the subject of discussion between the FEFC and the local authority associations. Certainly, very close collaborative arrangements will be necessary if confusion among students, parents and administrators is to be avoided. In addition, the absence in the FHE Act of any obligation on colleges to have regard to the needs of students with learning difficulties could lead to some very hard bargaining between colleges and the FEFC. Certainly, the nature of the assessment, counselling and placement of such students, the administrative systems needed to work effectively in the best interests of the students, and the means by which the transition from school to further education is managed will require careful planning and close dialogue between the FEFC, the LEAs and the colleges.

Unreasonable exercise of functions and mismanagement

s.68 of the 1944 Education Act provides that if the Secretary of State is satisfied that a local education authority or the governors of a county or voluntary school have acted or propose to act unreasonably in relation to the discharge of duties or powers, he may give directions to the authority or governors as appear to him to be expedient. The FHE Act 1992 extends the scope of the Secretary of State's power to the FEFCs and the governing bodies of colleges within the new further education sector (FHE Act 1992 Schedule 8 para.9) and s.57 of the Act extends the circumstances in which such directions may be issued to those involving a failure to discharge duties imposed upon the FEFCs and governing bodies.

Additionally, under s.57 of the FHE Act, the Secretary of State may, on the recommendation of the FEFC, remove and replace members of college governing bodies and modify college instruments of government if he is satisfied that the affairs of any college in the new sector have been or are being mismanaged.

Supplementary powers of FEFCs

An FEFC is empowered to provide financial support to the governing body of any institution within the further education or higher education sector. It may therefore fund further education provision in the universities and colleges of higher education. It may also fund higher education provision in further education colleges.

An FEFC is also empowered to provide resources for the establishment of new colleges, and for the provision of training, advice, research and other activities relevant to the provision for further education.

Financial support may be provided by the FEFC in the form of grants, loans or other payments on such terms as the FEFC thinks fit. The FEFC must not fund colleges in such a way as to discourage them from maintaining or developing funding from other sources. In addition, no conditions may be stipulated by an FEFC in respect of the application of income obtained by FEFC-funded institutions from other sources. This is an interesting limitation in so far as it precludes an FEFC from any direct influence in what are commonly regarded as college income-generating activities, including the provision of customised training for industry.

Continuing functions of local education authorities

Reference has already been made to the continuing function of local education authorities in respect of the provision of adult non-vocational education falling outside the scope of Schedule 2, and to LEAs' Youth Service responsibilities. Non-Schedule 2 provision may be made by authorities in their own adult education institutions which are not to become incorporated bodies, schools, colleges in the new further education sector and independent institutions. The FHE Act does not place any limitations on the kinds of institutions which may provide LEA-funded further education.

In respect of LEA maintained or assisted institutions which provide further education, authorities have a statutory duty under s.55 to keep under review the quality of education provided, the educational standards achieved and the efficiency of financial management, and have power to inspect such institutions. LEAs do not, however, have formal powers to cause inspections of provision which they fund in the new further education section, though inspections, audits, and the setting of performance targets in respect of such provision are matters to be settled between individual LEAs and colleges.

Under s.55, Her Majesty's Chief Inspector has a duty to keep the Secretary of State informed about the quality of education, standards and financial management provided in institutions maintained or assisted by LEAs, and must inspect and report on such institutions when invited by the Secretary of State to do so. These functions apply to all provisions made by authorities under further education statutory duties and powers, and include Youth Service provision.

In addition, the powers of local education authorities under s.2 of the Education Act 1962 to make discretionary awards in respect of students attending courses of further education is not affected by the FHE Act, and it remains for authorities to determine their own policies relating to the students to be supported and the level and duration of that support.

The powers and duties of LEAs relating to the provision of transport from home to school or college, contained in s.55 of the Education Act 1944, are extended to students in the new further education sector by the FHE Act (Schedule 8 para. 5). Authorities are obliged to make transport arrangements for full-time students in the new sector which are no less favourable than those made for pupils of the same age who attend LEA-maintained schools. Similarly, LEAs must make transport arrangements in respect of students with learning difficulties whose provision is funded by the FEFC which are no less favourable than those which are provided for such students directly by the authority in schools or other institutions. It is expected that the Secretary of State will make regulations requiring LEAs to publish information about transport arrangements for students aged 16–18 in the new further education sector, including those which have special educational needs.

Local education authorities at present have statutory responsibility under the Employment and Training Act 1973 to make the Careers Service available to pupils and students. The statutory basis of the Careers Service is, however, to be changed radically upon enactment of the Trade Union Reform, and Employment Rights Bill. National responsibility will be exercised by the Secretary of State for Employment, who is likely to authorise a multiplicity of local arrangements for delivery.

In addition, the FHE Act amends the Local Authorities (Goods and Services) Act 1970 (FHE Act 1992 Schedule 8 para. 71) in such a way as to enable local authorities to provide goods and services to colleges in the new further education sector. The FHE Act also enables local education authorities to lend money to higher and further education corporations and companies formed by such corporations (Schedule 8 para. 21).

Local education authorities also retain their responsibilities for the local organisation of schools. Before they, or the governors of voluntary schools, publish any proposals for a school closure, change of character or significant enlargement to premises, where such a proposal will affect the provision in schools for full-time 16–18 year olds, s.59 of the FHE Act requires them to consult the FEFC. Similar consultations must also be carried out before an LEA gives notice to the Secretary of State of proposals to close a special school or make changes in arrangements for provision in a special school which would affect the education of full-time 16–18 year olds, and LEAs must serve written notice on the FEFC if they intend to cease to maintain a special school.

Similarly, under s.51 of the Act the FEFC may not propose the establishment or dissolution of a further education corporation unless details have been published in a manner prescribed by the Secretary of State, the FEFC have considered any representations relating to such proposals, and details of the proposal and the representations have been sent to the Secretary of State. An amendment to the FHE Bill proposed in the House of Lords which would have obliged the FEFC to consult LEAs before such proposals were put to the Secretary of State was not accepted by the Government. However, Regulations [Education [Publication of Draft Proposals and Orders] [Further Education Corporation] Regulations 1992 SI No. 2361) made in October 1992 prescribe the time and manner of publication of proposals to establish or dissolve further education corporations, and the contents of such proposals. These Regulations also specify that the draft proposal must be sent to the local education authority in whose area the proposal would be implemented, the governing body of any further education sector college, or maintained or grant-maintained school providing full-time 16–18 provision, in the locality, or any other person who appears to the FEFC to have an interest in the proposal. There must then follow a period of one month in which representations may be made to the FEFC.

The provision of further education in schools

S.12 of the FHE Act gives powers to the governing bodies of county and voluntary schools to provide part-time education for over-16 year olds and full-time education for over-19 year olds. Maintained special schools may also admit such students but not without the consent of the local education authority. Provision of this kind will not constitute a change of character to the school, for which statutory notices and other procedures apply. Nor is the school prohibited from making tuition charges at its own discretion for such students. LEAs may not include the costs of such provision within the general schools budget or the formula used to allocate resources to schools. Governors may not meet any of the costs of such provision from their delegated budgets provided by the LEA.

Where governing bodies make provision of this kind which falls within Schedule 2 of the FHE Act, it is open to them to apply to the FEFC, via a sponsoring college within the further education sector, for financial support.

LEAs are not prohibited from funding further education provision of this kind in schools. Indeed, the FHE Act enables authorities to provide milk, meals and other refreshments for further education students in schools (Schedule 8 para. 17). However, the decision to make such provision and the means by which it may be planned and funded are entirely matters for determination by school governing bodies.

It is the intention of the Secretary of State to issue Regulations and guidance to governing bodies on these provisions, which come into force in August 1993.

Schedule 2 provision in LEA-maintained institutions

Arrangements for FEFC funding recognise that some of the provision for which it has a statutory duty is provided in institutions maintained by LEAs which do not form part of the new further education sector, notably adult education colleges and community schools and colleges. Under the terms of s.6(5) of the FHE Act, governing bodies of such 'external institutions' may apply for FEFC funding for the provision of Schedule 2 courses. This application must be made via a college within the new sector (a sponsoring body).

The arrangements for this level of funding were the subject of wide consultation by the FEFC and are outlined in the FEFC Circular 92/15 (October 1992). For 1993/94, the FEFC does not expect to fund any increase in Schedule 2 provision in external institutions, and the Secretary of State has asked that sponsoring colleges in the new sector should exercise caution in seeking to change existing patterns of provision in the short term. However, the criteria to be employed by sponsoring colleges in judging future applications, set out in s.6(5), are likely to have the effect of reducing Schedule 2 provision in external institutions over the next five years as such provision is increasingly likely to be made within the new further education sector.

The new further education corporations

Colleges and schools which initially fell within the new further education sector were either specified or designated by the Secretary of State under the provisions of s.15 and 28 of the FHE Act. s.16 enables the Secretary of State to make further specifications, including the specification of institutions maintained by a local education authority or a grant-maintained school which may be proposed for incorporation by the FEFC.

In general, provisions in the Act relating to the powers and duties of former aided schools which fall within the new sector differ from those which apply to former county, controlled and grant-maintained institutions, the former having been designated as eligible to receive FEFC funding and the latter having been specified as institutions to be conducted by a body corporate.

Further education corporations are given wide ranging powers relating to the provision of further and higher education and the supply of goods and services. They may acquire and dispose of land and property, enter into contracts, borrow and invest money, accept gifts, and provide scholarships, grants and prizes.

Each corporation must have an instrument and articles of government which comply with the provisions of Schedule 4 of the Act and associated Regulations (Education Regulations 1992 SI No.1963 and SI No.1957). The Regulations make detailed provisions relating to the membership and responsibilities of the corporations, the responsibilities of principals, the appointment and dismissal of staff and the conduct of any student union. Regulations relating to former further education colleges (SI No. 1963) envisage that membership of the corporation will evolve from the pre-April 1993 membership. All existing members of such governing bodies are expected to transfer to the new corporation with the exception of any elected member or employee of a local authority but, where not already provided for, with the addition of a nominee of the local training and enterprise council. The corporation may then determine its future size and composition, subject to specifications made in the Regulations, one of which provides that each body may have up to 5 co-opted members, of which no more than 2 may be elected members or employees of a local authority (other than teachers or members of a fire brigade).

At least half of the members must be 'business members' and the membership determined by the corporation must be achieved by the second meeting of the corporation which takes place after 1 April 1994. Regulations relating to former sixth Form colleges (SI No. 1957) make broadly similar provisions but do not assume a continuation of membership from old to new governing body.

In practice, these arrangements provide for a significant reduction in membership of governing bodies by local education authority elected members. Restrictions on local government elected members and employees apply equally to those from local authorities other than local education authorities.

Transfer of assets and staff

The FHE Act transfers to the corporations all land and property currently owned by local authorities and 'used or held for the purposes of the institution'. These transfers will be made through the Education Assets Board, which has powers to make directions where agreement is not reached between the authority and the Board. The Act also provides that any liability in respect of loans relating to such property or land shall not transfer to the corporations. The FEFCs are given powers to make payments to authorities in respect of such loans, the type of loan and the amounts to be paid being subject to determination by the Secretary of State.

The Act also provides for the transfer of college staff from local education authority employment to that of the corporation. Any person employed by the local education authority immediately before the date the new corporation becomes fully responsible for the governance of the college, 1 April 1993, and is either employed solely to work at the college, or is employed to work at the college (and elsewhere) and is designated by the Secretary of State, will automatically transfer to the new corporation. The individual's contract of employment shall have effect from that date as if it had been made originally between the individual and the corporation, and all the LEA's related rights, powers, duties and liabilities connected with such a contract are transferred to that corporation.

In 1992, the National Association of Teachers in Further and Higher Education (NATFHE) sought judicial review of the way in which further education employees' employment and collective bargaining rights were affected by the FHE Act. The High Court held that the provisions of the EEC Directive 77/187 — the 'Acquired Rights Directive' — had direct effect in relation to staff transfers under the FHE Act. The main implication of this ruling was that collective agreements relating to trade union recognition and negotiations would continue to have effect between the corporations and the unions after 1 April 1993.

The future

The FHE Act will bring about significant changes in the roles of the funders, planners and providers of further education. Governing bodies will have greater managerial and financial responsibilities and freedoms. Local education authorities will retain diminished but nonetheless important further education functions. The TECs will achieve greater involvement in the local planning and management of further education. And the FEFCs will have the massive task of responding to the needs of a £2.5 billion system, and of ensuring local adequacy of provision. And all of these activities will be expected to develop in a system in which the priorities of Government will be to increase participation whilst achieving efficiency gains through lower unit costs.

The system will not function effectively for the benefit of students if the actors in this unfolding drama do no more than comply with the law of further education. If, for example, the Government continue to expect the TECs to be responsible for the monitoring and achievement of national training and education targets, this will require wholehearted co-operation with the further education sector, the LEAs and the FEFCs. If the FEFCs and the LEAs between them are to secure provision which is coherent to parents, students and employers this will require an accord which recognises that these bodies share statutory responsibilities, particularly for those with special educational needs. If there is to be any coherence in the local planning and provision of further education, the TECs, the FEFCs, the colleges and the LEAs have much to gain by recognising the new dependencies which the FHE Act has created. In particular, the impact of LEA policies relating to discretionary awards and home-to-college transport on levels of college participation could be considerable. The LEA/FEFC responsibilities relating to the future organisation of local schools and colleges need to be sustained by a high level of mutual understanding and co-operation if adequate local educational opportunities are to be maintained and enhanced. And the need for colleges and LEAs to co-operate in the provision of an adequate local range of adult non-vocational provision will need to be fully reflected in local planning arrangements.

It will also need to be recognised that the FHE Act and the intentions of Government have created ambiguities. To what extent can the FEFC act as a securer of adequate local provision without explicit planning powers? How feasible is it to expect that a national FEFC and a local education authority can share statutory responsibilities for a common clientele? How will the FEFCs reflect local and national curriculum priorities in their funding methodologies? How will LEAs react in difficult financial times to the needs of colleges which are no longer part of their bailiwick? How will the TECs seek to resolve their ambiguous position of being both competitors with colleges and major participants in the planning of college provision? And how intense will be the competition for students among colleges and between colleges, schools and the TECs? How will schools respond to their new power to provide for adults and will there be any local planning of such provision? And will all these questions be answered by action which benefits students and employers and leads to an extension of educational opportunity and an enhancement of quality?

Further education's next five years will provide uncertain but interesting times.

References

FEFC (1992a) *Circular 92/19 Quality Assessment.*
FEFC (1992b) *Circular 92/09 Incorporation Matters.*
President of the Board of Education (1943) *Educational Reconstruction* HMSO Cmd 6458.
Secretaries of State for Education and Science, Employment and Wales (1991) *Education and Training for the 21st Century* Cmnd 1536 (2 volumes); HMSO.
Thompson, N.B.W. (1981) *The Legal Basis of Further Education — A review by officers from the Department of Education and Science, the Welsh Office and the Local Authorities* (unpublished but circulated to local education authorities).

Index